DIANA JOHNSTONE was born on 23 June 1934 in St Paul, Minnesota. Her childhood was spent in Washington DC and most of her adult life in Europe — France, Germany, and Italy.

   She obtained her Ph.D. at the University of Minnesota, where she was active in the large campus movement against the war in Indochina. She organized the first international contacts between American citizens and Vietnamese representatives in Paris. European correspondent for *In These Times* since it was founded in 1976 she has also written for *The New Statesman* and *Le Monde Diplomatique*. She now lives in Paris.

Diana Johnstone

Verso

The Politics of Euromissiles

Europe's Role in
America's World

British Library
Cataloguing in Publication Data

Johnstone, Diana
 The politics of Euromissiles: Europe's role
 in America's world.
 1. Cruise missiles   2. Europe — Military policy
 I. Title
 358'.1753'094   UG1312.C7

First published 1984
© Diana Johnstone 1984

Verso
15 Greek Street London W1V 5LF

Filmset in Baskerville by
PRG Graphics Ltd
Redhill, Surrey

Printed in Great Britain by
Thetford Press Limited
Thetford, Norfolk

ISBN 0 86091 0822
0 86091 787 8 pbk

Contents

Contents

Foreword

Amidst the controversy over deployment of nuclear missiles in Europe, we have been living through one of those strange moments in history when the world 'changes colour'. One meaning, which seemed clear, slides into another, and all our acquired common sense seems in danger of being swept away. These engines of death are first of all levers hastening the collapse of public reason. Human beings are being reduced to superfluous squatters on 'strategic' pieces of land, surrounded by 'strategic' bodies of water. The atmosphere and space are also 'strategic'. The missiles are props on a planet that is being set as a stage for war.

This time, the magnitude of the looming catastrophe no longer authorizes the comforting thought that 'History will decide' who was responsible. Unless we grasp very quickly the direction of events, and move to alter it, we have no grounds for assuming that adequate evidence and competent historians will survive to tell the tale. For we are threatened not only by nuclear war, but also, and more immediately, by institutionalized lies.

The customary journalistic approach to the Euromissiles affair is anecdotal. Events tumble over each other in wondrous succession. Europe is enjoying (more or less) détente. Then all at once Herr Schmidt, in his now legendary October 1977 speech in London, alerts the Atlantic Alliance to the threat of Soviet SS-20s targeted on Western Europe, with nothing similar staring back at them from the Western side. There is a moment of consternation, and then, as usual, Uncle Sam comes to the rescue: some brand–new cruise and Pershing 2 missiles will be stationed in five NATO countries to glower back at the wicked SS-20s. NATO leaders heave a sigh of relief, but the peoples of their countries take to the streets in protest against the mass of lethal hardware. To calm them down, the Americans go to Geneva in search of a deal with the Russians.

The secrecy of military matters sets up a peculiar dependence upon 'official sources', and a career-minded journalist would be well-advised not to challenge their version too closely. Since, moreover, any arms drive requires a degree of bluff, and since military strategy belongs to the domain of the imaginary, with 'scenarios' characteristically starring 'madmen', it is hardly surprising that political life is infected with even more than the ordinary deceit. In the midst of this process, in January 1981, the rearming Free World was given a new leader, Ronald Reagan, who, contrary to his image, did not prepare for the job by working as an honest cowboy, or even as an honest cowboy actor. He had spent his mid-career as a professional huckster, selling consumer goods on television and simple right-wing ideas on the businessmen's dinner circuit.

It is not easy to sort out the real from the play-acting. It is not obvious how American strategic policy is determined, nor what its true purposes may be. Other governments are scarcely more transparent.

Some people who write on these subjects can claim to be insiders. Men in power confide in them. But in order to receive even selective and motivated confidences, it is usually necessary to be in one of two states of grace. First, one may be a real insider, who shares the outlook, purposes and contempt for the ignorant masses of the men in power. Then one may learn a lot, but one will take care to pass along to the public only what it is good for the public to know. Or else, one may be disposed to believe what one is told, and then manipulation is easy.

'They are all lying', Bruno Kreisky has said of political leaders, advising journalists to 'watch what they do'. But the problem is not simply one of lies, of deliberate deception. More insidious is the consensus which grows around groups in power by a process of subtle social aping, so that the insiders themselves may not fully realize what they are doing and where they are taking us.

This book is the effort of an outsider to analyse current developments. It belongs to the 'Don't tell me, let me guess' school of journalism. What we are obliged to guess—or, more precisely, to work out for ourselves—is where things are heading, where the real dangers lie, what leaders are really up to, and whether they fully know it or not. The search for answers is a necessary part of living actively and responsibly in the present.

Our necessarily speculative analysis of the conflicting political tendencies involved in the Euromissiles affair is intended as a contribution to informed discussion, especially in and around the peace movement. Any errors will be due to honest misinterpretation of incomplete information, not to manipulation by 'authoritative sources'.

We are granted little time to understand these matters before the consequences are upon us. The need to be rapid and concise must leave open the extent to which the real tendencies coincide with deliberate intentions. One intention may slide into another, and there is reason to believe that important shifts in purpose have already taken place more than once in the Euromissiles affair, and may take place again. It is on these shifting sands that we must try to find our bearings.

As European correspondent for the American weekly *In These Times*, I have been observing the political scene in France, Italy and Germany for a number of years. This overview is at the origin of this book. As an American, I had long been struck by the degree to which European peoples are, politically, strangers to each other. Nevertheless, as the Euromissiles controversy developed, I was frankly amazed to see how the same set of facts were perceived in diametrically opposite ways in France and in Germany, especially among people calling themselves socialists. It was the struggle to explain this puzzle which made clear the most essential political significance of the Euromissiles.

This book, then, focuses on the politics of continental Europe. I hope it may usefully complement material already available to English-speaking readers about the significance of cruise missiles in Britain.

1
Politics and Strategy

The Decision

On 12 December 1979, at a special meeting in Brussels, the foreign and defence ministers of the North Atlantic Treaty Organization member countries reached a decision that would set the political agenda for the 1980s. Billed as the 'modernization of NATO's Long-Range Theatre Nuclear Forces (LRTNF), it appeared to be a technical matter of little interest to the general public. Indeed, few people outside specialized circles had a clear idea of its import, and even the cabinet ministers who gathered to approve it may not have been aware of its implications. The decision had been prepared for them by a group of high level officials — mainly at the Secretarial level in their various defence ministries — well versed in arcane questions of nuclear strategy.

In the closing years of the 1970s, a a certain consensus was reached in the restricted circles of top NATO officialdom on the need to revise NATO's nuclear capacity with the help of newly developed technology. President Jimmy Carter secretly obtained a general agreement from British Prime Minister James Callaghan, West German Chancellor Helmut Schmidt and French President Valéry Giscard d'Estaing, at a January 1979 summit meeting in Guadeloupe from which the other allies were excluded. All the NATO cabinet ministers then gave their stamp of approval at the Brussels meeting in December 1979. But, as a 1981 report[1] to the United States Congress pointed out, this hard-won consensus 'was restricted to the level of government officials and did not extend to parliamentary and public opinion.' And so, 'the consensus that had been carefully developed at the official level was seriously threatened by domestic political reaction in several countries.'

The actual motives behind the decision partook of different logics that did not always mesh. The oldest and coldest were purely technological: cruise and Pershing–2 were products of improved industrial capabilities under development for a decade and looking for military markets. The organizational logic of the Alliance itself was calling for the symbolic boost of modern weapons and renewed American commitment. And certain European leaders were concerned that Soviet–American strategic arms control had done nothing to diminish the weight of Soviet forces in Europe — that, on the contrary, it had given them free rein while limiting America's strategic retaliatory capacity. These technological and military motives were dominant among NATO experts who developed the details of LRTNF modernization.

At the top decision-making level, more general political considerations undoubtedly came into play. There was the German desire, embodied by Chancellor Schmidt, to play an international political role more in proportion to the Federal Republic's economic strength. There was the American desire to make the Europeans pay more of the price — both economic and political — for the world-wide defence of the capitalist system from which they (and especially the Germans) had been deriving a growing share of the profits. The compromise and clash between these two motives had provided most of the intra-Alliance drama in the Euromissiles controversy.

Once the decision was taken, it had to be sold to the peoples of Western Europe by more simple arguments than those of either the experts or the political leaders. The simplest was that the Soviet Union was threatening Western Europe with a dangerous new nuclear missile, the SS-20, which had to be 'balanced' by deployment of comparable weapons on the NATO side. Such arguments were rejected and refuted, on both technical and moral grounds, by a growing peace movement with its own body of experts.

Insofar as the NATO modernization was intended to restore and strengthen the unity of the Atlantic Alliance, it was a signal failure. In all the countries directly concerned, massive popular protests were registered not only against the nuclear arms race, but also against the undemocratic way in which the decision had been taken and against the growing assertion of military methods and priorities. Yet deployment has been pushed through, and has appeared more and more clearly as the opening wedge for a new electronic armada that will adapt NATO strategy to the dangerous offensive posture of 'Air Land Battle', as outlined in the August 1981 US Army Field Manual.

The main effect of the decision was to allow the United States to deploy 572 new nuclear missiles in five NATO countries. The US Air Force would install 464 'Tomahawk' ground-launched cruise missiles (GLCMs) in the Federal Republic of Germany, the United Kingdom, Italy, Belgium and the Netherlands. (The cruise is a sort of electronically navigated low-flying pilotless aircraft, whose computerized terrain-reading devices theoretically enable it to zigzag through enemy defences and even to switch targets on its way.) In addition, the US Army would deploy 108 Pershing–2 missiles in Germany, on launching sites originally built for the Pershing–1 missile which had been deployed since 1962.

Because the new Pershings would replace old Pershings, and because a thousand old US nuclear warheads were to be 'withdrawn from Europe as soon as feasible', NATO ministers insisted that the modernization programme would not increase NATO's reliance on nuclear weapons. However, the significant point about the new 'Euromissiles' was not their number but their range and capacity. The strengthening was not quantitative but qualitative. Unlike the weapons they were supposedly replacing, they could strike targets within the Soviet Union itself, and with much greater accuracy than the sea-based French, British or US missiles assigned to NATO. They also had a much better chance of penetrating Soviet air defences than the Europe-based bombers of the US Strategic Air Command — the so-called 'forward-based systems'.

There was a precedent. In 1957 NATO decided to deploy sixty Thor missiles in England and forty-five Jupiter missiles in Italy and Turkey, to strengthen deterrence and reassure allies worried by the new Soviet SS–4 and SS–5 missiles. In those days, the German Social Democrats were at the forefront of the movement to keep nuclear weapons out of Germany (a movement that failed utterly to prevent the stationing of thousands of short-range 'tactical' nuclear weapons), and in fact those first Western intermediate-range ballistic missiles were not stationed in West Germany, although, as we shall see, the US secretly installed some intermediate-range cruise missiles there throughout the sixties. In 1961, in *Defence and Retaliation,* Helmut Schmidt wrote that the deployment of enemy ballistic missiles on its very threshold must be a psychological 'provocation' to a great power. 'One need only imagine how the Americans would react if the Soviets were to station intermediate-range ballistic missiles in Cuba,' Schmidt wrote.

The very next year, one no longer needed to imagine: a demonstration was provided by the Cuban missile crisis. Europeans firmly believe that this dangerous confrontation, provoked by Soviet moves to instal missiles in Cuba, stimulated the official American imagination and led the United States, in a more or less tacit deal with Moscow, to phase out, in 1963, the Jupiters that had first been deployed in Turkey in 1959. After the failure of the 1963 American proposal to create a 'multilateral force' of sea-based nuclear missiles involving West Germany, it was argued that the Soviet missile threat to Western Europe could be adequately countered by NATO's Polaris submarines, and, more recently, by the five United States Poseidon submarines assigned to NATO, each with sixteen ten-warheaded missiles (eight hundred nuclear warheads).

Why, after twenty years, return to the idea of targeting Soviet territory with American missiles stationed on European soil? The hostile Soviet reaction, the domestic controversy — especially in Germany — were absolutely predictable. What were the political, military or strategic advantages justifying such a controversial decision?

The conflicting answers provided have only enlarged the question. NATO's simple official reason, 'to restore nuclear theatre balance', suffers from three visible weaknesses. First, the very concept of 'nuclear theatre balance' turns out to be very much less simple than it first appears, and its credibility as a motive for the Brussels decision cannot survive a careful study of the expert literature on the question. Secondly, if it is accepted that Soviet armaments in general, and the SS-20s in particular, pose a problem for Western Europe, the American cruise and Pershing-2 missiles do not in any way constitute a logical response or solution to the problem, but rather a sort of dangerous non sequitur. As a military deterrent, invulnerable sea-based forces would obviously make more sense than systems placed in heavily populated areas where they could draw enemy fire. Thirdly, NATO justifications have been increasingly overshadowed by the new American strategic doctrine, which has incorporated the Euro-missiles into a global US posture having little to do with the defence of Europe from a hypothetical Soviet invasion.

The political explanations are as uncertain as the military ones. NATO leaders have indeed 'shown their resolve' by going ahead with deployment in the face of massive protest. But to what end, precisely? The bitterness of the controversy has certainly not 'strengthened the Alliance', in the promised sense of closing ranks between Western Europe and the United States. On the contrary. But as the dust clears, a new factor is becoming visible: nuclear weapons capable of striking Soviet territory are being stationed on West German territory, and the Soviet Union has apparently been able to do nothing about it. A taboo has been lifted.

Was this foreseen? Was it a major political purpose from the start? For four years, there was little scrutiny of political purposes that might be hidden behind the proclaimed goal of 'getting the Russians to negotiate' — a task far less arduous, in reality, than getting the

Russians to accept long-range nuclear weapons in Germany.

'Double track' or double talk?

In their communiqué of 12 December 1979, NATO ministers had concluded that the overall interest of the Alliance would best be served 'by pursuing two parallel and complementary approaches of TNF (theatre nuclear forces) and arms control'. NATO asked the United States to deploy new nuclear missiles, and at the same time to hold talks with the Soviet Union in order to reach a more 'stable' military balance and to 'avert an arms race in Europe'. Because of this two-pronged approach — missile deployment and arms control talks — the December 1979 decision is called the 'double track', decision. However, real relationship between those two 'tracks' was ambiguous from the start. In the minds of NATO military planners, the arms control track was to a large extent merely the sugar coating to get European politicians to swallow the arms modernization pill.

The trouble started with the second round of Strategic Arms Limitation Talks (SALT II) between the USA and the USSR, begun under the Nixon administration in 1972 and wound up after Carter in 1979. SALT II aroused strong political opposition, which eventually succeeded in blocking US Senate ratification of the proposed treaty. Not the least of this opposition came from the lobby of enthusiasts for the new electronic cruise missile, which they saw as a relatively cheap (about one million dollars per vehicle[2]) and all-purpose answer to almost every Western military problem and which, they feared, was being foolishly sacrificed in order to reach an agreement with the Russians. In particular, cruise fans worried that a SALT II agreement might block cruise 'technology export' — that is, sales to America's European allies.

If it is defined by its distinctive means of locomotion — that is, jet propulsion — the cruise missile has been around for a long time. Its ancestor was the German buzz bomb (V-I) of the Second World War. Later, both the Americans and the Russians developed a series of models, but they were overshadowed by the faster, more accurate and much more powerful rocket-propelled missiles. However, unknown to the public, the United States maintained about 150 Matador and Mace cruise missiles in West Germany throughout the sixties. Over ninety of these were Mace missiles, whose range of a thousand miles put them within striking distance of Soviet territory. Although the Thor and Jupiter ballistic missiles were phased out of Britain, Italy and Turkey in 1963, the cruise missiles were kept on secretly in West Germany until 1969.[3] (Willy Brandt has said that it was only in 1972 that he obtained the right to be informed about what the United States was putting on German soil.)

Shortly afterwards, a new generation of much smaller cruise missiles was developed. 'The fact that cruise missiles are not covered in SALT-I motivated their development,' wrote one expert.[4] 'The major technical factor which gives the cruise missile an edge over rocket-powered missiles is that, since it breathes air, it does not have to carry an oxidizer and therefore has substantially longer range than a rocket-powered missile of equal weight.' Miniaturization was already being achieved by 1970. Since the light, slow but long-winded cruise can easily be blown far off its programmed path, a number of ultra-sophisticated electronic guidance systems have been developed to assure in-flight course correction. This is the really interesting part of the cruise boom, as it channels vast sums in research and development funds into the newest technologies. In 1977, the Pentagon estimated that a thousand million dollars had been spent in research, development, testing and evaluation for the long-range cruise missile (LRCM).

On 22 June 1979, after seven years of negotiation, President Carter submitted the SALT-II treaty to the Senate for ratification. The next day, at the Senate Armed Services Committee, Republican Senator John Tower of Texas set the tone in an opening blast against recent Carter administration decisions: the cancellation of the B-2 bomber, the halting of Minuteman missile production, and the delays in neutron-bomb, Trident, cruise and MX development were all denounced as 'unilateral arms control'. Senator Tower raised what he called a fundamental question: 'Does the treaty allow the United States sufficient latitude to make timely transfer of cruise missile technology to our NATO allies?'

The answer was not entirely clear-cut. Limitation of cruise technology was a major Soviet demand. Chief negotiator Paul Warnke has often said that without it, no agreement was possible. However, cruise was left out of the main SALT-II agreement, scheduled to run until 31 December 1985. It was mentioned in a protocol valid only until 31 December 1981, which banned in-flight tests of mobile intercontinental missiles, in-flight tests and deployment of air-launched ballistic missiles with a range of over 600 kms, as well as deployment of land- or sea-based cruise missiles with a range of over 600 kms. This was such a slight obstacle that even without ratification, the Reagan administration could claim to observe SALT-II and still go ahead with

its missile programme. But in the long run, cruise missile development was incompatible with the whole arms control process. The
trouble with cruise missiles was that they were not verifiable by the
'national' methods — satellites — used so far. Any other form of
effective verification of cruise was also hard to imagine.

Cruise missiles could carry either nuclear or conventional
warheads — a factor which, while adding to arms control problems,
was a main selling point for the Europeans. European NATO experts
were taken with the idea that cruise technology could achieve the
military effectiveness of nuclear weapons without their political draw-
backs. Thus the cruise missile, to a certain extent, paradoxically
pitted arms control against the desire to reduce reliance on nuclear
weapons.

Enthusiasm for cruise was propagated from America to Europe
through elite defence intellectual haunts such as the International
Institute for Strategic Studies in London and think-tank veteran
Albert Wohlstetter's less known but highly influential European-
American Workshop.[5] The suspicion that they were perhaps being
deprived of the wonder weapon of the eighties naturally whetted
European interest in the cruise.

General European distrust of the US–Soviet tête-à-tête was ex-
acerbated by the widespread impression that the Carter presidency
was incompetent and ineffectual. Helmut Schmidt had a particularly
low opinion of Carter. As Brandt's defence minister, Schmidt had
taken special interest in NATO nuclear policy, reportedly expressing
concern over a defence based on tactical nuclear weapons that would
be exploded on the territory of the Federal Republic of Germany
itself.[6] Finally, in his long speech of 28 October 1977 to the International Institute for Strategic Studies, he publicly voiced his concern
that Carter's SALT negotiators were not paying sufficient attention to
European interests. But although that speech later became famous as
a sort of Paul Revere's ride, which aroused slumbering Europe to the
growing Soviet missile threat, Schmidt did not once mention the
Soviet SS-20s, nor call for any new American missiles to build up
Western forces. On the contrary, his point in criticizing SALT was to
demand comparable efforts to reduce and balance conventional
forces in Europe. 'SALT codifies the nuclear strategic balance between
the Soviet Union and the United States,' Schmidt said. 'To put it
another way: SALT neutralizes their strategic nuclear capabilities. In
Europe this magnifies the significance of the disparities between East
and West in nuclear tactical and conventional weapons.' He concluded that 'we must press ahead with the Vienna negotiations on

mutual balanced force reductions (MBFR) as an important step towards a better balance of military power in Europe.'

For Schmidt, fulfilment of the 'principle of parity' had to be 'the aim of all arms-limitation and arms-control negotiations' with respect to 'all categories of weapons'. This was later interpreted as a call for 'parity' in the special category (unmentioned by Schmidt) of land-based intermediate-range nuclear missiles in the European theatre. However, such an interpretation is either very subtle or distorted. In the context of the speech itself, the 'categories' seem clearly to be the more simple ones of nuclear and conventional weapons. Schmidt recalled that at the Western summit in London the previous May he had said that 'the more we stabilize nuclear parity betwen East and West . . . the greater will be the necessity to achieve a conventional equilibrium as well.' He stressed the need for Europeans 'to recognize clearly the connection between SALT and MBFR . . . ' Schmidt's complaint about the Russians also seemed intended to prod them toward progress at the Vienna talks. 'Up to now the Soviet Union has given no clear indication that she is willing to accept the principle of parity for Europe, as she did for SALT, and thus make the principle of renunciation of force an element of the military balance as well.'

All these remarks on military matters were, in fact, a digression from the main subject of Schmidt's speech: the 'new dimensions of security'. Schmidt's point was that economic 'dimensions', such as full employment, adequate investment in the Third World and East–West trade, were as important to 'security' as the purely military dimensions. It could be ironic, or it could be a brutal assertion of power, that out of this speech American leaders chose to hear only a call for more hardware.

Although Schmidt did not mention the SS-20, the new Soviet missile targeted on Europe was the perfect concrete example of the limitations of arms limitations. It owed its very existence to SALT. To the Americans and Russians, 'strategic' weapons meant weapons that could strike the United States or the Soviet Union. Other kinds were left out of the SALT process. The Soviet Union had developed a mobile intercontinental-range missile system, called the SS-16 in the Western arms nomenclature. American SALT negotiators feared verification would be difficult and asked the Soviets to get rid of it. The Russians obliged and transformed it from a three-stage intercontinental missile into a two-stage intermediate-range missile. The SS-20 was born. In its new form it was no longer covered by SALT. It came in handy to the Soviet military as a deterrent on the Chinese front, and as a replacement on the Western front for the twenty-year-old SS-4 and SS-5s, considered obsolete and even dangerous to their surroundings by arms experts.

It is simply not true that Schmidt alerted the West to the Soviet SS-20 threat, whereupon NATO came to the rescue with new Euromissiles.

First, it was not Germans but Americans who first raised a hue and cry about the SS-20. Or to be precise, it was Swiss-born Fred Ikle, a veteran cold warrior of the strategic consultancy circuit, who as President Gerald Ford's Arms Control and Disarmament Agency Director in September 1976 drew NATO attention to the SS-20 in a semi-private speech. 'The spectre of such weapons grows like a towering cloud over Europe and Asia,' said Ikle. 'Why are they adding to this arsenal? What, must we ask with deep concern, is the possible political purpose?' This first cry of alarm introduced an idea that would be often repeated by champions of the NATO modernization: that the SS-20 buildup was not to be explained by the usual military logic of the arms race, but had some dark 'political purpose'. That presumed political purpose later came to be identified as 'nuclear blackmail', a capacity to bring political pressure on Western Europe that would result in its 'Finlandization'.

Second, the NATO modernization process was already underway when Schmidt made his speech.

The cruise lobby had been busy. Its most active champion was Richard Burt, then an assistant to the director of the International Institute of Strategic Studies and later a key figure in the Reagan administration's international security policy. In early 1976, Burt called attention to the many potential uses of the cruise missile, such as replacing aircraft on vulnerable deep-strike missions through increasingly effective anti-aircraft defences. Sea-based, it might supplant the need for aircraft carriers: land-based, it might do the job now assigned to tactical nuclear weapons.

The main *bête noire* of the cruise lobby was chief SALT negotiator Paul Warnke, apparently willing to sacrifice this technological marvel to arms control. Burt helped rally European NATO support to save the cruise from Warnke. In a pioneer article on 'The SS-20 and the Strategic Balance' (in *The World Today*, January–February 1977), he warned that the 'most interesting military option available to the West for countering the expansion of Soviet Euro-strategic capabilities is already under discussion at SALT — the long-range precision-guided cruise missile. In deciding whether to exploit cruise missile technology in this manner, the United States must therefore once again choose between placing priorities on strengthening the alliance ties and quickly obtaining a SALT agreement.' Burt further developed this idea in a *Foreign Affairs* article in the summer of 1978: 'Over time, many Europeans may conclude that the United States — in order to reach an agreement — has mortgaged systems that are most likely to serve Western rather than American interests.'

It was not yet clear whether or when cruise missiles would work as claimed, or how much they would cost. But European defence establishments were largely convinced that the technology was indispensable and did not want to see it snatched from them by selfish superpowers bargaining over their heads at SALT. 'In this sense, cruise missile application in the theatre nuclear role provided the most politically visible and immediately justifiable rationale for their exclusion from negotiating constraints and became the means for safeguarding the technology for future application.'[7]

The Pershing-2 had a long, separate history, which has been recounted in various public and private papers by Christopher Paine. In this case technological innovation and aggressive industrial marketing seem to have taken the lead, pulling along military planners and strategists and finally presenting political authorities with the *fait accompli* of the first nuclear weapon clearly designed not to wreak havoc but to make a 'surgical strike'. As with the cruise, research and development date back to the late 1960s, when the frustrations of counter-insurgency in Vietnam fuelled the aspiration towards a clean and distant 'electronic battlefield'. It was in 1969 that the Orlando division of Martin Marietta, which had been manufacturing Pershing-1 and Pershing-1A missiles for the US Army, proposed an improved version that would constitute the first precision-guided re-entry vehicle. Martin Marietta offered to build an original radar guidance system (RADAG) and later, in 1971, took up an Army suggestion to develop precision earth-penetrator warheads for selective use against hardened targets.

Five years after the programme began, the Pershing-2 appeared in the February 1975 Army budget and Congress began to ask questions. The project was defended at congressional budget hearings by Army Secretary for Research and Development Norman R. Agustine, who later went on to become a vice president of Martin Marietta for technical operations.

Later it was claimed that the United States in the mid seventies, paralysed by its 'Vietnam syndrome', had unilaterally stopped arming while the Soviets forged ahead. In reality, the cruise and Pershing-2 programmes advanced during these years, before the appearance of the SS-20s and protected by powerful lobbies. Early in his allegedly pacifistic presidency, at the May 1977 NATO summit, Jimmy Carter called for increased allied defence efforts, including theatre nuclear forces modernization. A long-term defence programme (LTDP) was to be worked out. For the modernization of theatre nuclear forces, NATO's Nuclear Planning Group, at its October 1977 meeting in Bari, Italy, set up a High Level Group (HLG) composed of senior defence ministry officials from eleven member states and chaired by US Assistant Secretary of Defense for International Security Affairs David McGiffert. The HLG had no staff of its own and depended in fact on Pentagon staff work. The strategic concepts and the weapons it finally adopted naturally came from the Pentagon.

What exactly was the European, and more precisely, the German input into nuclear planning? This is hard to determine because, faced with the unpopularity of the missile development, Germans and Americans each tend to blame the other. This tendency already began to emerge in the 'neutron bomb' episode of 1977, which by all accounts contributed to the mood of intransigence in NATO leadership circles when it came to ramming through the 'double decision'.

NATO's Nuclear Planning Group had been given a major briefing on the development of enhanced radiation (neutron) warheads by the American Defense Secretary Donald Rumsfield in January 1976,[8] a year before Carter took office. The public first learned of the 'neutron bomb' when the *Washington Post* of 4 June 1977 reported on a Pentagon appropriations request for the new warheads. News of the weapon that supposedly killed people but spared real estate roused movements of protest throughout NATO countries. Opposition was strong in Schmidt's own Social Democratic Party (SPD), and the SPD's Ostpolitik specialist, Egon Bahr, called the neutron bomb 'a symbol of the perversion of thought'.

Despite, or because of, the uproar Jimmy Carter was intent on getting his allies, and especially the Germans, to ask publicly for the neutron bomb. If the allies wanted a greater say in nuclear policy planning, then they should show readiness to take public responsibility. This unusual attitude evidently fitted Carter's general post-Vietnam policy of furnishing the United States with a clearer image more geared to human rights, and of giving NATO allies only the weapons for which they asked.

It is not clear whether Schmidt himself ever really wanted the neutron bomb, but some of his army officers did, and he backed them up. This was explained by Theo Sommer, editor of *Die Zeit*, in July

1977: 'Under various headings (death rays, 'mini-nukes'), the neutron bomb has been under continual discussion in the Nuclear Planning Group since 1973, with Bundeswehr representatives showing a positive attitude. Understandably, for they are permanently haunted by the thought that, in the event of hostilities, the Soviets might make a bold thrust towards an industrial area (the Ruhr, for example) where the use of tactical weapons would entail destruction of the defenders' own territory and plant.'

Bonn was puzzled by Carter's attitude. With over five thousand nuclear warheads already lying around in West Germany, why suddenly insist on making a big public fuss about a few more? Schmidt disliked Carter from the start, and, according to Ulrich Albrecht, now suspected him of deliberately trying to land him in bad political trouble. 'What the devil could Carter have up his sleeve, with his crazy request for public approval of this strange weapon, other than to put the Chancellor in an impossible position with the left wing of the SPD?'[9] Nor would a public request for the neutron bomb do much to help Schmidt's relations with the Soviet Union and East Germany. Nevertheless, he publicly gave his lukewarm endorsement. 'Until we see real progress on MBFR, we shall have to rely on the effectiveness of deterrence,' he said in his October 1977 London speech. 'It is in this context and no other that the public discussion in all member states of the Western Alliance about the "neutron weapon" has to be seen.' The allies had to consider not only its value 'as an additional element of the deterrence strategy' but also its relevance and weight 'in our efforts to achieve arms control'.

Five months later, after luring his allies into public (though qualified) support for the neutron bomb, Carter suspended the project. Schmidt was furious. From then on he filled his background briefings to American journalists with complaints about Carter's inability to understand European problems.[10] Schmidt's fury against Carter's indecisiveness eventually helped set the stage for Reagan. Did Europeans want 'strong leadership'? They would get it. And they'd better like it. By the end of the seventies, Schmidt had used up their complaint quota.

The legacy of the neutron bomb provided a final political rationale for the NATO LRTNF modernization decision. 'In the opinion of some observers,' wrote Dutch Labour MP Klaas de Vries at the time, 'the "neutron bomb" episode constitutes a self-inflicted wound which the Alliance has yet to heal.' Thus the LRTNF modernization decision is regarded 'as an opportunity to demonstrate the Alliance's ability to cope with the demands of coalition decision-making. In its most

extreme form, this perspective holds that whatever military programme is eventually decided upon will, in the long run, be less
important than the fact that the Alliance can decide.'[11]

Schmidt recounted later[12] that in 1977 he had strongly admonished
the Carter administration not to overlook the SS-20s in SALT-II, but
Carter and Warnke had replied that there was nothing to worry
about, since Soviet intermediate-range missiles were held in check by
the American intercontinental strategic capacity. 'But I told them
then,' Schmidt recalled, 'you will never issue an intercontinental
strategic military counter-threat just to ward off a medium-range
threat aimed at Germany.'

Getting no satisfaction from the Carter administration, Schmidt in
his October 1977 London speech 'called attention only to the
problem, not to any solutions'. These were supplied by Carter when,
to the SPD Premier's 'relative surprise', he invited Schmidt, Callaghan
and Giscard d'Estaing to Guadeloupe in January 1979 to tell them
that the SS-20 was indeed becoming a problem, and that the United
States should station new weapons in Western Europe to counter it.
Callaghan thought there should first be negotiations with the
Russians. Giscard said the Russians would negotiate seriously once
they knew that new missiles would otherwise be deployed. Schmidt
recalls agreeing to all this. But was it clear to the leaders in Guadeloupe precisely what they had agreed to?

Meanwhile the High Level Group was working out the details. Its
major new proposal was that the modernized NATO systems should
have sufficient range to strike targets in the Soviet Union. This was
justified by a supposed need to 'fill a gap in the escalation spectrum'
between short-range tactical nuclear weapons and strategic intercontinental missiles.

As late as February 1978, the chief of the Pershing-2 project, Army
Colonel Larry Hunt, told Senators that a conscious decision had been
made not to increase the range of the new missile beyond the 400 mile
(700km) range of the old Pershing-1, precisely in order to avoid the
'political implications' of a system that could strike Soviet territory.
However, during the NATO debate in autumn 1979, NATO officials
attributed a range of 1,800 kms to the Pershing-2, putting it within
striking distance of such western Soviet cities as Leningrad and Kiev.
The Pershing-2 had grown into a new missile, with not only a
precision-guided re-entry vehicle but also new first and second stage
rockets. Its range has continued to increase. Christopher Paine
learned from European aerospace industry sources that the United
States had informed NATO leaders of a new version of the Pershing-2,

with a range of 4,000 kms, that would probably be developed if the Geneva arms control talks broke down.

The High Level Group insisted that a highly visible land-based system would enhance the credibility of the new missiles, and that a mixture of cruise and Pershing-2 would increase its effectiveness by confusing Soviet defences. Such a mix would also allow the two rival branches, Air Force and Army, to have a piece of the action — no insignificant detail in Pentagon politics. In pushing through the American position, McGiffert was strongly supported by Norwegian Under-Secretary of Defence Johan Holst, a devoted habitué of Wohlstetter's European-American Workshop and the International Institute for Strategic Studies.[13]

The responsibility and reasoning behind the increase in Pershing's range has been the most mysterious and controversial part of the NATO modernization decision. Some Germans have suggested it was an American idea, and some Americans have suggested it was a German idea. But the real question behind the 'Who?' is 'Why?', as the realization has grown that American reasons and German reasons were not the same. In simple terms, the Germans had a vital interest in preventing nuclear war on their territory, whereas the Pentagon was increasingly interested in improving its means to wage nuclear war against the Soviet Union. These cross purposes had to be concealed from Western public opinion and the Russians by a great show of NATO 'resolve'.

While the High Level Group was working up its missile brew, the political pitfalls began to dawn on some NATO officials. Such a major escalation in the arms race could not just be sprung on Europeans accustomed to détente. In particular, the social democrats in various NATO government coalitions would raise strong objections and demand that, if indeed there was a 'gap' somewhere, it should be closed downwards through negotiations rather than upwards through new missile deployments that the Soviet Union would certainly regard as aggressively provocative. 'Public and parliamentary support for modernization could only be assured if the alliance demonstrated a willingness to close the gap through arms control negotiations. It was important to underline the continued commitment of the alliance to the twin objectives of defence and détente. In addition, alliance officials perceived that it would not be in NATO's interest to engage in an unrestrained arms race with the Soviet Union in theatre systems.'[14]

Thus in April 1979, when the High Level Group's work was already far advanced, NATO set up a Special Group (SG) to second it by developing a compatible approach to arms control. The SG guidelines, which were not published, put modernization ahead of negotiation. An eventual arms control agreement was evidently conceived as a way of regularizing and stabilizing the new situation created by introduction of Pershing-2 and cruise missiles.

It was the joint report of these two groups, the HLG and the SG, that formed the basis of the NATO ministers' 'double track' decision in Brussels on 12 December 1979. From the start, the arms control component was highly ambiguous and tainted by ulterior motives. In its December 1981 Interim Report, the North Atlantic Assembly's Special Committee on Nuclear Weapons in Europe noted: 'At the public level, the ambiguity of the precise objectives of the NATO decision has led to a degree of misunderstanding. The integral relationship between modernization and arms control has not been clearly understood. In some countries, the emphasis on arms control may have created the impression that negotiations can solve the problem of deployments.'

If there was, indeed, confusion on 'the public level', it had been deliberately created by defenders of the double track decision. The most simple justification, echoed by the media, was that the NATO modernization was necessary to correct an 'imbalance' created by the recent Soviet arms buildup, especially SS-20 deployment. The Pershing and cruise missiles would enable NATO to catch up with the Russians, or at least force them to negotiate. If an excess of Russian missiles was really at the heart of the Euromissile problem, this could surely be worked out in arms control talks.

Strategic Reasoning

The notion of a Russian threat to Europe, of balance or imbalance in the European theatre, belongs to the primary level of NATO reasoning, which is not necessarily the most operative.

NATO was founded in 1949 as a formal structuring of the American protectorate of Western Europe that emerged from the Second World War. On the most ostensible level, it was intended to defend the Western European member states from military aggression by the USSR. A few years later, the Soviet Union organized the Eastern European buffer states into a parallel protectorate of its own, formalized by the 1955 Warsaw Pact. The official *raison d'être* of each of these military blocs was to defend itself from the other. Fortunately for Europe, this was never necessary. The division symbolized by the

Yalta conference was tenaciously clung to by the Soviet Union, and grudgingly accepted by the United States. The actual wars were in Asia: the unfinished partisan wars in China, Korea and Vietnam.

In Europe, the real danger felt on both sides was to the inner stability of the post-war social order, or orders, in East and West. The alliances helped to assure the internal coherence of the two rival protectorates. This does not imply that the two had much else in common. With the help of Marshall Plan funds, it is obvious that the American protectorate was willingly, even eagerly, accepted by a majority of people in Western Europe — which was hardly the case with the Soviet protectorate in the Eastern buffer states. The Warsaw Pact and the theoretical danger of 'German revanchism' helped to justify Soviet military occupation of Eastern Europe. But even in the West, the designation of the external totalitarian enemy was useful in isolating and weakening Communist Parties in the countries where they were strong — Italy and France — and more generally in holding the Left and the labour movement to a defensive, circumspect posture during the period of postwar economic recovery.

Another essential purpose of NATO and the American protectorate was to establish a stable system of mediation among the Western European powers — especially between France and Germany, whose rivalry had triggered both world wars of the twentieth century. NATO was a way of maintaining the division of Germany, of allowing West Germany to arm, but not too much, and keeping it tied to the West. It was a way of preventing new arms races between the Western capitalist powers, since NATO provided a forum for the allocation of military tasks and resources, with the United States as final arbiter.

Last but not least, NATO kept available for conflict in the Third World the basic pool of European and North American military strength: it facilitated American support to the French war in Indochina before the United States took over the job; and it helped Portugal to retain its colonies — South Africa's buffer zone — until the mid-seventies. The great novelty of the Reagan administration has been to insist on giving official recognition, and even top priority, to this dimension that used to be virtually unmentionable.

The internal and North–South dimensions have arguably been the most operative, year in and year out. However, the formulation of NATO policy and NATO strategy has habitually been conducted in terms of East–West relations, with the Russian threat to Europe as the permanent basic assumption. At first everything was perfectly simple: the United States had the absolute weapon, the atom bomb; and anyone who laid a finger on America's allies would be blasted to smithereens. Although the security provided by their 'nuclear umbrella' was soon undermined by the Soviet bomb and missiles technology, the underlying mentality remained for a very long time in the popular consciousness. It is probable that until about 1980, most people in Western Europe more or less vaguely assumed that the Russians were held at bay by the threat of what used to be called 'massive retaliation' back in the 1950s. Only the Euromissile crisis has brought to public attention the evolution of American nuclear strategy over the past twenty years.

Of course, Sputnik, and then the Kennedy–Khrushchev crises over Berlin and Cuba, had a considerable public impact, but the strategic consequences have only recently become a matter of general knowledge. In that period, American leaders got scared. To a large degree, they scared themselves by their imaginings, but the fright had lasting effects.

First there was the famous 'missile gap', denounced by Senator John Kennedy in the late Eisenhower years on the basis of post-Sputnik military intelligence estimates projecting a force of from five hundred to one thousand Soviet intercontinental ballistic missiles by the start of the sixties. After Kennedy was elected President, his men rushed to scan fresh spy-satellite photos for visible proof of the dread Soviet ICBM armada. They looked and looked and finally found, not one thousand, not five hundred, not even fifty, but precisely four. There was no haste to relieve public anxiety by publishing this figure, although Defense Secretary Robert McNamara let slip that there was no missile gap. But he gave out no embarrassing details.[15]

The real missile gap of the period was heavily in America's favour, and Kennedy administration officials knew it when the famous 1961 Berlin crisis reached its peak. Khrushchev had long been pressing for a stable settlement of the status of the two Germanies and Berlin. If the West refused to negotiate, the USSR would make its own settlement, he warned. With tunnel vision, American officials chose to interpret this pressure solely as a threat to US occupation rights in West Berlin. White House memoirs concur in their description of the peculiar psychological atmosphere of that crisis. Kennedy, and apparently his closest team, seem to have experienced the whole episode in an extraordinarily subjective manner, as a personal challenge from Khrushchev to the young American President. Seen in this light, Kennedy came through with flying colours as usual, standing fast and not losing his nerve. The crisis came and went, and West Berlin was still part of the free world. Yes, but it was surrounded by an ugly wall. Had the Americans seen this coming? Had they done anything to prevent it? Had they (as many Germans believe) tacitly or explicitly given their consent? If so, no written evidence has come to light. Indeed, accounts of the crisis indicate that the top American leadership was so absorbed in the possible military aspects of the confrontation that they ignored the political heart of the problem. In public, at least, there was little American recognition that Khrushchev had a more down-to-earth aim: namely, to stop the drain of skilled labour that was undermining Communist East Germany.

Berlin is the only spot along the East–West frontier whose status is disputed, the only place where a traditional territorial war might break out. The West Berlin enclave could not be successfully defended in case of serious attack, and through much of 1961 American leaders wrestled with the problem of how to use the threat of retaliation to defend Berlin. By this time, it was known that the 'missile gap' was a false alarm and that the United States had a clear nuclear superiority over the USSR.[16] First Dean Acheson and then Paul Nitze worked on contingency plans, the latter devising a stage-by-stage escalation to full-scale nuclear war in case the Russians should block the Autobahn access to Berlin. The experience brought out some of the inherent difficulties in the threat of nuclear retaliation, which is so drastic that it may not be believed until it is too late. Nitze's contingency plan therefore included a nuclear warning shot along the way, to show serious intent. This was in fact 'flexible response', which during the sixties replaced 'massive retaliation' as United States and eventually NATO doctrine.

By this time, the Russians had nuclear missiles able to strike Western Europe, and they soon followed the USA in building enough ICBMs to obliterate everything. All this time the United States was still officially planning to respond to non-nuclear Soviet aggression with a nuclear attack, just as in the early days of American monopoly of the atom bomb. This no longer made much sense, but American leaders could not bring themselves to give up the absolute power seemingly conferred by mastery of nuclear weapons. At this point, the job of the nuclear strategists was to preserve this power, or the illusion of this power, by devising theoretical ways in which it might be used.

Of course, everyone preferred to use it without actually *using* it. The idea was to convey a credible threat. But the more one thought about it, the less credible it was that the United States would actually opt for 'mutual assured destruction', in the form of a full-scale nuclear exchange with the USSR, for the sake of some piece of European real estate. The French, not prone to undue sentimentality about the generosity of others' intentions, were first to reach this conclusion and act on it, when De Gaulle chose to equip France with its own nuclear *parapluie*. But this was all very theoretical. There was no serious risk of war in Europe once the Berlin crisis was past, and the American doctrinal incoherence on nuclear strategy did not seem to matter. Political attention shifted to conflicts in the Third World, and the whole problem of nuclear weapons faded from public consciousness in the sixties.

In their think tanks, however, the nuclear strategists continued to play war. Simply knocking all the pieces off the board does not make much of a game, so they did not play 'mutual assured destruction' but rather, 'flexible response', to see how it might go. Elaborate war games, with Blue (the United States) against Red (the Russkies), were the rage in the American defence community in the fifties and sixties and tended to shape conceptions of a war, which fortunately was only imaginary, and an enemy who was perhaps real but alien and secretive. The nuclear strategists preferred to play war with the imaginary enemy of the war games.

The Imaginary Enemy

A war game has certain characteristics which distinguish it from a real war:

—it follows an orderly sequence: time between alternate moves allows for reflection;

—both sides play the same game: they agree to the rules and communicate in a common language;

—each side is exclusively motivated by the desire to win;

—it is, after all, only a game.

The development of 'game theory' reinforced 'worst case' assumptions about the adversary. The essence of game theory, explains Fred Kaplan, is to 'find out your opponent's best strategy and act accordingly.' You assume your opponent will do his worst, then you work out by sophisticated calculations what this worst will be and act accordingly. Conservative and pessimistic, 'game theory' was 'the perfect intellectual rationale for the Cold War, the vehicle through which many intellectuals bought on to its assumptions.'[17]

This pessimism has its consolations for those absorbed in the exercise of power. The enemy who always does his worst is theoretically *calculable*, and therefore can eventually be manipulated and controlled. Game theory totally excludes and replaces the real world of human motivations with an abstract construct. It eliminates politics altogether. Instead there are statistical probabilities. It creates a perfect surrogate enemy, always absolutely hostile. It spares America's strategists (many of whom, incidentally, are anti-communist Eastern Europeans) from actually having to think about the real enemy and how it might be possible to get along with him.

The game theory hothouse, where every little movement has a meaning all its own, has helped to keep 'flexible response' as official NATO doctrine to this day. Flexible response has been summarized as follows: 'We will fight with conventional forces until we are losing, then we will fight with tactical weapons until we are losing, and then we will blow up the world.'[18] Obviously the final outcome leaves much to be desired. The trick is to control the sequence so that it stops somewhere along the way, while you are ahead. Or more precisely, since *deterrence* is still the objective, you must so obviously control every stage of the escalation sequence that the adversary, seeing the way the game would go, decides not to play.

It is this type of thinking that produced such concepts as 'gap in the escalation spectrum', which in turn generated the demand for Pershing-2 and cruise missiles in Europe. The idea is that strategic parity between the United States and the Soviet Union, codified in SALT, has cancelled out the US strategic nuclear force except as a deterrent to protect the sanctuary of United States territory. The nuclear umbrella protecting Europe has been folded up. Tactical nuclear weapons are still there, however, in abundant supply, ensuring that any European war would rapidly become nuclear. But as it escalated, it would reach a level where the Russians, with their SS-20s, would have an edge.

The Real Enemy

The High Level Group's deliberations 'initially concerned the deficiencies of NATO's own capabilities', according to the North Atlantic Assembly's Special Committee.[19] 'However, in the public discussion, attention increasingly focused on the SS-20.' Some specialized observers think the SS-20 might be used for political intimidation in times of crisis, others doubt it. 'The over-emphasis on the SS-20 was perhaps inevitable because it is easier to discuss publicly the need for LRTNF modernization by pointing to visible Soviet capabilities than by explaining somewhat esoteric NATO doctrine. However, while understandable, this emphasis has contributed to some of the current ambiguity concerning the precise objectives of the NATO decision.'

The Special Committee noted that 'the precise relationship between arms control and modernization remains ambiguous and consequently uncertainties exist concerning the precise objectives of the NATO decision. To be precise, what degree of modernization is necessary and to what extent should this be influenced by SS-20 deployments? This uncertainty reflects different perceptions of the cause and hence its solution. Put simply, if the main cause of the gap is a deficiency in NATO's own capabilities, then modernization is necessary irrespective of Soviet deployments: but if the principal cause is SS-20 deployments, then in theory, arms control could provide the solution through reductions.'

Advocates of the NATO modernization have expressed irritation with the whole idea of the 'zero option' and the expectations it raises of abolishing both the SS-20s and the Pershing and cruise missiles. Modernization advocates would clearly rather have both than neither. The reasons for this insistence are far from crystal clear. The important 1981 report[20] to the House of Representatives concluded that 'while the military rationale, and particularly the threat of the SS-20, was used consistently to gain public support for LRTNF modernization, political and psychological factors provided the predominant criteria for the final proposal. Most officials conceded that the strictly military rationale — other than the renewal of old systems — were not convincing.' The report noted that Walter Slocombe, principal deputy assistant secretary of defence for internal security affairs, had emphasized the 'psychological aspect of deterrence'.

Confusion over the real purpose of the NATO Euromissiles has been compounded by a dawning realization that just as the NATO decision was being taken, the whole underpinning doctrine of 'flexible response' was collapsing under the weight of its own absurdity.

Nuclear Warfighting

In the American policy-making establishment, the war of doctrinal succession raged in the early eighties. On the liberal side stand the advocates of 'no first use', ready to eliminate the whole unmanageable 'escalation spectrum' of tactical and intermediary nuclear weapons in favour of conventional arms, preserving a reduced nuclear arsenal only as a deterrent against other nuclear arsenals. This school of thought led by Robert McNamara began to elaborate its views in opposition to the Reagan administration.

The initial victories in the war of doctrinal succession have thus been carried by the opposing school of nuclear warfighting, or 'nuclear use theorists', a label yielding the acronym NUTS, in contrast to the older school of 'mutual assured destruction' (MAD).²¹ Nuclear warfighting is one way to resolve the long-standing ambiguity in the 'flexible response' doctrine between deterring war and winning it. This resolution first emerged in the last year of the Carter presidency, when Presidential Directive 59, issued in the summer of 1980, explicitly endorsed a 'countervailing strategy'. In reality, operational plans for tactical nuclear weapons as well as strategic targeting had been 'counterforce' for decades — that is, aimed at destruction of the enemy's military strength. In the days of massive retaliation, the idea was to blow up everything — the civilian population of cities, the economy, military forces, the works. As aim improved, targeting could be more precise, and it seemed more professional to knock out military targets rather than random urban centres. This was the beginning of a slippage toward the notion that nuclear explosions could be used, not just as threats of dire punishment, but to win a war in the old-fashioned military sense.

Nuclear warfighting scenarios developed along the lines of war games and 'flexible response' — first you move in your conventional forces, then it's my turn and I take out your tanks with tactical nukes, then it's your move and what do you do? In game theory logic, if you know that escalation to your strategic nuclear forces would leave me with enough to destroy you, you may recognize you're beaten and quit. But suppose the opponent doesn't see it that way: suppose he is poorly informed, or stupid, or confused. Then we might just blow each other up and neither side would win or even survive. Based on such considerations, a major aspect of nuclear war planning has been to convey signals and messages to the other side, to help him play the game correctly.

The leading nuclear use theorist, Colin S. Gray, has pointed out the flaws in this system. 'Most of what has been portrayed as war-fighting strategy is nothing of the kind,' Gray wrote in a 1980 article that aroused great interest in some circles and consternation in others.²² 'Instead, it is an extension of the American theory of deterrence into war itself.' Difficulties could arise through 'inability to communicate or through Soviet disinterest in receiving and acting upon American messages.'

Gray recalled that former Defense Secretary James R. Schlesinger had adopted 'limited nuclear options (LNOs) — strikes employing anywhere from a handful to several dozen warheads' as a 'compromise between the optimists of the minimum deterrence school and the pessimists of the so-called war-fighting persuasion.' LNOs were supposed to be used if a war broke out to show that the United States meant business. 'But what happens once LNOs have been exhausted? If the Soviets retaliated after US LNOs, the United States would face the dilemma of escalating further or conciliating . . . . Deterrence may fail to be restored during the war for several reasons: the enemy may not grant, in operational practice, the concept of intrawar deterrence and simply wage the war as it is able; and command, control and communications may be degraded so rapidly that strategic decisions are precluded and both sides execute their war plans.'

Gray emphasizes the 'self-deterrence' inherent in flexible targeting that could lead to unmitigated disaster. 'No matter how well designed and articulated, targeting plans that allow an enemy to inflict in retaliation whatever damage it wishes on American society are likely to prove unusable.' Gray points out two flaws in the flexible response strategy of the seventies: first, 'the United States would be initiating a process of competitive escalation that it had no basis for assuming could be concluded on satisfactory terms.' And second, the strategy did not include any 'persuasive vision of how the application of force would promote the attainment of political objectives.'

Here lies the major novelty of the nuclear use theorists who have invested the Reagan administration: nuclear weapons are no longer limited to the *military* function of deterring aggression, but are to be used to attain *political* objectives.

Gray argues for a shift from economic and military to *political* targeting, and from 'warning shots across the bow' (as the expression goes), signals to enemy leadership, to *destruction* of that leadership. He advises US strategic planners to 'exploit Soviet fears insofar as is feasible from the Soviet perspective' and notes: 'Only recently has US nuclear targeting policy been based on careful study of the Soviet Union as a distinct political culture.' That was written in the last months of the Carter administration: since then, Pentagon planners have undoubtedly moved rapidly down the new strategic path. By the summer of 1981, Gray was able to boast that the arguments of his recent articles were 'about as close to current US official (if still substantially private) thinking as one is likely to find anywhere in the public domain.'[23]

Gray maintains that the best way to frighten Soviet leaders is to have a plausible strategy for destroying the Soviet state and surviving with 'acceptable' casualties of, say, twenty million American dead. 'The most frightening threat to the Soviet Union would be the destruction or serious impairment of its political system,' Gray wrote in conjunction with Keith Payne in the celebrated 1980 article. 'Thus, the United States should be able to destroy key leadership cadres, their means of communication, and some of the instruments of domestic control. The USSR, with its gross overcentralization of authority, should be highly vulnerable to such an attack. The Soviet Union might cease to function if its security agency, the KGB, were severely crippled. If the Moscow bureaucracy could be eliminated, damaged, or isolated, the USSR might disintegrate into anarchy . . . Judicious US targeting and weapon procurement policies might be able to deny the USSR the assurance of political survival.' There at last is a nuclear targeting strategy to warm the heart of an American President who believes, to hear him talk, that Moscow is the centre of an 'evil empire' causing all the troubles of this troubled world.

The major achievement of the new American strategists is to put *political purpose* back into war planning — nuclear war planning, that is. And here appears a second slippage, parallel to, and even more dangerous than, that from deterrence to 'flexible response' to 'counterforce': namely, the slippage from planning to stop a dangerous aggressor to thinking that after all, if we can do it, why not just go in and get rid of him once and for all.

Of course, Ronald Reagan's simplistic utterances must be understood as the public packaging of his administration's attitude toward the Soviet Union, which was shaped mainly by Professor Richard Pipes, former director of Harvard University's Russian Research Center who spent a couple of years on Reagan's National Security Council. Pipes's influential position was laid out in an article that appeared in *Commentary* in July 1977, entitled 'Why the Soviet Union Thinks It Could Fight and Win a Nuclear War.' His view of the Russians provides a basis for Gray's ideas on how to 'exploit Soviet fears'. Pipes turns around the standard belief that Russians hate war because they suffered so much in the Second World War. On the contrary, says Pipes, if the country lost twenty million and still won the Second World War, its leaders can easily contemplate losing thirty million (the population of major targeted cities) in the next war. Thus American deterrence policy, targeting Soviet cities, does not frighten Soviet leaders at all. Americans would consider such losses frightful. 'But clearly a country that since 1914 has lost, as a result of two world wars, a civil war, famine and various "purges", perhaps up to sixty million citizens, must define "unacceptable damage" differently from the United States,' concludes Harvard's top specialist on the USSR.

What frightens the Russians is any evidence that the United States may be switching from deterrence to counterforce. This 'throws Soviet generals into a tizzy of excitement,' writes Pipes, who also admits: 'We know surprisingly little about the individuals and institutions whose responsibility it is to formulate Soviet military doctrine.' The matter is handled with 'utmost secrecy'. But extrapolations from published texts enable him to conclude with certainty that the Soviets have a war-fighting strategy, look on American deterrence with the contempt reserved for the feeble-minded, and fear only that the innocent Americans will get smart and take up counterforce too. 'In its essentials,' concedes Pipes, 'Soviet nuclear doctrine as it finally emerged is not all that different from what American doctrine might have been had military and geopolitical rather than fiscal considerations played the decisive role here as they did there.' Thus Pipes's denunciation of Soviet nuclear war-fighting strategy turns into a plea for the United States to have one too.

Pipes was chairman of the 'Team B' appointed by President Ford, under right-wing pressure, in order to prepare a more menacing estimate of Soviet strategic objectives then the one tabled by the CIA. Pipes also helped lead the attack on détente, arguing that Russians lack the sense of fair play which, in American eyes, is capable of producing a reciprocal response. Pipes is too much of a conservative in his way to take communist ideology very seriously: what is really wrong with the USSR is the slyness, cunning and belief in force of the Russian peasantry brought to power by the Bolshevik revolution. He muses that some great shock might be more useful in overcoming this cultural backwardness than détente could ever be. 'Nothing short of a major cataclysm that would demonstrate beyond doubt that impulses rooted in its history have lost their validity is likely to affect the collective outlook of the Russian nation and change it, as defeat has caused the German and Japanese to turn away from dictatorships, and the Nazi massacres have caused the Jews to abandon their traditional pacifism.'[24] Could nuclear holocaust give to the Russians the historic boost that Hitler's holocaust gave to the Jews?

Such reflections led to the notion of 'decapitation'. Gray and Payne recommended that the United States should target Soviet military power and the political, military and economic 'control structure' of the USSR. 'Striking the USSR should entail targeting the relocation bunkers of the top political and bureaucratic leadership, including those of the KGB; key communication centres of the Communist party, the military, and the government; and many of the economic, political and military records. Even limited destruction of some of these targets and substantial isolation of many of the key personnel who survive could have revolutionary consequences for the country.'[25]

These interesting, even exciting prospects coincided with the development of the very weapons that might be able to do the job. If they could be made to work as promised, cruise missiles, and especially the Pershing-2, would be able to zero in on the Communist Party and KGB leaders, allowing the USSR to 'disintegrate into anarchy'. The Pershing-2 could even be equipped with Earth Penetrator warheads able to plunge twelve metres underground and wipe out command bunkers. This is the weapon that NATO ministers decided in December 1979 to station in West Germany, only some five minutes' flight time from targets in the Soviet Union.

When Reagan took office in January 1981, the nuclear-war-fighting or, more specifically, the nuclear-decapitation school was absorbed into the new administration. They had made their point, and there was no further need for polemical articles to appear in public journals like *Commentary* and *Foreign Policy*. Actual details of United States strategy and targeting remain, as always, top secret. But from all that has been said in the public debate it is obvious enough that somewhere along the way, the rationale for the Pershing-2 and cruise Euromissiles underwent a decisive shift. They were never meant to defend Western Europe from the threat of the Soviet SS-20. Their purpose is no longer anything so abstract as to fill a 'gap in the deterrence spectrum'. They are there as decapitation weapons, a gun pointed at the head of the Soviet Union.

And the gun is being eased into European hands. As if in preparation for the perfect crime.

Horizontal Escalation

Once the Western Europeans are equipped for war, which war will it be?

The war for which American strategists have been preparing since the late seventies is the war of the Persian Gulf. As one of them, Robert W. Tucker put it, 'the centre of gravity of American interests in ths world today is not to be found in Europe but in the Persian Gulf.'[26] This is because the 'loss of the Gulf could be expected to form an almost certain prelude to the effective end of the American position in Western Europe and Japan.' Thus whereas at the start of the cold war, when NATO was first founded, Europe was the bone of contention between the rival superpowers, today 'the Gulf provides *the* critical

source of conflict between the United States and the Soviet Union.'
One could fill a volume with quotations from the Reagan administration's strategic thinkers to this effect; the consensus is overwhelming.

The tales of sudden waves of Soviet tanks overwhelming Western
Europe are designed to frighten children and other naïfs. As perceived
by American strategists at the start of the 1980s, the real Russian
threat to Europe — or more precisely, to American predominance in
Europe — is quite different. It was described in 1980 by Paul Nitze,
one of the most powerful figures in American strategic planning for
over three decades, as 'the now-emerging possibility that the Soviet
Union may offer to join West Germany and France in joint negotiations with Persian Gulf suppliers for long-term oil-purchase contracts
in adequate volume and at stable prices.' Nitze observed that it might
'not be unrealistic on the part of West Germany and France to see
advantages in negotiating in partnership with the Soviet Union
rather than as an opponent.'[27] This was something to be forestalled,
and the moral quarantine imposed on Moscow as punishment for the
invasion of Afghanistan provided the means.

On a visit to India in December 1980, Leonid Brezhnev proposed
an agreement between the USSR, the West, China, Japan and the
Persian Gulf states to ban foreign military bases, nuclear or other
mass destruction weapons and any threats of force or foreign intervention in the Gulf or the adjacent islands. The agreement would
guarantee free trade and use of sea routes, in a spirit of respect for
non-alignment and for the rights of states to their natural resources.
Only Kuwait showed any interest. The danger of international agreement seemed to be receding.

But the problem of military control of the Gulf area remained. A
verbal net was cast over the region by the 'Carter doctrine', and a
Rapid Deployment Force created for on-the-spot intervention.
Various intermediary bases were secured for its use, notably in the
Sinai, thanks to the device of a 'multinational peace-keeping force' in
the Egyptian Sinai after Israeli evacuation. Such successful ex-
pedients could not disguise the stubborn fact that the Gulf was very
far away from the United States, and considerably closer to the Soviet
Union. 'We must recognize,' wrote Tucker, 'that we cannot defend
the Gulf against a determined Russian assault — not now, not in the
immediate years ahead, and perhaps not ever. Beyond a certain level
of conventional threat, we must either rely on the threat of responding
with nuclear weapons or concede that there is no response we can
make.' But the nuclear threat runs up against 'the now familiar
problems of credibility'.

The most sophisticated strategic thinkers[28] argue that the eventual solution will involve the Soviet Union as a junior partner to the United States in the maintenance of world order. But first the USSR must be taught to give up its 'insistence upon being treated as an equal of America'.[29] How? The answer may be the same as to the question of how to defend a vital region, the Gulf, where the United States is inherently and permanently in a position of weakness.

Albert Wohlstetter noted in 1979[30] that the existence of a policy 'proposed, or more usually hinted at, by those who think it inherently impossible to overcome the advantage in conventional strength which the Russians are supposed to achieve simply by having their home-land nearby, would rely implicitly or explicitly on a threat to escalate — that is, to start a war outside the region or to use nuclear weapons.' Wohlstetter notes that some such possibility 'is always there'. But he cautions that 'the actual execution of a threat by the United States as leader of the alliance to start a war elsewhere — for example, on the northern flank of NATO — might only worsen matters for us and for our allies. It is not likely to be welcome "elsewhere".' Wohlstetter, in close touch with the European defence elite, had grounds for his misgivings. Nevertheless, the policy of threats to 'start a war elsewhere' was adopted more or less discreetly a couple of years later by the Reagan administration as 'horizontal escalation'.

An April 1982 report[31] to the US Senate Foreign Relations Committee noted that an alternative proposal to NATO's traditional doctrine, 'recently advanced by the Reagan administration, would place a far greater premium on the global flexibility of US forces and hold open the option of responding to aggression in one region (such as the Central Front in Europe) by retaliating in other regions. The key to this strategy, known as "horizontal escalation", rests in the reassertion of US maritime superiority. Although the Administration staunchly reflects a moving away from NATO, many critics are not so sure.' This report tactfully reverses the probable procedure of 'horizontal escalation' in the example it offers, suggesting that aggression in Europe would lead to retaliation elsewhere, when in reality the thought is apparently to respond to aggression elsewhere (and specifically, in the Gulf) by retaliating in Europe.

Defense Secretary Caspar Weinberger made this perfectly clear in his Annual Report to Congress for Fiscal 1983: 'In recent years,' he wrote, 'it has become increasingly clear that the members of the Alliance in the northern, centre and southern regions are bound together as one and critically depend on each other and even outside the NATO treaty boundaries — notably the Persian Gulf . . . The strategy we have been developing seeks to defend Alliance interests in such other regions. For the region of the Persian Gulf, in particular, our strategy is based on the concept that the prospect of combat with the US and other friendly forces, coupled with the prospect that we might carry the war to other arenas, is the most effective deterrent to Soviet aggression. This strategy, thus, has two dimensions. First, we must have a capability rapidly to deploy enough force to hold key positions, and we must be able to interdict and blunt a Soviet attack . . . . Second, this strategy recognizes that we have options for fighting on other fronts and for building up allied strength that would lead to consequences unacceptable to the Soviet Union' (I–14).

These 'unacceptable consequences' could evidently be inflicted by 'allied strength' in the form of cruise missiles. The Weinberger report indicates where this strength might be applied: 'A wartime strategy that confronts the enemy, were he to attack, with the risk of our counteroffensive against his vulnerable points strengthens deterrence and serves the defensive peacetime strategy.' Not just any old place will do for the counteroffensive. 'If it is to offset the enemy's attack, it should be launched against territory or assets that are of an importance to him comparable to the ones he is attacking. Some important Soviet vulnerabilities have to do with the fact that the Soviet empire, unlike our alliance, is not a voluntary association of democratic nations. Thirty-seven years after free elections were promised at Yalta, the imposition of martial law in Poland makes clear how such elections would turn out if they were permitted. Our plans for counteroffensive in war can take account of such vulnerabilities' (I–16).

That is about as clear and explicit as such a strategy can be in public documents. The details must be kept secret. But the general thrust is made public as part of the deterrent message to the Russians.

However, even some details have been leaked, and prior to Weinberger. The *New Statesman* reported in December 1982: 'In some highly classified contingency plans, the United States has envisaged launching a "pre-emptive attack" and an invasion of Eastern Europe in order to "liberate" East Germany and Czechoslovakia. This EUCOM operations plan, or OPLAN number 100–6, was leaked to various Western European media during 1980, but did not receive wide attention.' (One can bet that the Russians pricked up their ears, however.) 'OPLAN 100–6 envisaged circumstances in which the US European Command would need to have its own command bunkers separate from NATO, since it recognized that "all of NATO may not elect to participate in these operations." It was, however, expected that Britain would remain loyal to the US even in the event of a pre-emptive American nuclear attack on Eastern Europe.'[32] This report fits ominously with US plans to establish fallback war head-quarters for EUCOM (the United States European Command) at High Wycombe in Buckinghamshire. The EUCOM commander, currently General Bernard Rogers, is also head of Supreme Allied Command Europe (SACEUR) in charge of NATO forces, operating from Supreme Headquarters Allied Powers Europe (SHAPE) at Castau, near Mons, in Belgium.

It is the presence of the new precision weapons, cruise and Pershing-2, that make credible the threat to lop off the head of Soviet power in Poland, East Germany or Czechoslovakia. These are weapons theoretically adapted to 'political targeting'.

In early 1983 a classified National Security Decision Directive 75, written by Richard Pipes and issued to government officials, reportedly set internal changes in the Soviet system as a US policy goal. This was confirmed in the testimony given by Secretary of State George P. Shultz on 15 June 1983 to the Senate Foreign Relations Committee. 'We take it as part of our obligation to peace,' he said, 'to encourage the gradual evolution of the Soviet system toward a more pluralistic political and economic system.' Shultz said the doctrine of global opposition to the Soviet Union was intended to replace the outdated policies of containment and détente.

A few days later, after a festive dinner in Williamsburg, Virginia, at a summit meeting supposedly devoted to economic affairs, the leaders of the major industrialized capital nations unexpectedly endorsed the Reagan administration of indivisible global security. European NATO leaders had originally endorsed a missile deployment that was supposed to prevent Europe's 'decoupling' from the American strategic deterrent. Instead, they found their security 'coupled' to a United States global strategy outside their control.

Notes

1. 'The Modernization of NATO's Long-Range Theater Nuclear Forces', report prepared by the Library of Congress Research Service for the Subcommittee on Europe and the Middle East of the United States House of Representatives Foreign Affairs Committee, Washington, US Government Printing Office, 1981.

2. The real cost, hard to calculate, is no doubt much higher. See Desmond Ball, 'The Costs of the Cruise Missile', *Survival*, November–December 1978.

3. Michel Tatu, *La Bataille des Euromissiles*, Fondation Pour les Études de Défense Nationale, Paris 1983 p. 93; slightly different figures are cited by Eugenia Osgood in the *Bulletin of the Atomic Scientists*, December 1983.

4. Air Force Major-General (retired) John C. Toomay, 'Technical Characteristics', in *Cruise Missiles*, edited by Richard K. Betts, Brookings Institution, Washington 1981.

5. Fred Kaplan, 'Warring Over New Missiles for NATO', *New York Times Magazine*, 9 December 1979.

6. Paul Buteux, *The Politics of Nuclear Consultation in NATO 1965–1980*, Cambridge 1983.

7. 'The Modernization of NATO's Long–Range Theater Nuclear Forces.'

8. Buteux, *The Politics of Nuclear Consultation in NATO 1965-1980*.

9. Ulrich Albrecht, *Kündigt den Nachrüstungsbeschluss!* Frankfurt 1982, p. 90.

10. Ibid.

11. Klaas de Vries, 'Responding to the SS-20: An Alternative Approach', *Survival*, November–December 1979.

12. In an interview with the *Frankfurter Rundschau* reproduced by Erhard Eppler in his book, *Die tödliche Utopie der Sicherheit*, Berlin 1983. A more succinct account was provided in a letter to the *International Herald Tribune*, published 21 December 1983, from Jens Fischer in Helmut Schmidt's office in Bonn. In response to an editorial asserting that Helmut Schmidt had 'requested the new weapons in compelling terms', Fischer wrote: 'This is absolutely wrong. What Mr Schmidt really asked for in 1977 was to have the question of the growing Soviet INF forces, especially the SS-20 fleet, included in the SALT-II negotiations between the United States and the Soviet Union. This was rejected by the Carter administration. Later on, President Carter made (at the Guadeloupe meeting in January 1979) the proposal to deploy medium-range missiles on West European soil to counter the SS-20 buildup. This was modified by the leaders of Great Britain, France and West Germany in a way that led to the NATO double-track decision in December 1979.'

13. Kaplan,'Warring Over New Missiles for NATO'

14. 'The Modernization . . . '

15. Fred Kaplan, *The Wizards of Armaggedon*, New York 1983.

16. Nitze took a Soviet diplomat out to lunch to make sure there was no misunderstanding on the point. (Paul H. Johnstone, unpublished memoir.)

17. Kaplan, *Wizards*.

18. Morton Halperin quoted by Rik Coolsaet, 'US changes rules of war', *END Journal*, London, June–July 1983.

19. 'Interim Report on Nuclear Weapons in Europe', prepared by the North Atlantic Assembly's Special Committee on Nuclear Weapons in Europe (Chairman, Senator Joseph Biden, USA; Vice Chairmen: Klaas de Vries, Netherlands; Alois Mertes, Federal Republic of Germany; Rapporteurs, John Cartwright, UK; Julian Critchley, UK), submitted to US Senate Foreign Relations Committee on 10 November 1981, Government Printing Office, December 1981.

20. 'The Modernization . . . '.

21. Paul Joseph, 'From MAD to NUTS', *Socialist Review*, number 61, Oakland, California, January–February 1982.

22. Colin S. Gray and Keith Payne, 'Victory Is Possible', *Foreign Policy*, summer 1980.

23. Colin Gray, letter to the editor, *Bulletin of the Atomic Scientists*, June–July 1981.

24. Richard Pipes, 'Détente: Moscow's View', in *Soviet Strategy in Europe*, 1976.

25. In *Le Monde*, 16 October 1983, Michel Tatu wrote that 'while McNamara wanted to spare Soviet political command centres . . . today the "Nomenklatura" seems very

clearly targeted: the Pentagon has more or less catalogued the 110,000 people who make it up — including 6,300 at the regional level — as well as the shelters they have built for themselves.'

26. Robert W. Tucker, 'American Power and the Persian Gulf', *Commentary*, November 1980.

27. Paul H. Nitze, 'Strategy in the Decade of the 1980s', *Foreign Affairs*, Fall 1980.

28. Notably George Liska, author of *Russia and the Road to Appeasement*, Baltimore and London 1982.

29. Robert Tucker, 'The Purposes of American Power', *Foreign Affairs*, Winter 1980–81.

30. Albert Wohlstetter, 'Half-Wars and Half-Policies', in *From Weakness to Strength*, Institute for Contemporary Studies, San Fransisco, 1980.

31. 'NATO Today', Report to the United States Senate Foreign Relations Committee, US Government Printing Office, 1982.

32. Duncan Campbell, 'America's Base Motives', *New Statesman*, 17 December 1982.

2

Germany's Political Awakening

The Euromissiles controversy has gone a long way toward awakening Germans politically to their present situation, while shedding a fresh light on their past. Some of the younger generation are beginning to examine the founding myths of the Federal Republic and of NATO.

The First Berlin Crisis and the Origin of NATO

The long-standing consensus in West Germany was forged above all around events, most notably the Berlin Airlift of 1948.

In 1945 Germany was thoroughly defeated and occupied by the richest country in history and its allies in the West, and in the East by a vast, poor nation largely destroyed by the German invasion. The United States had no need of reparations. On the contrary, the policy-making establishment[1] had already decided that this time, defeated Germany must not be ruined by reparations but included in a 'grand area' (later to become the 'free world') of open economies, as a prosperous trade partner for the United States. A reparations burden must not stand in the way of Germany's ability to buy American goods.

The Russians wanted reparations. They wanted reparations not just from their own occupation zone, relatively small and poor, but from all of Germany, and especially from the industrial Ruhr in the British zone of occupation. For this reason of self-interest, the Russians wanted to maintain Germany's economic unity. There is every reason to suppose that the Soviet Union would have conceded German unity in return for the thousands of millions of dollars in reparation it was seeking from the Western occupation zones. Or to put it somewhat differently, had United States negotiators wanted to secure German unity in return for war reparations to the Soviet Union, they could surely have swung the deal. But this was not their aim.

The French also wanted reparations. But they did not, like the Russians, seek to extract them from Germany as a whole. Rather, they wanted to gain economic control of contiguous regions in the occupation zone allotted them in the Rhineland–Palatinate, and even hoped to annex the Saarland. As the Russians opposed this approach, the potential Franco–Soviet alliance on the reparations issue collapsed.

Some confusion was introduced into early US occupation policy by the unworkable Morgenthau Plan to pull Germany's industrial teeth and turn the country into peaceful pasture. The only practical effect of this punitive approach was a short-lived tolerance of the Soviet policy of dismantling industrial plant in Eastern Germany. However, the course was soon corrected as the United States military government under Lucius Clay went all out to preserve and strengthen capitalist free enterprise. The German left was essentially excluded from any in-depth 'de-Nazification', which would have tended to diagnose the Nazi illness in terms of the 1930 crisis of capitalism, the six million unemployed, the complicity of industrial magnates and international financiers in bringing Hitler to power to crush the German working-class movement. Efforts by the local population, as in Hesse, or by the British Labour government, as in North Rhine Westphalia, to socialize industry or otherwise limit free enterprise were quashed or undermined by the Americans.

These economic choices required an ideological explanation. The American diagnosis stressed single-party rule and state economic planning as the key aspects of the Nazi system, interpreted as but one version of the more general malady, totalitarianism, now being spread by the Soviet Union in its newly conquered sphere of influence in Eastern Europe. As the only known cure for totalitarianism was the one that had just been administered to Nazi Germany, the American ideologues ruled out non-military ways of dealing with the 'totalitarians', so that instead of political compromise, which might have been possible through patient negotiations between the principal victors, the Second World War was rapidly followed by the stalemate called 'Cold War'.

American needs in Germany were simply contrary to Russian needs. Without a prosperous Germany — and Western Europe — to absorb American goods and capital, the United States was heading for a crisis of overproduction that would soon bring back the massive unemployment of depression years. The European Recovery Programme, announced by General George Marshall in his Harvard speech on 7 June 1947, was no doubt the best possible way to solve the problem in a capitalist system, boldly redistributing the cards to bring the partners into the game and keep it going. The only condition was that governments on the receiving end should maintain an open, private enterprise economy. The Marshall Plan thus made definitive the division of post-war Europe between the economic systems of the two principal victors. Unable to gain reparations from Western Germany, the Russians set about rebuilding their ruined country with what they could get from occupied Eastern Europe.

These opposing economic policies, which from a distance might seem the simple function of material self-interest, necessitated on both sides frantic campaigns of political self-justification and propaganda against the other side. In Western Europe opponents of the Marshall Plan — that is, the Communist Parties — were driven from coalition governments in France and Italy, while in Eastern Europe, those receptive to the Marshall Plan were purged. For propaganda purposes, both the Russians and the Americans justified the imposition of their own economic logic in terms of defence against a purely hypothetical military threat from the other side. In order to dare vote the thousands of millions of dollars of Marshall Plan aid, American Congressmen in particular had to be able to tell the voters that Europe and the 'Free World' were threatened by a new expansionist peril in the style of Hitler's Germany. The Russians' brutal retraction to their own occupation zones was portrayed as symptomatic of this military threat. The Russians, for their part, portrayed the American-sponsored reconstruction of West Germany as an encouragement of German 'revanchist' ambitions towards the territories lost to the Soviet Union, Poland and Czechoslovakia.

Later, few people in the West would remember the series of developments that led to the Berlin Blockade and the Berlin Airlift. On 20 June 1948, in connection with the European Recovery Programme, the United States had carried out a draconian currency reform which rendered the Reichsmark valueless in the Western zones of occupation. Three days later, the Russians carried out a currency reform of their own in their Eastern zone of occupation, Berlin included. The next day, on 24 June, the Americans introduced the new Deutsche Mark as legal tender in the Western occupation sectors of Berlin. To the Russians it seemed that the Western powers, having excluded them from their rightful share of the West German economy, were intent on disrupting the East German economy under Soviet control. The Soviet military command immediately cut rail traffic through the Soviet zone to Berlin. There had never been an Allied agreement covering Western access to Berlin, and to Moscow this probably looked like a good bargaining chip. Instead, the United States and its Western allies organized the Berlin Airlift — a smashing propaganda victory which, together with Marshall Aid prosperity, offered the West Germans an honourable place in the new Cold War imagery of the Free World, standing up heroically to the Soviet threat. The Berlin Airlift was the founding myth of the Federal Republic of Germany. The confused and corrupt 'de-Nazification' process was now left more or less in a shambles: the past could be forgotten, as Germans were offered a new and politically virtuous identity based on anti-communism.

The dispute among the Allied powers entailed that Germany, alone among the defeated Axis powers, was never granted a peace treaty. West Germany, like East Germany, remains an occupied country with limited sovereignty. It is true that, under the terms of the German Treaty of 26 May 1952, as revised in Paris on 23 October 1954, the three Western powers — the United States, Britain and France — granted the Federal Republic the 'full powers of a sovereign state over its internal and external affairs'. However, this was accompanied by the stipulation that the three powers retained their rights regarding Berlin and Germany as a whole, including reunification of Germany and a peace treaty settlement, as well as their *rights to station armed forces in the Federal Republic*. Thus as a matter of strict legality, the United States has always had the right to station Pershing-2 nuclear missiles or anything else it chooses on West German territory. West German political leaders are of course fully aware of this, but for the sake of domestic political morale and their own prestige try their best to act as if they enjoyed full sovereignty. The German Treaty further limited the Federal Republic's sovereignty by committing it to the 'common goals of the Free World' in full association with the 'community of free nations'.

The North Atlantic Treaty was concluded on 4 April 1949, one month after the lifting of the Berlin Blockade. But it was only on 23 October 1954, after five years of French objections, that the Paris agreements revised the German Treaty to bring the Federal Republic into NATO. At the same time, West Germany became a member of the Western European Union that had originally been set up in March 1948 between France, Britain, Italy and the Benelux states to consult on mutual defence issues, with Germany designated as potential aggressor. The WEU took note of Adenauer's pledge to ban production of atomic, chemical or biological weapons, as well as a designated list of heavy armaments, on West German territory, and took over the task of monitoring West German rearmament. The Federal Republic was thus allowed to rearm — indeed enjoined to do so — but all its new military forces were in NATO, under American command, and its arms industry was to be held within certain limits under joint West European control.

This limited sovereignty could be overlooked by the general public, because the Federal Republic seemed so much more independent in its actions than the Soviet satellite state in East Germany. Moreover, as German productive capacity revived and expanded, West German business had every interest in access to the vast 'Free World' market. West Germany became the 'first in the class' of the Western capitalist system under American hegemony.

The Second Berlin Crisis and the Origin of Ostpolitik

Throughout the crass fifties, West Berlin was the 'showcase of the Free World', serving to shame and destabilize the surrounding Communist regime while reinforcing Western convictions of superiority. American newspaper editors and columnists regularly made the pilgrimage to savour the contrast and to write the inevitable article on freedom's showcase and its drab Soviet antithesis. Tourist buses carried these Dantes for an afternoon through the circles of Communist hell to try to spot the political vices responsible for the fall, before returning to enjoy the apolitical vices of the showcase.

For East German rulers, West Berlin was the wide open exit draining their country of badly needed professionals and skilled labour.

Right after the war, the Soviet zone of occupation had to take in the majority of destitute refugees driven out of the Eastern territories. As the Allies stalled on the original Soviet demand for ten thousand million dollars in reparations, the Russians helped themselves to the 40 per cent of industrial equipment in their zone granted at Potsdam. In June 1946, the Soviet military administration took possession of the most concentrated 25 per cent of East German industry, whose production served to pay war reparations until it was given to the German Democratic Republic at the end of 1953.

Politically, the Soviet occupiers carried out a more thorough and coherent de-Nazification and granted Germans more political and administrative responsibility sooner than the Western Allies. Land reform broke up the old Junker estates and gave small plots to poor peasants and to the refugees driven out of East Prussia. On the grounds that the opposition between Socialists and Communists had enabled Hitler to come to power, the Soviet occupiers encouraged the Social Democratic Party (SPD) and the Communist Party (KPD) to merge as the Unified Socialist Party (SED) on 21 April 1946. The SED got 47 per cent of the vote in elections held in the Soviet zone in September 1946, and led to the formation of a coalition government.

From then on, however, the Soviet Union matched every move of the Western powers to cement the division of Germany into two separate states: the Western zone currency reform was followed by an Eastern zone currency reform: the establishment of the Federal Republic of Germany was followed by the establishment of the German Democratic Republic (DDR); and finally, when it became apparent that the Western allies were preparing West German rearmament, Moscow allowed the SED to proclaim the 'construction of socialism' in July 1952.

Work speedups led to worker protests and the East Berlin riots of 17 June 1953. Walter Ulbricht came to power with a less ambitious 'new course', but the population drain through Berlin meant that socialism was being built on moving sands. Ulbricht urged Khrushchev to do something about it.

In November 1958, Khrushchev began to demand an end to the Allied occupation of Berlin and its 'normalization' as 'capital of the German Democratic Republic'. That was the maximal position. More seriously, he suggested negotiating a special status of free city for West Berlin, with a four-power guarantee and perhaps United Nations protection. This was accompanied by the threat to turn over Soviet occupation powers in Berlin to the DDR, an entity the West refused to recognize. Khrushchev set a time limit of six months: which turned out to be just the time the American Secretary of State, John Foster Dulles, had left to live.

Two years later, the question was still up in the air. Before expiring, Dulles had launched a 'political offensive' which used Berlin's power of attraction to try to bring down Ulbricht's regime and roll back Communist power in Eastern Europe.[2] The exodus from the DDR quickened, while on the other side, in May 1959, the United States and the Federal Rpublic of Germany signed an agreement to co-operate in nuclear matters for defence needs. If that weren't enough to stimulate Eastern paranoia, Bonn in 1960 announced plans to recruit for the Bundeswehr in West Berlin and to allow several organizations of *Vertriebene*, ethnic Germans driven Westward, to hold meetings in West Berlin demanding the return to Germany of territories taken over by Poland and the Soviet Union at the end of the war. *Revanchism*, in a word. Ulbricht was losing patience, but Khrushchev preferred to wait for the new American president John Kennedy to take office in January 1961.

On 6 January 1961, Khrushchev gave a speech to party intellectuals vowing unreserved support to ' "sacred" wars of national liberation'. Here was just the planetary challenge which, as we saw in the last chapter, the Kennedy team was itching to meet. In March and April 1961, Khrushchev came back to the Berlin question. In a long interview with columnist Walter Lippman, the Soviet leader suggested the possibility of some kind of reunification of the three elements of Germany: the two German states and the 'free city of West Berlin'. Otherwise, Moscow would conclude a separate peace with the DDR.

Nothing in the American documents and memoirs of the period suggests that the substance of this proposal was seriously considered even for a moment. The competitive climate of Washington would probably have stifled instantly any thought that, after all, the Berlin situation was bizarre and potentially dangerous for everyone and that some adjustments might be negotiated that could benefit everyone all around. In London, the mood was different; Macmillan favoured negotiations. But Washington chose to see Khrushchev's proposals as nothing but a challenge to American power.

Khrushchev, it seemed, wanted to force the Allies to leave West Berlin. Thus the crisis would break out when the East Germans, recognized as in charge and supported by the Soviets, would stop Allied military convoys on the Autobahn between West Germany and West Berlin. Throughout 1961, Pentagon experts and the President's highest advisers worked on scenarios to deal with that fateful moment. Centrally involved in these exercises was Paul Nitze, who had helped invent the Cold War in 1949 with his famous National Security Council position paper NSC-68, warning that negotiation was a waste of time with the Soviet Union, whose inner nature as a communist slave state drove it toward implacable expansionism and destruction of freedom. Later, in the seventies, Nitze was a prime mover in the Committee on the Present Danger that played a key role in refuelling the nuclear arms race.

In late June, Kennedy received a report on Berlin by Dean Acheson, who interpreted Khrushchev's proposals as a simple effort to destroy American influence in the world. It was a 'contest of wills'. This was happening because American nuclear deterrence had lost its credibility. Thus the United States must restore its nuclear credibility, and to do so, it was necessary to 'accept the risk' of nuclear war. One must convince oneself first.

In the latter half of 1961, the upper spheres of the Kennedy administration seem to have been absorbed in the psychodrama of convincing themselves of the real danger of nuclear war the better to convince the adversary. In their memoirs, Kennedy's aides stress that he disliked the Acheson report and would have preferred to negotiate. But negotiate what? The State Department had no ideas. Washington was defending the status quo in Berlin and was not pursuing any negotiable goals. In the existing political culture, it was hard to see the problem other than as a 'contest of wills'.

At the Pentagon, where Nitze was deputy defence secretary in charge of international security questions, scenarios continued to be concocted for confrontations on the Autobahn. Thus American leaders were apparently completely taken by surprise when the Wall began to close around West Berlin on the night of 13 August 1961. Unbelievable as this may be to many Europeans, dismayed American officials have always insisted that their burgeoning intelligence services had no report of the three Soviet divisions that had surrounded the city. Plunged into their apocalyptic scenarios, the American strategists neither foresaw the real event, reacted to it, nor even grasped its significance. Only when West Berlin's mayor, Willy Brandt, issued an urgent appeal did Kennedy send Vice-President Lyndon Johnson to ensure the shocked inhabitants that America was still with them.

Failing to realize that the Wall had closed the issue, the Pentagon went on turning out scenarios. In October the master himself, Paul Nitze, went to work in collaboration with Foy Kohler of the State Department. The result was a document, approved by Kennedy on 23 October 1961, which laid out a series of reactions, including 'selective' nuclear attacks intended as 'demonstrations' and culminating in general nuclear war. At the end of November, American officials obtained what they considered Allied consent in appropriately ambiguous consultations. But the crisis petered out . . . after the Kennedy circle had given itself a good scare. Some months later, with the Cuban missile crisis, they had a chance to share their good scare with the whole world.

The Berlin Crisis was subsequently celebrated as a great victory for American 'resolve', whereby Kennedy had stood up to Khrushchev and preserved West Berlin for the Free World. American leaders could even consider the Wall a propaganda victory, since it disgraced the East German regime and its Soviet protectors. Score plus one for our side, and minus one for their side. A zero sum game: if it's bad for them, it's good for us.

Berliners didn't see it that way. Propaganda advantages were poor compensation for the grim reality of the Wall. All American toughness had accomplished was to rule out any negotiated accommodation that might have offered the East German regime a less brutal way to check the population drain encouraged by the West.

Willy Brandt has recalled 13 August 1961 in his memoirs as a day of 'horror, anguish and confusion' which 'forced me to mediate on the external factors on which German politics and that of Europe would depend in the years to come'. Either Western intelligence had been caught napping by the huge wall-building project, or else (as was rumoured at the time and is still widely believed) there was a more or less tacit complicity between the Americans and Russians to solve the crisis this way. Neither hypothesis was particularly reassuring. More than that, Brandt was struck by the way the Allies had been absorbed in their fear of the wrong crisis. The perspective Brandt gained from the eperience of that day lay behind what came to be called his *Ostpolitik*.

Brandt's close colleague Egon Bahr has also recalled the impact of that day.[3] When the Wall went up, 'power politics showed how truly weak it was'. The West was militarily superior, but even then the risk of military action was too great. To 'those who today take up the cause of a politics of power', Bahr says: 'Remember 1961'. Experience showed that 'Berliners had to look after their own interests, and so we did . . . responsibility for Germany had to be borne by Germans themselves.'

The Americans were, in fact, ready to risk war to defend their own great power rights to access to their occupied sector of Berlin. But the rights of Germans could not be a *casus belli*.

As to the long-range political significance of the Wall, apart from mere propaganda value, the Americans also seemed unaware or indifferent. The days of the 'showcase of the Free World', paradise of vulgar consumerism and double agents, were ending, and West Berlin began its evolution into something quite different, a sort of experimental terrain for contemporary political and cultural contradictions.

With the population drain stopped, the East German Communists were finally able to construct a prosperous economy and a strong state. Thus the DDR had not dared to echo the Federal Republic's introduction of compulsory military service in 1956: only in January 1962, when young people were no longer able to flee through West Berlin, did it feel strong enough to bring in conscription.

With United States attention increasingly riveted to the strategic confrontation with Communism in Asia, space opened in Europe in the sixties for Europeans to take greater initiative in their own external affairs. *Ostpolitik*, however, far from involving a course independent of the West, followed the example of de Gaulle and the hints and proddings of the Americans and their allies. Détente was the Western policy of the period, and a reversal of Bonn's foreign policy was necessary to détente in Europe. The Adenauer government's righteous refusal to recognize the East German regime or the new boundaries of the Polish state, shifted westward by the Soviet Union at the expense of German territory, had kept alive Eastern European fears, both real and propagandistic, of 'German revanchism'. In the late sixties and early seventies, Willy Brandt opened diplomatic relations with the states of Eastern Europe, and a series of treaties normalizing relations laid the ground for an improvement of economic and human relations. For the German people, the most important aspect was the new possibility for West Germans to visit their relatives in the East.

Egon Bahr has observed that anyone dealing with the Russians needs an ample supply of time and patience. By Russian time standards, détente was just getting underway by the mid seventies. Those in the West, notably in the United States and France, who were soon declaring that 'détente has failed' may be suspected of lacking the patience required, or of having second thoughts about letting it work.

Convergence of Two Systems?

As it was shaping up in the mid seventies, détente seemed to favour, among Western nations, Germany, and among Western political forces, Social Democracy.

From about 1973, social democracy seemed to be emerging as the single universally attractive political alternative. In Europe, détente nourished hopes of an eventual peaceful convergence of Eastern and Western systems, in a form that would combine the social benefits of socialism with the political freedoms of Western democracy. The bitter half-century-long feud between Communists and Social Democrats had been calmed considerably by the German Social Democrats' exercise in self-control in dealing with the Eastern European Communist regimes. Whereas Social Democrats had been among the most vehement anti-communist cold warriors in the post-war years, in the West a number of Communists and Social Democrats began to see possibilities of returning to the common historic roots of the

European working-class movement, which had been shattered and split by the 1914–18 war and the Bolshevik revolution.

The 'Eurocommunism' of the mid seventies was an attempt to contribute to this convergence through a process of a social democratization that would integrate the CPs more fully into Western parliamentary democracy, while at the same time lending political support to kindred currents in Eastern Europe, notably the defenders of the 'Prague Spring' in Czechoslovakia. Thus in 1976, some Western Communists joined with non-communists in attempts to use the agreements reached at the Helsinki Conference on European Security and Cooperation to promote some modest liberalization of political rights in Eastern Europe.

This was also the period when the fall of Allende in Chile showed the impossibility of even a peacefully 'radical' left to survive American-backed pressure, while murderous military dictatorships flourished in all the southern cone of the western hemisphere on the ruins of revolutionary movements. Revived politically and financially by the SDP, the Socialist International, under the chairmanship of ex-Chancellor Willy Brandt, found Latin Americans ready to turn to European social democracy as their last political hope. Détente gave the revived Socialist International the space to preach democratic development in North–South relations and disarmament in East–West relations.

During the Schmidt years, West Germany expanded its international presence with what amounted to three different foreign policies. The official policy corresponded to the consistently pro-Western, pro-American outlook of foreign minister Hans-Dietrich Genscher's Free Democratic Party. Meanwhile, acting on his own from the solid Bavarian power base of his Christian Social Union (CSU), Franz-Josef Strauss maintained friendly relations with the military dictators of South America's southern cone as well as far-right forces in the southern NATO states and Spain. A third, more humanitarian foreign policy was run by the SDP through its Friedrich Ebert Foundation and the Socialist International.

The main share of the budget of the revived Socialist International was paid by the SDP, followed by the Swedish and Austrian parties, whose leaders shared Brandt's approach to North–South and East–West relations. This approach was also behind the two independent commissions headed by Willy Brandt and Olof Palme whose respective reports on North–South relations and on disarmament attempted to establish standards of international common sense capable of rallying a consensus. It could be said that the promotion of East-

West détente and third world human rights was in the interests of certain business sectors in central and northern Europe unable to use force to obtain markets or investment space, as well as of a European labour movement concerned by the flight of industrial investment to countries with repressive rightist regimes. (After the SPD government fell in 1982, Brandt's leadership and line in the Socialist International were increasingly challenged by southern European parties in office, notably the French Socialist Party on East–West and disarmament issues, and the Portuguese Socialist and Italian Social Democratic Parties on the SI's alleged opening to revolutionaries and 'Cuban influence' in Latin America.)

Social democracy was able to appear in the seventies as a centrist approach to world problems capable of promoting compromises based on universal humanist values. At the same time, however, the social basis of social democracy was being eroded by the long recession in the industrialized countries where unemployment appeared incurable by the eighties and the welfare state was plunged into a growing financial crisis. The pressing questions facing the industrialized societies were the reorganization of work and, even more fundamentally, the discovery of a social *purpose* to inspire a new phase of economic production. The preservation and expansion of Europe's democratic political culture required the involvement of ever larger sectors of the population in the definition of human and social needs, corresponding to new forms of production and new forms of technology. Yet the very appearance of a naturally evolving consensus around social democracy only reinforced essentially conservative and defensive postures in the working-class movement. Labour wanted to hang onto its golden age even as it slipped away.

The Left's timidity in proposing, and even more in pursuing, democratic responses to the deepening world economic crisis left the way open for the Right to shift the centre of political debate from social-economic to military and strategic questions. This very shift, however, involves a social-economic programme.

The proximity of the Soviet bloc, with its repressive political systems justifying themselves by an official ideology inherited from the same working-class movement, is a source of great political problems for European social democracy and an inhibiting factor in the development of bold new approaches. At every stage, the question arises of clearly marking the difference between social democracy (or Eurocommunism) and Soviet-bloc Communism, and this exercise could only become more delicate if and when there should be any real signs of peaceful convergence between the two systems.

For this and other reasons, the German Social Democrats' general approach was to fasten themselves ever more tightly to their Western anchor, NATO and the United States, even as they ventured deeper into the *terra incognita* of *Ostpolitik*. By accepting Belgian Foreign Minister Pierre Harmel's 'Report on Future Tasks of the Alliance' in December 1967, NATO had officially defined its goals as both defence and détente. Deterrence was supposed to strengthen détente, and vice versa. This did not seem contradictory in Bonn, but it could appear so in Washington to leaders who saw less and less interest in paying to protect West Germany's economic and political projects in Eastern Europe.

Schmidt's exasperation with Carter was symptomatic of a more basic problem facing Social Democratic leaders: the drastic decline of their best political friends in the United States. The SPD had long counted on Democratic Party liberals to understand its problems and to protect its basic interests in international affairs. In the seventies, however, the social democratic tendencies in the Democratic Party underwent an erosion of their social base, and thus contributed to the election in 1980 of an administration which virtually excluded the SPD's liberal friends in the Eastern establishment from any say in policy making.

The Missiles Strike German Politics

Helmut Schmidt emerged as the most prestigious of Western leaders — a clever, tough man, under whose leadership the Federal Republic was no longer 'an economic giant and a political dwarf', but was beginning to gain a normal amount of political weight. But just when it seemed that Schmidt was able to make his views heard even on strategic nuclear questions, he began to fall, or to be led, into the Euromissile trap that would be his undoing.

When, at the Guadeloupe summit in January 1979, Carter announced America's forthcoming gift of Pershing-2 and cruise missiles, to Europe, Schmidt evidently did not see the trap. It was all decided very hurriedly and the information about the Pershing-2 was vague. Nearly five years later, at the SPD's special anti-missiles congress in Cologne in November 1983, Horst Ehmke confessed that the SDP leadership, and especially old Herbert Wehner, had had an overwhelmingly critical response to Schmidt's report-back from Guadeloupe.

'We all made mistakes', said Ehmke, explaining that in politics, decisions have to be made promptly and 'not everything can be foreseen'.

Whether or not SPD leaders were quick to spot the strategic trap, they obviously had their work cut out to win rank-and-file acceptance of what would surely be denounced as a gratuitous and provocative escalation in the nuclear arms race. Beyond these party concerns, it was necessary to save détente despite the predictably angry and suspicious reaction of Soviet leaders to the NATO modernization.

The SPD had a tradition of opposition to nuclear armament. On 22 March 1958 Helmut Schmidt, then the young defence policy spokesman for the SPD faction, made an impassioned speech in the Bundestag against NATO plans to arm the Bundeswehr with tactical nuclear weapons. Schmidt warned that 'the decision to arm the two parts of our fatherland against each other with atomic bombs will in history look as grave and fateful as the bill granting full powers to Hitler.' In the fifties, the SPD and the trade union confederation DGB led a mass movement against the nuclear arming of the Bundeswehr.

However, any governing party in the Federal Republic must adjust its policies to American requirements, while the party leadership must seek to ensure that they do not provoke the disaffection of voters and of its own rank and file. The function of mediating between voters' expectations and opposing forces, of rationalizing concessions and compromises, is common to all Social Democratic — and other — parties. But is is made particularly essential and delicate in the Federal Republic by the country's limited sovereignty.

The SPD's loyalty to NATO is a prime example of this function at its most accomplished. Social Democrats have been persuaded that NATO, by integrating the Bundeswehr into an international force under American command, was the best safeguard against any resurgence of German militarism. This argument enables SPD leaders to present themselves to the Americans, in all sincerity, as the most faithful of allies, and at the same time, with equal sincerity, to justify their position to anti-militarists within their own party as well as to Warsaw Pact governments.

After Guadeloupe, Schmidt succeeded in getting the missile deployment 'doubled' with an arms control negotiations 'track'. This allowed the whole package to be rationalized as another step forward in the NATO policy, as defined by the Harmel Report, of combining defence with détente. The Pentagon had already persuaded NATO's High Level Group to accept its plan to station 672 nuclear missiles in Europe when, in April 1979, a Special Group was set up at Schmidt's request to work out possible terms of an arms control agreement that could accompany (and perhaps reduce) the deployment, so as to keep the arms control process alive and prevent a runaway arms race in Europe. Schmidt could thus maintain to his party that he was exercising a decisive influence on his American friends and guiding them toward negotiations with the Soviet Union that would provide better than SALT-II had done for European security needs. Indeed, the NATO modernization decision was justified as a necessary incitement to a fruitful SALT-III.

This was the line put forth to an incredulous and increasingly restive SPD — the first occasion being the party congress held in Berlin on 3–7 December 1979, only a few days before the fateful Brussels decision. Although the Berlin congress ruled out any 'exclusive stationing of medium-range nuclear missiles on German soil', SPD defence minister Hans Apel went on to accept the NATO plan to station Pershing-2 exclusively on German soil.

When the double decision was being taken by NATO, Major-General Gert Bastian was commander of the twelfth tank division which, like all West German forces, is under NATO command. Disturbed by the haste and superficiality of the debate, General Bastian sent an eight-page memorandum to Defence Minister Hans Apel complaining that discussion in Germany had been biased by terminology which made it seem that the NATO arms buildup (*Nachrüstung*) was a follow-up to a Soviet advance (*Vorrüstung*). The prevailing arguments made it impossible to recognize what a decisive switch was being made, a switch that 'would result in a highly significant new distribution of nuclear capacity and risk among the allies themselves, as much as between the superpowers.'

General Bastian insisted that nuclear deterrence depended on global balance between the two superpowers, which the new missiles, far from rectifying, threatened to undo. The United States had understandably considered Soviet plans to station medium-range missiles in Cuba in 1962 as an intolerable provocation. 'Now today, isn't it to be expected that the Soviet Union would likewise take the stationing of US medium-range nuclear weapons aimed at its vital centres as a provocation?' It was obvious that 'such a conspicuous nuclear force' on German soil, able to cause strategically significant damage to the USSR within a few minutes, inescapably raised the question whether in a situation where war seemed imminent the Soviet Union might not feel 'flatly obliged to get rid of this new risk through a preventive nuclear strike'. The danger was only increased, General Bastian added, by all the public conjecture that United

States strategic forces could no longer be counted on to protect non-American interests. 'By the new distribution of nuclear strike capacity, decided in Brussels last December 12, Central Europeans' prospects of survival in case deterrence breaks down have been made even slimmer than they were, that is, reduced to zero!' Moreover, the chances of breakdown in deterrence had been considerably increased.

Apel tried to muzzle General Bastian by transferring him to an obscure desk job. The General was eventually able to retire and in November 1980 co-sponsored the Krefeld Appeal against the missile deployment, which within a year gathered over two million signatures. That was the beginning of the mass peace movement whose strength was first displayed on 10 October 1981, when three hundred thousand demonstrated in Bonn against nuclear weapons. In March 1983 General Bastian entered the Bundestag as one of the first nationally elected representatives of the new Green Party.

In 1980, however, criticism of the NATO modernization was inhibited by the Soviet invasion of Afghanistan and by residual confidence in the Democratic administration in Washington to pursue arms control negotiations with the Russians. Moreover, 1980 was a German election year, and not only Social Democrats but even much of the left that would later turn to the Greens rallied around Schmidt after the Christian Democrats chose the Bavarian right-wing leader Franz-Josef Strauss to head their ticket. The Euromissile controversy would become the overarching public controversy only after officials of the new Reagan administration began to talk of being in a 'pre-war period' and to suggest the possibility of limited nuclear war.

SPD leaders sought to contain the protests rising within their own party and to channel the debate toward demands for arms control negotiations that might strengthen Schmidt's hand vis-à-vis Washington and Moscow. Party leaders Brandt and Herbert Wehner cracked down hard on dissent that went outside certain bounds of decorum and political rationale. Thus outspoken Bundestag member Karl-Heinz Hansen was even expelled from the SPD, ostensibly for rude statements about Schmidt. But the content of Hansen's criticism, denouncing the drift toward military spending and arms exports at the expense of Third World development aid, was also offensive. This was not the kind of approach the SPD leadership was prepared to tolerate.

Nonetheless it stands to reason that some SPD leaders, notably Willy Brandt, secretly welcomed the development of a West German peace movement against the nuclear missiles. The United States Senate had refused to ratify SALT-II, and the Reagan administration showed no interest in arms control negotiations. However, German leaders sincerely wanted arms control, and were beginning to have doubts about the Pershing-2. The existence of a large and growing peace movement might help Schmidt persuade American officials of the need to assuage German fears by negotiating with Moscow.

The peace movement was also an asset in dealing with the Russians. Given the grave potential dangers of the Pershing-2 deployment, it could be essential to show the Russians that the German people, far from nursing a warlike spirit of revenge, had learned from their dreadful past and become truly peace-loving.

The major voice against the missiles within the SPD was the Protestant leader Erhard Eppler, an eloquent speaker who analysed the strategic logic behind the Pershing-2. At the Young Socialist (Juso) congress in the summer of 1981, Eppler asked why there was suddenly all this talk about the Soviet SS-20. Soviet SS-4 and SS-5 intermediate-range missiles had been aimed at Western Europe for twenty years, and no one had paid attention. Why now were the Americans so worked up, so intent on deploying missiles of their own? 'It has nothing at all to do with the SS-20s,' said Eppler. 'There is absolutely no logical connection between the deployment of the SS-20s on one side and the deployment of the Pershing-2 and cruise missiles on the other.' The Pershings provide, if anything, a target for the SS-20s, but certainly not a defence. In reality, he said, the Pershings belong to 'an entirely different context' from the SS-20s, the context of new American strategic thinking about the possibility of waging and winning a limited nuclear war with numerous, smaller warheads and more accurate missiles. Specialists were currently discussing the fact that, in a tense situation, the fear generated by the thought that an enemy first strike might largely disarm one's *own* side would be too much for human nerves. 'And when, in addition, missiles are stationed in the German Federal Republic that can strike Soviet command centres in the Kremlin and elsewhere within five minutes, then tension will naturally rise.' Eppler noted that Bonn defence officials justified the Pershings with the argument that because the USSR had 'taken the German population hostage' with its SS-20s, NATO must take part of the Soviet population hostage. 'Then don't be surprised if a new conflict begins with a super-Mogadishu with the Russians freeing their hostages.'[4]

The matter could have been put even more bluntly. By embedding their most deadly first-strike weapons in densely populated Baden-Württemberg, the *Americans* were actually taking the *German* population hostage. For in case of a crisis, the USSR could not 'take out' the

Pershing-2 first-strike missiles without taking out a substantial part of the German civilian population, thus committing a massive crime that could justify even more massive retaliation. From the American point of view, there could be no safer place to put their missiles. This began to dawn on SPD leaders when they learned that American objections to stationing the missiles at sea rather than on land were not founded technologically or militarily.

By the time the SPD held its next congress in Munich in April 1982, the dangers of the NATO double decision were much clearer to more people than they had been in 1979. In the security debate, a majority of delegates was clearly convinced by the critics of the missiles, led by Erhard Eppler and Oskar Lafontaine. The only way the party leadership kept the congress from voting then and there against the Euromissile deployment was by shifting the debate from the substantial question (missiles: yes or no) to the tactical question of when and how the party decision could be most effective. Egon Bahr, considered a major architect of the SPD *Ostpolitik* for his work in negotiating the treaties with Eastern Europe, was given the task of defending the leadership resolution to postpone the Euromissile decision until another congress in the autumn of 1983. Bahr argued that since saying 'yes' or 'no' to the missiles was the only decision the Federal Republic had the legal and especially political weight to make, the decision should be held off as long as possible to put maximum pressure on both the Soviet Union and the United States to reach a satisfactory agreement in the Geneva intermediate-range nuclear forces (INF) talks. Bahr tried to make it seem that the INF talks were a necessary and normal extension of détente, following a long-range plan envisaged back in 1969. This required three stages. First came a bilateral stage of Bonn's treaties with Eastern Europe, then a multilateral stage (the Helsinki accords) and, finally, a third step of 'transferring détente to the military field'. The INF and the Mutual Balanced Forces Reduction (MBFR) talks in Vienna were necessary to complete the work of détente, which could not survive the arms race. Whatever the impact of Bahr's speech, we can be sure that the fear of openly defying the United States was a powerful unspoken motive underlying the decision to postpone a decision.

Schmidt's speech at the end of the debate, described by *Le Monde* as a display of the Chancellor's ability to master his troublesome party, was largely a boast of his power to master his troublesome allies. Schmidt said although he had been the main target of a recent spate of anti-European editorials and cartoons in American newspapers, blasting European reluctance to go along with anti-Soviet economic sanctions, he was able to stand up to it and had the best existing credentials for successfully influencing the Americans 'through four different administrations'.

An April 1982 report to the US Senate Foreign Relations Committee entitled 'NATO Today: the Alliance in Evolution' confidently predicted that should the SPD congress in Munich that month 'reject Schmidt's position, either Schmidt would govern without SPD support on this issue or a centre–right coalition would be formed.'

So the party never really had anything to say on the matter.

The following October, Schmidt was forced out of office when the SPD's junior partner in the governing coalition, the Free Democratic Party (the tail that wagged the dog), switched over to the Christian Democrats. After that, it was inevitable that the SPD's long-inhibited opposition to the NATO double decision would finally be clearly expressed. At one regional assembly after another in the summer and autumn of 1983, Social Democrats voted overwhelmingly against any Pershing-2 or cruise missiles on German soil. This was finally formalized at a special party congress in Cologne in November.

The Peace Movement

By that time, the peace movement which sprung up in protest against the missile deployment had transformed the West German political and cultural landscape. It grew so rapidly, into the most significant popular movement in the West, by tapping important existing intellectual, moral and political sources.

In October 1983, Protestant peace movement leader Volkmar Deile was able to observe — at the end of a DGB conference at which trade unionists argued down Defence Minister Manfred Wörner on the fine points of AirLand Battle, 'horizontal escalation' and the Pentagon's 'decapitation' strategy — that the peace movement had succeeded in 'democratizing defence policy' — or at least the debate.

The German peace movement has by no means relied solely on moral or emotional appeals, however compelling these may be. A movement based on 'Protestant *Angst*' (in Richard Perle's memorable phrase) would not necessarily have had any clear focus or direction, and it would have been hard put to counter the fear — of the other side — that was constantly evoked to justify the new weapons. Indeed, in 1980, the Schmidt government came under attack less from the left than from the right, which accused it of failing to react vigorously to the SS-20 threat. Political rhetoric aside, however, Germany's exposed position was conducive to serious curiosity about the real strategic significance or potential uses of all the mass destruction weapons stationed on its soil or pointed at it. The Euromissile controversy thus stimulated an outpouring of well-reasoned, thoroughly documented books and articles, whose readers in and around the peace movement now comprise a large minority of citizens extraordinarily well informed about military and strategic questions.

An important contribution to this public understanding came from the Peace Research Institutes established in years past to promote détente — in keeping with the Federal Republic's constitutional commitment to 'serve peace in the world' — with the backing of *Land* governments, churches or foundations. Several of the most influential peace researchers, such as Alfred Mechtersheimer and Count von Baudissin, are former Bundeswehr officers with inside knowledge of NATO. It soon became possible, then, to argue credibly that the Americans were imposing on NATO a new strategy which did not enhance the defence of the Federal Republic but actually imperilled its survival. While most of the West German press is in the hands of conservative publishers (above all, the notorious Springer chain), much of this criticism was made available to the broader public by the liberal weeklies *Stern* and *Der Spiegel*.

From an initial concentration on the Euromissiles, the intellectual work stimulated by the peace movement has broadened out to questions of alternative defence, arms industry reconversion, and especially the relationship between the arms race and the Third World.

In October 1983, the Bonn public library listed 115 recent books on the theme of 'peace', many of them dealing directly with the missiles and related military or strategic questions. A few were concerned with psychological problems of aggressiveness and the 'enemy image'. Some had a Christian ethical basis. The influence of Protestantism on the German peace movement is too pervasive to be readily measured, and goes beyond church support. Germany is unique in the contemporary West in that theology, largely in the sense of imperative ethics is part of the intellectual mainstream and an aspect of left culture.

Protestant theologians have been prominent speakers at all major peace rallies. At its national church meeting in Hamburg in June 1981, the Protestant Church gave its backing to the growing movement, under the influence of the Dutch. The large-scale Protestant commitment in turn encouraged grassroots Catholic peace activity, in spite of the conservative attitude of the German Catholic hierarchy. But it is the Lutheran theme of duty to the dictates of conscience that predominates, evidently strengthened by the national disgrace of the Hitler period. There is widespread determination among Christians to resist from the start any tendencies to involve Germany in projects to bring war to other peoples, so that never again will 'good Germans' be reproached with having made evil possible by passive acquiescence.

A system of tithing, by which a portion of individual tax payments goes to the designated church, gives German churches the means to support international programmes devoted to root causes of war such as hunger, apartheid and third world exploitation. The high rate of conscientious objection provides able young volunteers for such programmes. The Action Reconciliation Peace Service (ASF), supported by Protestant Churches, with a strong international awareness and influenced by the disarmament campaign of the Dutch Inter-Church Peace Council (IKV), was the vanguard of Protestant participation in the peace movement of the eighties.

The West German churches have a special sensitivity to he situation of the churches in East Germany and of the need for détente in order to combat the excessive militarization of life in the East.

The peace movement also grafted itself onto a remarkably vigorous environmental protection movement. In the late seventies, there had grown up some forty thousand local 'citizens' initiatives', *Bürgerinitiativen*, whose national coordinator, young Social Democrat Jo Leinen, went on to become chairman of the national Coordinating Committee that planned the main actions against Pershing-2 and cruise missile deployment. It was not hard to persuade civic-minded citizens, ready to protest against an atomic power plant or other local nuisance, that a Pershing-2 base across the playground from their suburban school would not enhance the quality of life.

The protests against Pershing-2 and cruise gave the German Communist Party (DKP) a unique chance to emerge from its isolation, and it zealously lent its organizational skills to such campaigns as the Krefeld Appeal, collecting literally millions of signatures. At rallies, DKP speakers tend to dwell on the past; the terrible destruction visited by Nazi Germany on the Soviet Union and Eastern Europe, the fatal disunity of the German Left that let Hitler come to power, and so on. In the name of that past, they stress the need for left unity (meaning a place for the DKP) and Germany's duty to leave its Eastern neighbours in peace. Communists tend to interpret this duty as precluding any criticism of the Eastern regimes, even of Soviet nuclear arms or arrests of unofficial peace activists in East Germany. This defensive pro-Sovietism and general political style have been a growing source of irritation to other elements of the peace movement, especially Greens seeking to build a peace movement that transcends blocs. On the other hand, the centrists in the peace movement — that is, the Protestants and left Social Democrats — sometimes have seemed to make use of the DKP presence as a sort of conservative ballast.

The battle against the missiles played an essential role in the recomposition of the German Left. It virtually created the Green Party, providing an issue of sufficient urgency to overcome the fragmentation inherent in the highly decentralized ecology movement. The Green experiment was the culmination of a long process that began with the Socialist German Student Association (SDS) in the sixties.

From Red to Green

On Christmas Eve 1979, just twelve days after the NATO double decision, the symbolic leader of the SDS, Rudi Dutschke, died in exile in Denmark. It had taken nearly a dozen years for the bullets fired into his brain in a West Berlin street on 7 April 1968 to put an end to his life. Dutschke was less a real leader than an emblem of the generation that re-created the German left out of moral indignation in the sixties. Like many German radicals of his generation, his political involvement grew out of a Christian moral sense. He refused military service in his native East Germany as a conscientious objector, and in 1961 moved to West Berlin, shortly before the Wall went up. He was then twenty-one. At the Free University he turned from Protestant theology to sociology, from religion to politics.

The West German New Left of the sixties was based on a double rejection: rejection of the 'actually existing socialism' of the Eastern European regimes, and rejection of the 'realism' of the SPD that had led it, at its 1959 Bad Godesberg congress, to abandon the goal of replacing capitalism with socialism. In the process of giving itself a more conservative image, leading up to Willy Brandt's accession to the Chancellorship in 1969, the SPD broke with the SDS, which went its own way to become the centre of an extra-parliamentary opposition concerned with principles rather than electoral compromises, and notably with solidarity for third world struggles.

Like many of his contemporaries, Dutschke was strongly influenced by philosopher Ernst Bloch, who helped to rehabilitate utopianism by showing the universal hopes for a better society expressed in religions. Dutschke was also influenced by Herbert

Marcuse's analysis of the ways in which advanced industrial society suppresses opposition through the authoritarian structures of state power, technological power and the mass media. Dutschke hoped that 'consciousness-raising' would eventually make it 'impossible for the elite to manipulate us'.

It was in effect the mass media that struck him down, through a 23-year-old house-painter, Josef Bachmann, who had read about 'Red Rudi' in the sensation-mongering Springer press and said he wanted to kill a 'dirty communist'. Bachmann was jailed for seven years after Dutschke's lawyers argued that he was only the unwitting tool of more powerful forces. Dutschke himself, who lost his memory as a result of the attack and had to relearn languages and his field of sociology, began a 'consciousness-raising' correspondence with Bachmann to help them both understand what had moved the young worker to try to kill him. Bachmann was apparently affected by this correspondence, and it was reportedly after not having heard from Dutschke for a while that he committed suicide in 1970.

The attack on Dutschke moved a minority of the movement to despair of peaceful political action. 'The bullets fired at Rudi put an end to the dreams of non-violence. If you don't take up arms, you die,' wrote Ulrike Meinhof, who two years later joined with Andreas Baader to found the disastrous Red Army Faction. The Baader–Meinhof saga, which ended with the surviving leaders' mysterious mass suicide in Stammheim prison in 1977, attracted worldwide media attention. The image of West Germany in the seventies was of a repressive, conformist society absorbed in hunting down a handful of extremist desperadoes.

Less conspicuously, the overwhelming majority of the veterans of the sixties new left, like Dutschke himself, preferred the 'long march through the institutions', notably the schools and the media, to try to spread anti-authoritarian awareness. Many ran foul of the *Berufsverbot* when they tried to get jobs. Some went into voluntary exile. Many more grouped together to create the most vigorous autonomous counter-culture in the West, moving away from traditional views of class struggle toward ecological issues.

Dutschke himself went to England with his American wife and baby son to convalesce and resume his studies, only to be thrown out as politically undesirable. West German universities were closed to him. Denmark let him take a university teaching job and settle in the town of Aarhus. In the late seventies, he began moving back into West German political life, commuting to Bremen to work in the anti-nuclear movement there. The month before he died, he took part in the foundation of the new nationwide Green Party.

The death of Dutschke, the NATO double decision, the change of decade, all mark a change of phase in the German Left. Throughout the long years of marginalization, the German New Left never let up its work of analysis and self-criticism. In no other radical movement is triumphalism more totally absent and the 'pessimism of the intellect' more systematically exercised. This perseverence meant that a substantial minority struggled through the sectarian desert of the seventies to the Green oasis of the early eighties.

The far left in the rich countries in the seventies was subject to two sorts of disintegration. The internal disintegration was precipitated by battles between rival 'vanguards', each with the correct revolutionary line, vying for leadership of a shrinking mass movement. The external disintegration took place as activists abandoned all-encompassing groups for new single-issue or special-interest movements, of which the broadest were the women's and ecology movements. The creation of the Green Party was a first stab at the recomposition of those movements into a unified political force.

By mid 1982, the Green Party had made it over the five per cent barrier into several *Land* parliaments and was scoring considerably more in federal opinion polls. The FDP 'betrayal' of Schmidt in the autumn of that year created a wave of popular sympathy for the SPD just as it was forced out of government. In late 1982, polls showed a potential majority for a new left coalition of the SPD with the Green Party, about to make its first serious bid to enter the Bundestag. For a brief interlude, this faint prospect provided Europe's beleaguered leftists with one of their wildest dreams: the colourful mirage of a 'red-green' coalition of old left Social Democrats and new left Greens able to block the rightward swing in Europe.

This hope was premature. Not ready for such an adventure, SPD leaders themselves dispelled the illusion midway through the campaign for the 6 March 1983 elections by announcing that they would not even enter into talks with the Greens, whose offers of conditional support to an SPD government were spurned. Instead, SPD candidates stressed their concern for peace and the environment in a vain effort to win enough potential Green votes to keep the newcomers out of the Bundestag.

SPD leaders cannot really have been eager to win an election that would have put them back in office with an ambiguous mandate to face the wrath of both the Reagan administration and business leaders in their own country. Both had made it known in no uncertain terms that they wanted to see the conservative CDU–FDP coalition returned under Chancellor Helmut Kohl. The economic blackmail was extraordinarily brutal. Business leaders let it be understood that the nation's investment capital was perched on the Swiss border, ready to flee abroad the instant a red–green coalition won the elections. Business contracts were written with an 'election clause' stipulating that all deals would be null and void if voters made the wrong choice. One civil court actually ruled, in the case of an employee who had been wrongly dismissed, that his employer would have to take him back, but only if the conservatives won the elections. Otherwise, it was implied, there would be no more orders to fill, no more jobs — the economy would grind to a halt on 7 March.

These were the elections that were described by a number of observers as the most fateful held in Europe since the Second World War, and which would be triumphantly interpreted as the German people's consent to missile deployment. But the leading parties did not make an issue of the missiles, and people could still hope that the Geneva INF negotiations would get rid of the problem. The majority voted above all for the favourable business climate which, they were told, would assure an economic upswing. Even in the SPD stronghold in the Ruhr, many working class voters went over to the conservative coalition, reckoning that free enterprise had to be given its way if the economy was to start moving again.

No upswing ensued, and employment prospects continued to worsen. In these circumstances, the legendary post-war patience of German labour could run out very abruptly. For that patience, that readiness to collaborate with the interests of capital, was based on an explicit social pact providing full employment and social welfare benefits.

Thus the last half of 1983 saw the slow but sure rapprochement of the peace movement with the eight-million-member German Trade Union Confederation, the DGB. So far, German union leaders have rejected the arms lobby claim that weapons production is good for employment — but it must be admitted that the arms lobby in West Germany has, for obvious historical reasons, long been more discreet than in other countries. This could change with the Reaganization of Europe. DGB leaders cite studies showing that arms investment creates fewer and less secure jobs than other kinds of investment, and support Willy Brandt's proposal to cut military spending by five per cent in all countries and to earmark the funds for economic development in the Third World. Theoretically, such a measure might help to save German export markets and thus, German jobs.

German labour has been coming around to the peace movement at a time when, as in other developed countries, it is severely weakened by unemployment. By loyally following the United States, the conservative coalition may hope to get for Germany a big share of the action in a new development cycle. But even this will not help labour. High technology economic growth no longer produces jobs. German economists envisage the development of a split economy, with a highly productive, technologically advanced and profitable capital-intensive sector on the one hand, and, on the other, relatively un-productive labour-intensive activities or simply people with nothing to do. This prospect raises the major political question of how, and to what extent, the wealth produced by the capital-intensive, largely automated sector would support the mass of people outside it. The right's answer — in order to keep the idlers as far as possible from the money-making machine — is a return to traditional values and above all the traditional family (or rather, the nineteenth century family) with one breadwinner who takes care of his dependants. At the other end of the spectrum, the Greens are groping at the idea of community control of the productive mechanism for socially and ecologically beneficial purposes.

Here, the issue of war or peace may be the key. History is full of examples to show that mass idleness, especially of young males, tends to be resolved sooner or later by recruiting them for war. On the other hand, if a widespread awareness develops of the need to reconvert the militarist section of the economy — simply in order to assure the most basic human and social need, survival — then a political culture could emerge which seeks to adapt the entire economy to democrati-cally defined human needs.

A recent consensus has formed on the left that workers' control is essential to democratic socialism. But attempts at workers' control have generally foundered on the indifference of most workers to the idea of exercising 'control' for its own sake, or for the sake of some-thing as abstract as 'socialism'. To start with the workers may be the wrong way around. The answer to the question *why* they should bother to control what they are doing should properly come from society at large — from a society able to speak up clearly for a new kind of demand, and ready to support workers who decide to stop harmful activities in favour of beneficial ones. This is a distant Utopia indeed. But under the deadly gun of the Euromissiles, its dim outline begins to be visible.

The German Question

For over thirty years, the overwhelming majority of West Germans accepted their country's limited sovereignty within the Atlantic Alliance without a murmur. It took the development of an American strategy for NATO that put the nation's very survival in jeopardy for the question of sovereignty to begin to be raised. It was raised only hesitantly. Unspoken, it underlay the long SPD struggle over 'the double decision': was the Federal Republic's right to say yes or no only a pretence, which would be kept up so long as it said 'yes' but would be exposed as a fraud if ever it dared say 'no'? And with what political consequences?

The Pentagon's busy champion of strategic superiority, Richard Perle, is quoted as saying flatly that the United States can station whatever it likes, since Germany in an occupied country.[5] Inevitably, then, the Euromissiles affair has called Germans' attention to the abnormal status of their nation. This was not, however, a main preoccupation of the movement to stop missile deployment, and the accusations of 'nationalism' voiced in some other countries were either prejudiced, malicious or, at the least, premature.

The alarm was sounded on the other side as well. When the second European Nuclear Disarmament (END) convention was being planned to take place in West Berlin in May 1983, the president of the official Soviet Peace Committee, Yuri Zhukov, sent a particularly irritable letter to over a thousand peace activists in Europe complaining that 'the organizers plan to bring a so-called "German question" into discussion at the Convention, thus trying to challenge the inviolability of the post-war European frontiers and to violate the letter and the spirit of the Helsinki Final Act.' The Soviet peace bureaucrat fancied he spotted 'an interference in the internal affairs of the German Democratic Republic, and a provocative attempt to force onto the anti-war movement an issue which has nothing to do with the movement for a nuclear-free Europe and which resuscitates revanchist sentiments.'

In reality, the German question has everything to do with the movement for a nuclear-free Europe — even if most of the movement prefers not to think about it — and the discussion at the West Berlin END Convention was a healthy step toward bringing it out of the closet. Theodor Schweisfurth, a specialist in international law from the Max Planck Institute, noted that everyone seemed to think the 'German question' meant reunification, when the problem would really be very complex. Normally, after a war, there is a peace treaty. After the Second World War, for example, one was signed with Italy. But not with Germany, because the victorious powers could not agree. Legally, said Schweisfurth, the Federal Republic could not withdraw from NATO. The Soviet Union and the United States have the right to remain with their troops. Schweisfurth therefore suggested that the demand should be put forward for a peace treaty.

The left, non-aligned 'national liberation' current in the peace movement, represented by a small group in West Berlin around Peter Brandt and Herbert Ammon, call for a confederation bringing together the two German states and West Berlin in a 'German community' which would sign a peace treaty with the victors of World War II and adopt a non-aligned policy 'on the Austrian model'.[6] Most of the German peace movement, however, regards this as a dangerous pipe dream that can serve only to arouse suspicion and hostility among Germany's neighbours. There is an awareness that, as Ulrich Albrecht has stressed, 'every other country has a fundamental interest in keeping Germany divided.'

'If Germany today could be towed away to the South Pacific, the United States and the Soviet Union would have to ask themselves what their quarrel is all about,' columnist William Pfaff wrote in February 1983. The formulation suggests impatience with Germany for causing so much trouble. Yet there has never been any serious effort on the part of the United States government to settle its quarrel with the Soviet Union over Germany. Many years ago, Soviet leaders more than once indicated readiness to negotiate a more stable arrangement. In 1953, after the death of Stalin, Georgii Malenkov made hints in that direction, and Churchill called for a summit conference. This was rebuffed by Washington. American diplomat Charles Bohlen said later that 'from what we know now, this would have been a very fruitful period and might easily have led to a radical solution in our favour of the German question . . . '

Again in the late fifties, in the period leading up to the Wall, Khrushchev's offers to negotiate a permanent and reasonable status for the two German states and Berlin were dismissed by Washington as 'threats' that had to be firmly resisted. After the right-wing furore over Yalta, with the accusations of Communist manipulation and betrayal, it seems that no American government ever dared even to think of negotiating seriously with the Soviet Union on the future of Europe. A policy of force, even if sterile, was always politically safer. The American military establishment grew used to Germany as a comfortable and indeed congenial forward base, the favourite overseas posting. America's allies, especially France, were satisfied with the situation and would be alarmed at even the slightest move toward German reunification.

Finally, Konrad Adenauer, the aged former mayor of Cologne

plucked by the victors from his rose garden to lead the West German government, was no enthusiast for reunification. The old Rhinelander did not really mind being cast loose from Prussia. He was only too happy to attach the Federal Republic firmly to the West. Moreover, without Protestant, Social Democratic Prussia, the Federal Republic could more easily continue to be predominantly Catholic, conservative and Christian Democratic.

The Federal Republic's constituion requires its government to pursue the goal of reunification. The Adenauer government did this verbally, by refusing to recognize in any way the existing separation or the new Eastern border of East Germany imposed by the Soviet Union when it moved the whole of Poland westward. Theoretically, Germany would be reunited when the Russians withdrew and the states it had set up in East Germany and Poland collapsed. How this was to transpire was never spelled out.

In practice, loyalty to NATO was the most effective obstacle to reunification. In 1957 renewed Soviet efforts to avoid nuclear rearmament of West Germany — through the establishment of a nuclear-free zone in Central Europe that would theoretically have preserved and even enhanced the possibility of reunification — were blocked by Western demands for all-German free elections for a government that would be free to join NATO. The Soviet Union could never agree to a reunified Germany as the spearhead of a military alliance against the USSR.

The SPD, throughout that period, was most earnestly concerned with reunification, in part perhaps for the same reason that the Christian Democrats were less eager: the Eastern territories were the traditional stronghold of Protestantism and Social Democracy. In the mid 1950s, SPD leader Fritz Erler came up with the idea of European 'security for and from Germany' that could take the form of a 'collective security system' involving all European states, instead of two hostile military pacts. To a large extent, NATO and the Warsaw Pact served precisely to achieve "security for and from Germany", especially *from* Germany, keeping the two German states permanently divided.

In the late 1950s, the SPD and the DGB supported the mass movement to keep nuclear weapons out of Germany, and specifically, to prevent the equipping of the Bundeswehr with weapons capable of carrying nuclear warheads, to retract the agreement to store NATO nuclear warheads in Germany, and to prevent the stationing of US short and medium-range missiles. In July 1958, over three hundred thousand people took part in anti-nuclear demonstrations.

There were significant similarities between the late fifties and early eighties. In both periods, the elite American 'crisis peddlers'[7] were taking advantage of technological breakthroughs to urge costly and ambitious arms programmes aimed at establishing American global strategic superiority, while publicly promoting the buildup as necessary to counter a threatening new 'Soviet superiority' which never in fact existed. In both periods, Soviet reluctance to be forced into an expensive new round of weapons development seemed to offer the prospect of negotiations in which Moscow might be willing to make some concessions, and northern European Social Democracy did what it could to support this possibility.

In particular, the SPD and the DGB had strongly supported the proposal put before the United Nations General Assembly on 3 October 1957 by Polish foreign minister Adam Rapacki for an atomic-weapons-free zone in Central Europe. Rapacki announced that if the two German states agreed to ban production and stock-piling of atomic and thermonuclear weapons on their territories, the Polish People's Republic was prepared simultaneously to impose a similar ban on its own territory. The Czechoslovak government sub-sequently expressed its willingness to do the same. In the West, Belgium's Christian Democrat foreign minister Pierre Harmel was interested in the proposal and made contact with Rapacki until discouraged by his NATO Allies.

The 'Rapacki Plan' fitted in with Soviet efforts to stop the Americans from equipping NATO's German forces with nuclear weapons. A few months earlier, on 20 April 1957, Marshal Nikolai Bulganin, the Soviet prime minister, had written to British Prime Minister Harold Macmillan on a loosely defined 'Eden Plan' for establishing a demilitarized zone in Europe and areas of restricted armaments. The tone of the letter was unmistakably conciliatory. Macmillan replied that no settlement of East–West issues was possible unless a reunified Germany would be free to join NATO. This stipulation, upheld by the Adenauer government, was clearly unacceptable to the Russians.

About the same time, on 27 April, the Soviet government sent a much ruder note to Bonn charging that West Germany was being converted into 'the main European springboard and chief NATO shock-force for atomic war in Europe'. 'It is quite obvious that the conversion of the Federal Republic into a NATO atomic base is bound in the event of war to make West Germany the immediate object of retaliation by all types of modern weapons, including rocket weapons,' the Soviet note said, thereby announcing the SS-4 and SS-5 missiles, ancestors of the SS-20, that would be deployed in the Western USSR in the early sixties. 'There is no need to dwell in detail on the consequences this would entail for the Federal Republic, which has such a density of population and concentration of industry that the vital centres of the country could be paralysed by a single hydrogen bomb,' the Soviet government wrote threateningly, adding that 'Germany would become one vast graveyard . . . ' 'If the policy pursued by the Federal Republic — a policy of remilitarization, accession to aggressive military blocs and suppression of democratic freedom[8] — has created great obstacles to the unification of Germany, the equipping of the Bundeswehr with atomic weapons and the conversion of West Germany into a centre of atomic war in Europe would strike an irreparable blow at the national reunification of the German people,' the note warned.

In the extremely acrimonious exchange that followed, Moscow accused the Bonn government of deceiving its own public opinion. It is noteworthy that Moscow's objections to the Pershing-2 were never couched in such brutally threatening terms. The memory of these pre-détente threats would explain the Schmidt government's insistence on not being the only country to accept missiles and its refusal of any 'double key' arrangement implying German control of their use.

In December 1957, on the eve of the NATO summit approving stockage of nuclear arms and IRBMs in Europe, Bulganin wrote to UN member countries proposing a demilitarized zone in Central Europe, comprising the two Germanies, Poland and Czechoslovakia, in which there would be no manufacture or stocking of nuclear weapons. This proposal was included in a seven-point peace resolution passed on 21 December. Then on 8 January, Bulganin sent notes to all nineteen NATO governments plus Sweden and Austria proposing summit negotiations and giving full support to the Rapacki Plan.

Contrary to the American dismissal of the Rapacki Plan as Soviet propaganda, many in Central Europe saw that the Polish government had its own good reasons for proposing a measure that would have eased Soviet pressure and prevented the subsequent militarization of both West and East Germany.

It was in the context of trying to prevent a nuclear arms buildup in West Germany that Khrushchev made his proposals for a three-state solution to the German question (the Federal Republic, the Democratic Republic and West Berlin as an internationally guaranteed free city) which Washington chose to interpret as threats and tests of strength. Finally, on 18 September 1959, Khrushchev made a truly sensational proposal to the United Nations General Assembly for a four-year general and complete disarmament programme under strict international supervision.

In March 1959, the SPD came up with its own Plan For Germany, to achieve German reunification and a European security system by stages. According to Rudolf Steinke[9], the SPD learned through 'intensive consultations in Moscow' that Soviet leaders had no more interest in this policy than did the Western allies and the reluctant Adenauer government. In its Godesberg Programme of that year, the SPD promised to 'strive for the inclusion of the whole of Germany in a European zone of détente and controlled arms limitations: foreign troops will be withdrawn from this zone as a consequence of the restoration of the unity of Germany in freedom, and no nuclear weapons or other means of mass destruction shall be either produced or stored or used in it.' Thereafter, the SPD dropped the mass protest movement against nuclear weapons as it sought ways to move from opposition into government.

The SPD's history of searching for accommodations made it a suitable party for government when, in the late sixties, the United States (in need of its own accommodation in Vietnam) decided to pursue a course of détente. By the time they were brought into coalition government in Bonn, SPD leaders had learned that despite what they might say in public, all European leaders (except for occasional flashes of British eccentricity) were firmly opposed to German reunification. In any case, the SPD never ruled alone and could never pursue any lingering yearning for daringly original policies.

Meanwhile, steps were taken on the Eastern side to make the division more irreversible. The Treaty on Relations between the German Democratic Republic and the USSR, signed on 20 September 1955, was extended in the Treaty on Friendship, Mutual Assistance and Cooperation of 12 June 1964, which committed East Germany to provide troops to assist the Soviet Union and allowed the USSR to station troops in East Germany *even after dissolution of the Warsaw Pact*, whose continuation is contingent on that of NATO. The treaty says that Berlin is to be regarded as an independent political entity, legally a part of the German Democratic Republic although still occupied by foreign powers and having a 'different social system'.

In this situation, Peter Brandt and Herbert Ammon see that 'a disengagement of the two German states from the two blocs, i.e., from the hegemonic powers, would hardly be possible without a massive movement from below. The beginnings of such a movement may be discerned in the emerging all-German peace movement. The new

German peace movement is in need of a goal such as has been prefigured for example, in E. P. Thompson's pan-European campaign.'

Any interpretation of the European nuclear disarmament movement as a step toward German reunification has aroused particularly strenuous objections from the Dutch movement's leaders in the Inter-Church Peace Council (IKV). Most of the German movement also considers that it would be politically disastrous to give itself goals that could boomerang by arousing the anti-German feelings that lie not very far below the surface in most of Europe.

There is far greater support for the quite contrary approach taken by Günter Gaus, who formerly represented the Federal Republic in East Berlin. Gaus maintains: 'The existence of clearly defined blocs in Europe is today the only chance for regaining as complete a guarantee of protection as possible for our own interests and for those of others.'[10] Like the SPD in general, Gaus would have West Germans work inside their own bloc to try to influence United States policy in the third world in particular. Gaus recognized: 'One day West German indifference to the national question will give way', but urges patience since: 'Only catastrophe walks on nimble feet and could rapidly be upon us in the form of war.'

This patience becomes harder to maintain as the Cold War is reheated. After the suppression of Solidarnosc by General Jaruzelski, the German Left and peace movement found their self-controlled discretion about Poland coming under vehement attack from the French Left, which seemed unaware of the dangerous sleeping dogs lying around the Polish question in Germany. Yet the delicacy of the matter is well known to the French political class.

'When Stalin decided to move the Polish border far to the West after World War II, the reason had little to do with blind expansionism,' writes Ulrich Albrecht.[11] 'The major political consideration was to solve the key Soviet security problem by creating a new Polish national state (on the ruins of the old one that had been destroyed by the Germans) with the Soviet Union acting as midwife. Stalin made a cynical, although extremely illuminating, remark to General de Gaulle in 1944: since the new Polish state was to arise on the former territory of the German Reich as far as the Oder and Neisse rivers, any hopes for a reconciliation between Germany and Poland would be permanently stifled, and the greatest threat to the USSR would be quashed. "Poland has regularly served the Germans as a corridor for attacking Russia," commented Stalin at that time. "That corridor must be blocked, and it can best be done by the Poles themselves." '

For twenty years of Christian Democratic government it was consistent Bonn policy to demand the return of Eastern territories 'under Polish administration', thus keeping alive fears of 'German revanchism' and helping fasten Poland to its Russian protector. While events in Poland in the early 1980s were presented by the French media, and consequently perceived by French public opinion, as a brutal revelation of dangerous Soviet expansionism, the very same events were understood in Germany as signs of the Soviet empire's weakness and eventual collapse — a development that should be allowed to proceed peacefully, without outside interference that could push the USSR into a defensive war. The German Left, like Ulrich Albrecht, considered that the far-ranging emancipatory developments in Poland were 'only conceivable, and indeed could only have become a reality, in the political setting created by Brandt's *Ostpolitik*.' West German restraint is the necessary condition for the emancipation of Eastern Europe.

It follows that the aggressive posture toward the East forced on the Federal Republic by the presence of Pershing-2 and cruise nuclear missiles will make any movement for Eastern European emancipation more difficult and more dangerous.

The necessarily discreet goal of northern European Social Democratic diplomacy has been the 'Finlandization' of Eastern Europe. 'The greatest achievement of Finnish politics,' writes Ulrich Albrecht, 'is that of having persuaded the Soviet Union that its vital interests were compatible with the existence of an independent Western-oriented Finland. The other Scandinavian countries contributed to the solution with their astute politics of consolidation. Sweden, despite earnest entreaties to join NATO, remained alliance-free, not because the Swedes were so enamoured of their own neutrality but, among other reasons, to relieve some of the Soviet pressure on Finland. . . . Although Norway and Denmark are members of NATO, their refusal to permit the stationing of nuclear weapons on their territory in peacetime helps further to buffer Finnish policy toward the East.' The 'Finlandization' of Eastern Europe would thus imply a certain 'Swedenization' of West Germany.

The consolidation of the German Democratic Republic is a fact that for any foreseeable future rules out a single German state.[12] The most for which anyone dares hope is some kind of very loose confederation, of which there are ample precedents in German history. But what seems most possible, at least as a first step toward a more united Europe, would be a southward extension of the Scandinavian model. 'Our movement is patriotic, not nationalist,' said peace movement coordination committee chairman Jo Leinen in answer to French accusations of 'national pacifism'.[13] 'There is no hidden phantasy of reunifying the "German nation". It is rather a new identity of the Federal Republic that is being brought out. I think we have the obligation, in the centre of Europe, with the history of the two world wars, to have progressive, even *avant garde* policies in the fields of disarmament, of political and military détente. Our new identity will be somewhat "Swedish" . . . '

Jo Leinen, a former full-time officer of the *Jusos* (Young Socialists, the youth organization of the SPD), was a leader of the three hundred thousand-member Federation of Citizens Initiatives for Environmental Protection before becoming involved in the peace movement. He said he had been able to see 'how a mass movement was in the process of forming on problems that the SPD was not prepared to deal with. And I felt that was going to change the culture and the political life of this country. So it was important to get involved in this mass movement outside the party, even if it meant going back in later to help it integrate that political reality.'

Rudolf Bahro, who was imprisoned and thrown out of East Germany for his criticism of the system in Eastern Europe, is vehemently opposed to such SPD recuperation of the peace movement. He considers that the working-class movement has become a conservative force in the advanced capitalist countries, and favours the entirely fresh political and social approach of the Greens. However, he too sees the peace movement as a chance for Germans to develop a new identity based on a new culture. Why, he asked rhetorically during a panel debate in Bonn in October 1981, was Europe now 'set up as a shooting gallery for both superpowers?' Why, even though there was no conflict, had the two superpowers put off withdrawing? Because, he answered, 'aggressive European culture' produced two world wars that started from Germany. 'And why now has this peace movement sprung up in such proportions? Because there they go again, planning to install new missiles that within a few minutes could cause as much damage to Russia as Hitler's armies in four years. That was a lesson we don't mean to forget. We don't mean to forget it, even though the Soviet Union is holding hostage European countries with no nuclear missiles. Both factors must be kept in mind. When people start talking about whether the Russians may be coming, well, twice in this century the Germans came, and in Germany this cannot be forgotten.'

Bahro added that so long as Germany was perceived as a potential military threat, the Russians had a perfect pretext to stay in Eastern

Europe and clamp down on every sign of dissent. But if Germany were demilitarized, both culturally and in fact, what excuse would the Russians have to stay on? This was the great historic opporunity for the peace movement to change Germans from the 'fright monsters' of the Western world into a people like any other.

The Horns of the Dilemma

At a special congress in Cologne on 19 November 1983, the SPD finally rejected the 'double decision', totally and overwhelmingly. Of four hundred delegates, only thirteen, including four former cabinet ministers, voted with Helmut Schmidt against the executive resolution opposing deployment of cruise and Pershing-2 nuclear missiles on German soil. The SPD did its best to make defeat painless for Schmidt, the better to go united, or nearly so, into the final Bundestag debate two days later. The official face-saving party line was that the 'double decision' might have ended happily in an arms control agreement instead of an arms buildup, if only Helmut Schmidt had stayed in office as Chancellor. With his incomparable influence as star member of the world leaders' club, Schmidt would surely have been able to bully Washington and Moscow into an agreement; instead, wishy-washy Helmut Kohl let the Nitze-Kvitsinski 'walk-in-the-woods' deal get away. This is the flattering myth that the SPD gave Schmidt to take home with him in retirement.

In his much-awaited hour-and-a-half-long speech to the Cologne congress, Schmidt asked whether enough had been done 'in the interest of Germans in both states' to bring the superpowers to an agreement. Clearly not. Therefore he would not support the government motion. Schmidt expressed his 'bitter disappointment' that the USSR had continued to roll out more and more SS-20s, after he and Brezhnev had agreed in May 1978 at a meeting in Brühl that a rough balance of forces existed. The USSR had then stationed fewer than fifty SS-20s. Why the subsequent over-arming? he asked. Schmidt acknowledged that the Russians wanted peace, but blamed them for refusing to understand that 'their drive for absolute security creates ever greater insecurity for everybody else.' The SS-20s were a 'big mistake', he said.

Schmidt acknowledged that the Pershing-2 was also a mistake. By earmarking for the Federal Republic a weapons system considered especially alarming by the Russians, NATO had violated the principle of avoiding German singularity. Schmidt also accused the Reagan administration of a 'serious violation' of the double decision in turning down the 'walk-in-the-woods' deal — which would have eliminated the Pershings and struck a balance between cruise and SS-20s — without consulting the European allies. There was 'no excuse' for failure to inform the NATO allies, he said.

Willy Brandt put it more plainly when, in his speech to the mammoth peace demonstration in Bonn on 22 October 1983, he said the trouble was that some very powerful 'people had got it into their thick heads that it was more important to station the Pershing-2 missiles than to get rid of the SS-20s.'

Three general considerations can be seen to have brought the SPD around to opposition to the NATO missile deployment. The first was the need to respond to the massive popular groundswell against deployment. SPD leaders virtually had to jump on a moving train, already packed with their own constituents and heading in a direction — nuclear disarmament — they had traditionally advocated. This was the forthright explanation offered by Willy Brandt for his presence on the speakers' platform at the Bonn rally. Green leader Petra Kelly said she hoped this did not mean the SPD was planning to take over the movement in order to betray it, as it had already done when it dropped the anti-nuclear weapons movement at the end of the fifties.

The second was the need to prevent the missiles from wrecking the carefully established relations between the two Germanies. It was already clear after Guadeloupe that the East Germans would have grounds to object strongly. The 21 December 1972 Treaty on the Basis of Relations between the Federal Republic of Germany and the German Democratic Republic includes (Article 5) a joint promise to support efforts 'to achieve arms limitations and disarmament, especially with regard to nuclear weapons and other weapons of mass destruction.' Chancellor Schmidt and his government considered that the second track of the double track decision, plus Schmidt's own efforts to promote Soviet–American arms talks, kept Bonn well within the spirit of that agreement. But in a major policy speech in Gera on 13 October 1980, the East German leader, Erich Honecker, made a carefully aimed thrust at Schmidt, remarking that it would not do to claim that 'the only subject worth discussing with the GDR was "the facilitation of travel" ' while simultaneously acting like 'the inventor and chief whip of the Brussels missile decision'. At the tenth congress of the ruling Socialist Unity Party on 11 April, 1981, Honecker warned that 'we do not dream of being able to maintain good relations with the Federal Republic of Germany, one of the strongest NATO states, when relations between the USSR and the USA are aggravated by an incalculable United States policy aiming at confrontation.'[14]

The third consideration was the shifting American strategic context. Schmidt had favoured the new missiles as a way to bind the United States strategic deterrent to the defence of Germany. But as a matter of fact, the Pentagon was moving away from deterrence strategy. And, as a matter of political psychology,[15] did it make any sense to attempt by some technical device to force a great power to do something it did not want to do? This could not be the American purpose. 'Europe does not want to allow America the freedom to decide when to put its own existence on the line, but rather wants to link the United States indissolubly, in an almost automatic manner, with Europe's own destiny,' Egon Bahr has written. 'But the United States has in fact rejected this option since it abandoned the strategy of mass retaliation with the declaration that the threat of using the ultimate weapon in the case of a limited attack is no longer credible. No one can force America to place its own existence on the line if it does not deem it to be directly threatened.'[16]

In a 1981 study[17] for the SPD's Friedrich Ebert Foundation, Eckhard Lübkemeier found the planned missile deployment incurably ambivalent from a military strategic point of view. He emphasized that it was 'imperatively urgent for the Federal Republic of Germany to seek a solution to her security problems primarily *in the political field.*' There was 'no alternative to a policy of détente' for West Germany.

But Lübkemeier pointed out that the missile deployment was not the only factor. The Pentagon was foisting on NATO a new strategy. 'AirLand Battle', which would involve the use of long-range 'smart' missiles to break up a massed 'second wave' of Soviet forces deep inside Eastern Europe. West German politicians initially reacted favourably to suggestions by NATO commander-in-chief General Bernard Rogers that the new weapons should replace short-range battlefield nuclear weapons. However, this was an obvious ploy to get Europeans to raise their defence spending for the purchase of new electronic American weaponry. Lübkemeier also spotted a less obvious pitfall: not only would AirLand Battle not dispense with nuclear weapons; it would substitute an offensive for a defensive strategy. To the Americans, it might make military sense to trade space for time, to allow German territory to be overrun while long-range missiles concentrated on Soviet forces in Poland. But from a German standpoint, an invasion had to be deterred or stopped at the border. Otherwise, there would be nothing left to fight for.

Others[18] pointed out later that the new Rogers strategy was all the more inappropriate for Europe in that the 'second echelon' which the American 'smart' weapons were supposed to attack no longer played an important role in Soviet military planning. The confusion around AirLand Battle was another sign that the Americans were going ahead with their own global strategic planning, with no concern for European defence needs or European views, and then imposing their schemes on their allies.

On 2 December 1982 NATO defence ministers agreed in Brussels that member countries with the means should take action outside Europe if need be 'to deter threats to the vital interests of the West.' The SPD's 'no' to the missiles was thus also a tacit refusal of the global Pentagon war-fighting posture being forced on NATO. The SPD's main emphasis throughout, however, was on Soviet–American arms control negotiations as an indispensable instrument of détente. Given this admitted dependence on the good graces of Washington and Moscow, SPD security policy might appear as friendly encouragement to some hypothetical future (Democratic) administration in the United States, or else as an admission of helplessness.

Rejection of the missiles was accompanied by moves to unify the badly split party around a new security policy. A Work Group on New Strategies was set up in 1982 under the chairmanship of Egon Bahr, with thirteen members ranging from Schmidt's defence minister Hans Apel, a prominent figure in the party's conservative leadership group, to the most ardent critic of NATO and the missiles, Saarbrücken mayor Oskar Lafontaine. Their report completed in June 1983 rejected AirLand Battle, 'horizontal escalation' and any extension of NATO activity outside treaty limits. In Germany's interest, NATO strategy must be 'visibly defensive'. Thus NATO must forego acquiring an offensive capacity to carry out 'long-range inter-diction'.

The Work Group Report accepted the idea of strenghening NATO's conventional forces to reduce dependence on early use of nuclear weapons. It noted that technological developments had improved the scope for a switch to conventional weapons. But it added that politics must dictate to technology, and not the other way around. 'The question must be: what possibilities does the development of arms technology offer for strengthening the defensive strategy of forward defence? And not: how can the strategy be adapted to the new weapons? Moreover, the consequences for arms control must be thought through. Not everything that is technologically feasible is necessary or desirable.' More generally, the Report stressed that the 'militarization of politics' was dangerous and had to be reversed. 'Keeping peace is a political task.'

The Work Group further observed that in the nuclear age, invulnerability is an illusion, and that security can no longer be achieved *against* the potential enemy but must be developed *with* him. Thus policy proposals must be based on the principle of 'security partnership' or 'common security'.

The SPD security policy committee headed by Andreas von Bülow adopted most of the Work Group's report to propose as official policy to the party congress in Essen in May 1984. But one omission and one ambiguity pinpointed areas of ongoing controversy. The omission was particularly conspicuous because it concerned a proposal first made by the Work Group's chairman, Egon Bahr, when he was working with the Independent Commission on Disarmament and Security Issues chaired by Olof Palme.

The 1982 Palme Commission report, *Common Security*, generally recommended the implementation of confidence-building measures — specifically, the establishment in Central Europe of a 300-kilometre-wide nuclear-weapon-free zone (150 kilometres deep on each side of the German–German and West German–Czechoslovak borders).[19] A less purely technical and more explicitly political proposal to achieve a large nuclear-weapons-free zone had been sympathetically entertained by the Palme Commission, but, owing to misgivings on the part of the four nuclear states,[20] was left out of the report (which had to be adopted unanimously) and put in an annexe in the form of a Comment by Egon Bahr. The 'Bahr Proposal' was that 'all nuclear weapons should be withdrawn from European states which do not themselves possess nuclear weapons.' 'Our sovereignty in security questions is no less than that of Italy and Norway or of the Netherlands and Belgium,' Bahr wrote.[21] 'The sovereignty of the non-nuclear states is limited to saying yes or no to the stationing of atomic weapons on their soil. After their "yes", others decide. With their "no" they undertake greater responsibility for credible conventional defence inside the alliance, covered through the strategic weapons of the nuclear states.'

The full Bahr Proposal also included the preservation of both alliances, and an approximate conventional balance of forces between NATO and the Warsaw Pact. However, the Reagan administration exhibited a violent allergy to his suggestions, and American newspaper articles singled out Bahr as a dangerous radical inside the SPD. Behind the scenes, the SPD's most conservative leaders managed to eliminate what was most offensive to Washington from the policy proposal.

On the other hand, von Bülow's commission took up with some gusto a proposal which, in the Bahr scheme, had been a concession in return for de-nuclearization — that is, the strengthening of conventional forces. Now a 'considerable' (*erhebliche*) strengthening was recommended, which could be understood as a way to prepare for eventual de-nuclearization, or else as a capitulation to the 'Rogers Plan' to boost spending on 'emerging technologies' (ET) weapons without any commitment to de-nuclearize. This was the major ambiguity hiding behind the 'second pillar of NATO', the newly fashionable phrase for Europe's military strength attributed to John Kennedy, as if to suggest that the world could be young again.

The SPD is unanimous on one thing: the rejection of any independent, nationalist go-it-alone approach. From left to right, German Social Democrats are resolutely internationalist, seeking points of support and coordination in friendly countries.

On the party's left wing, when Oskar Lafontaine suggests, not without irony, that the Federal Republic should 'follow de Gaulle's example' and consider leaving the NATO unified military command, he quickly adds that the Gaullist example should be followed . . .*except* for nuclear weapons, and *except* for nationalist independence. 'Whoever equates the peace movement in Germany with a newly arising nationalism has not understood its motives,' Lafontaine has written.[22] 'The peace movement knows that sovereign nation-states have seen in war a way to settle conflicts. The sovereign nation-state has been the fundamental factor in many centuries of wars. The peace movement has recognized that, in the age of nuclear bombs, this way of settling conflicts is finished. Whoever speaks out today for resolving bloc confrontations cannot have as his aim the restoration of sovereign states. Giving up atomic armament is precisely a partial abandonment of falsely understood sovereignty. Whoever has recognized that the atomic bomb can no longer serve any purpose, that there are no more winners and losers, must reach the insight that with the atomic bomb, which is a global threat no one can run away from, the idea of sovereign states is dying out.'

The fallout from a nuclear test, the radiation from a nuclear power plant malfunction will not stop at the boundaries of sovereign states. The superpowers have no right to terrorize the whole globe with their nuclear weaponry, Lafontaine maintained. 'The alternative to the idea of the sovereign nation-state is the Europeanization of Europe and with it the dissolving of bloc confrontation. The effort must be made to create an internationally agreed security system in the framework of the United Nations.'

Internationalism can flourish only if it has something to attach to in other countries. Lafontaine's does not, as yet, attach to anything. Even Willy Brandt's internationalism was in difficulty in 1983. The Socialist International's southern European member parties refused to go along with a unified disarmament policy condemning the NATO missile deployment, and the disarray of attempts to achieve an independent third world policy was dramatized by the assassination of Palestinian moderate Issam Sartawi at the SI congress in southern Portugal in April. The Brandt school of thought tended to fall back on Northern and Central Europe, where some consensus on disarmament policies still seemed conceivable.

Unless these efforts bear fruit, there is a danger that SPD internationalism may degenerate (once again) into simple subservience to the United States. The right-wing internationalist line is developed in the SPD by Karl Kaiser of the 'Seeheimer Circle' around Hans Apel, who condemns the Bahr Proposal as an anachronistic reversion to the notion of national states.

In the final debates over Pershing-2 deployment in late 1983, Willy Brandt insisted on the vital necessity of Franco–German understanding for the future of Europe, and urged the peace-movement wing of his own party to make patient efforts to understand French fears and explain German problems to French friends. Quite a number of Social Democrats were searching in some perplexity for ways to do this.

Since its ejection from the coalition government with the Liberals in 1982, the SPD has had to share the opposition with the Greens. There is a measure of agreement across the German left on the madness of the arms race and the need for new relations with the Third World, but the Green–SPD relationship is far from unproblematic. Thus, speaking after Brandt at the October 1983 anti-missile rally in Bonn, Petra Kelly attacked the contradiction in his opposition to the missiles and his acceptance of NATO. The following month, as the SPD Congress was at last saying 'no' to the missiles, the Greens also met and for the first time called for withdrawal from NATO, as part of the dissolution of both NATO and the Warsaw Pact. This is admittedly not a very immediate prospect. West German public opinion, while opposed to the missiles (by upwards of 60 per cent, according to various polls), has never seriously questioned NATO membership. Nevertheless, it provides a standpoint from which to criticize SPD positions as ultimately insignificant efforts to relate to factional disputes within NATO.

The SPD and the Greens also have divergent attitudes toward the Eastern bloc. The Greens' appealing idea of 'détente from below', borrowed from the Dutch peace movement, is still rather ill-defined since efforts to put it into practice have met with slammed doors and crackdowns designed to strangle it at birth. For their part, SPD leaders explicitly reject 'détente from below' as potentially damaging to their own 'détente from above'—a strategy which some Greens perceive as the basis for an eventual condominium of northern industrialized states. Green Bundestag member Roland Vogt, for example, has called 'security partnership' a 'dangerous concept that might be turned against the Third World'.

During the 21 November 1983 Bundestag debate, before the SPD and the Greens voted against the missile deployment, Social Democrat Karsten Voigt argued that next to a healthy patriotism, there was a rebirth of nationalism 'on the left, and not only on the right'. Urging the Greens to reflect on 'history, and our neighbours' concern', he warned that although it would be necessary in the long term to overcome the need for NATO, 'withdrawing from NATO today would be a step backwards to the nationalization of security policy.'

The fact that the conservative wing of the SPD may, as in the past, use this line of argument to justify subservience to the United States does not remove the element of truth in Voigt's warning. For, so long as the Greens, and the left in general, are too weak to carry through a genuinely 'internationalist' departure from NATO, such ideas may end up being recuperated by the right. This could happen especially if American policy continues to go so contrary to key German (and European) interests that some degree of rebellion becomes inevitable. A leader with the anti-communist reputation of Franz-Josef Strauss could be favoured to save West Germany's essential interests in Eastern Europe, because he would not arouse dangerous suspicions in Washington. A combination of business with the East and heavier spending on arms could satisfy the essential requirements of both Moscow and Washington, and a sauce of nationalist (or 'European nationalist') rhetoric could make the concoction more palatable all around. This is the 'Gaullist' recipe, and would perhaps include nuclear arms within a European force. The Reagan administration is the first American government likely to favour such a project. Indeed, beneath the insistence by some foreign critics of the German peace movement in 1983 that they could nonetheless 'understand' the 'nationalist' sentiments supposedly involved in it, there was also a certain willingness to see the nationalist right recuperate the sense of community and grievance created by the stationing of Pershing–2 and cruise missiles on German soil. But despite outside encouragement, such recuperation has been slow to appear.

Initially, the governing Christian Democrat–Liberal coalition headed by Chancellor Helmut Kohl could continue Schmidt's policy without having to try as strenuously as Schmidt to justify it. After all, it could plausibly be said that the Social Democrats had been responsible for the situation in which West Germany found itself. Kohl's initial task was to save both the Western alliance and the Eastern détente policies, to support the NATO modernization while maintaining the hard-won relations with the German Democratic Republic. This was successfully accomplished, and inter-German relations actually prospered in the wake of the first Pershing-2 deployments.

But the missile deployment was not the end of American demands on the alliance. Even Defence Minister Manfred Wörner, known as a pro-American NATO loyalist, had to object to Pentagon chief Caspar Weinberger's efforts to peddle Reagan's thousand million dollar 'star wars' gadgetry to NATO countries. The demanding, erratic, and belligerent behaviour of the United States has been creating a situation in which German moves toward military, and even nuclear, independence might no longer look like a gratuitous and threatening upsurge of nationalist 'revanchism', but appear as the most simple matter of self-preservation — even of concern for peace. There are signs that some in the Reagan administration hope for this effect.

Back in Cold War I, when Bonn and Moscow exchanged insulting notes, Franz-Josef Strauss openly coveted nuclear weaponry. Times and tones have changed. By the summer of 1983, when Strauss shocked the CSU true believers by working out a thousand million mark deal with Erich Honecker, his enthusiasm for nuclear weapons seemed to have cooled — or, at least, he was far more discreet on the subject than in the past. Speaking to the CSU defence policy group in Munich on 8 April 1984, Strauss called for greater European military independence from the United States, and at the same time invited greater 'clarity' from France on the use of French nuclear weapons. No satisfactory agreement existed on the subject, he noted. But, said Strauss, 'as it is obvious that French nuclear missiles are in part aimed at targets located on the soil of Germany — and Germany naturally also includes the DDR — there is a vast field, not only for

exchanges of information, but also for harmonization, a mutual clarification and joint planning.' An integration of European armies, he
said, would enable Europe to attain the measure of independence
necessary to be a 'balanced pillar' in the Atlantic Alliance.

The notion of clarification of French nuclear plans was also expressed by CDU Bundestag leader Alfred Dregger. The right seemed
to have found the tactful approach to the issue. On 17 April Christian
Democrat defence policy spokesman Jürgen Todenhöfer called for a
merger of the expanded French and British nuclear systems with US
cruise and Pershing-2 missiles into an integrated force under the
command of an executive body representing the United States and all
the European NATO members. Todenhöfer complained that the
capacity of Britain and France to use their nuclear deterrents without
consulting Bonn left West Germany with third-rate security. 'The
time has come for German security interests to be taken into account,'
he said.

Soviet international affairs specialist Vadim Zagladin reacted
immediately with a statement in Brussels: 'I think it must be absolutely excluded that West Germany gain access to nuclear weapons.
There are still some quite powerful revanchists there, and they must
be absolutely excluded from getting their hands on nuclear arms.'

Speculation was growing on how to pool the nuclear and other
military strengths of the European big three, Britain, France and
West Germany. Some on the left had seen this coming. 'I think the
world does not need yet another atomic superpower,' Willy Brandt
told his party in Cologne. And in the Bundestag debate a few days
later Brandt stressed: 'So far as we understand and want it, there can
and will be no Europe formed against the United States, a Europe
possibly with the ambition of being another atomic superpower.
Instead, Europe as a moderating force and, eventually, a stabilizing
power will be able to contribute to advantageous changes in world
political power structures.'

A sign that the broad consensus in West Germany was for détente
and disarmament was the choice of the Christian Democrat mayor of
West Berlin, Richard von Weizsäcker, as the new president of the
Federal Republic in May 1984. Rather than present a candidate of its
own, the SPD supported the choice of a man friendly to the peace
movement and devoted to the deepening of human relations with East
Germany. The new President's older brother, Carl von Weizsäcker,
was the first prominent West German to analyse nuclear deterrence
and to conclude that nuclear weapons could not defend but only,
eventually, destroy a country like Germany.

If Germans manage to find in their present difficult situation a national vocation to promote peaceful international relations, they will need patience to overcome residual anti-German prejudice even, or especially, on the left in other European countries. Fortunately, Germans in the peace movement seem quite aware of this and prepared to take their time.

Notes

1. See Laurence H. Shoup & William Minter, *Imperial Brain Trust*, New York 1977, pp. 188–95.

2 Robert M. Slusser. 'The Berlin Crises of 1958–59 and 1961', in *Force Without War*, eds. Barry M. Blechman & Stephen S. Kaplan, New York 1978.

3. Egon Bahr, in the collection *Germany Debates Defense: the NATO Alliance at the Crossroads*, eds. Rudolf Steinke and Michael Vale, New York 1983.

4. The reference was to the successful German commando raid that killed three of four hijackers and rescued a Lufthansa airliner held at Mogadishu airport in October 1977.

5. This is apparently nothing new. According to Paul Buteux in *The Politics of Nuclear Consultation in NATO 1965–1980*, Cambridge 1983, p. 139: 'The nadir of inter-allied relations in this period was reached in October (1973) when the Arab–Israeli war created acute differences between the United States and its allies . . . . When the German government requested that the United States cease moving military supplies from Germany for shipment to Israel, the American ambassador, Martin Hillenbrand, is said to have stated that the United States regarded Germany's sovereignty as limited, and reserved the right to take any action it deemed proper in the interests of international security. This message was reinforced in Washington by the Secretary of State in an interview with the German ambassador.'

6. *Germany Debates Defense.*

7. See Jerry W. Sanders, *Peddlers of Crisis*, London 1983.

8. Evidently an allusion to the outlawing of the Communist Party in the Federal Republic in 1956.

9. *Germany Debates Defense.*

10. Ibid.

11. Ibid.

12. Reunification is generally assumed to imply that capitalist West Germany, by far the richer and more populous, with over 61 million inhabitants, would dominate Socialist East Germany, with a population of less than 17 million. Reunification from East to West, as a function of 'Communist expansionism', is a nightmare that haunts some sectors of the West particularly lacking in self-confidence, notably in France. Brian May, author of *Russia, America, the Bomb and the Fall of Western Europe*, argues succinctly that German reunification would be not a goal of, but an obstacle to, any Russian expansionism westwards.

'1. Russian occupation of a substantial part of Western Europe would require the prior occupation of Western Germany—and its consequent communization.

'2. A communist West Germany would inevitably become reunified with East Germany.

'3. There is nothing in the world that the Kremlin dreads more than a reunified, armed Germany, communist or not' (*The Guardian*, 6 February 1984).

May adds that 'the thought of being sandwiched between a communist China . . . and a communist Germany, with its restless dynamism, would be a nightmare.' Moscow, he believes, 'could certainly not control a reunified communist Germany.'

13. Interviewed by Jean-Pierre Ravery, *L'Humanité*, 25 October 1983.

14. Quoted by Wilhelm Bruns in *The NATO Two-Track Decision and German/German Relations*, Bonn 1981.

15. What exactly did Schmidt think he had obtained from the Americans in the NATO 'double track' decision? The search for an answer, or answers, to this question leads to the dark side of German–American relations.

Christopher Makins (in 'TNF Modernization and "Countervailing strategy"', *Survival*, July–August 1981) suggested that the NATO modernization had started out, more or less, as 'a set of weapons without a corresponding strategy'. Under the strong influence of the military–industrial complex, and the cruise lobby, the modernization was initiated as part of the Long Term Defence Programme proposed by Carter in May 1977, when the missiles were indeed being developed, but when the strategy for their use was simply the vague old grab-bag 'flexible response'. According to Makins: 'Although the issue was discussed mostly in terms of counteracting the expanding Soviet threat to Western Europe, notably from the SS-20, this was in large measure a result of the fact that many of the deeper, intra-Alliance anxieties about the credibility of extended deterrence in Europe were too difficult and sensitive to raise openly between governments.' Schmidt's share of 'deeper, intra-Alliance anxieties' was related to Germany's position as potential nuclear battlefield, something that had worried him while he was defence minister. With five thousand tactical nuclear warheads lying around, in 'use them or lose them' positions, a war in Germany would quickly become a nuclear holocaust. Since the USA and the USSR had worked out 'strategic parity', this holocaust might be limited to Germany, since both the Americans and the Russians would hold back their strategic forces for self-protection. The fact that it could be limited to Germany might reduce the zeal of both the Americans and the Russians for preventing it.

Two kinds of remedy could be envisaged. One would be to accept the elimination of 'extended deterrence'—that is, the American nuclear umbrella over Europe—and reduce the threat of limited nuclear war in Germany through disarmament negotiations, notably the mutual and balanced force reduction talks in Vienna. This is what Schmidt actually suggested in his famous October 1977 London speech. However, for several years NATO apologists have insisted that that is not what he *meant*. What he meant was the other remedy: restoration of strategic deterrence, a patching-up of the American nuclear umbrella. New missiles could 're-couple' Germany to the US strategic deterrent. How this would supposedly work was explained in a very revealing article in the Winter 1983–84 issue of *Foreign Policy* by Steven Canby and Ingemar Dörfer, who blamed German strategists, and by name, Uwe Nerlich, for cooking up the notion of a 'gap in the escalation spectrum' in order to lure the United States into a trigger mechanism that would assure its own destruction in the case of nuclear war in Germany. The Pershing-2 and cruise missiles 'would act as a trigger for US strategic weapons should the United States hesitate to keep its promise to defend Western Europe'. How would this work? By three conditions. First, they must be 'land-based nuclear missiles capable of reaching Soviet territory to ensure that the Soviet Union would not be a nuclear sanctuary in a European war.' Second, they had to be 'unambiguously owned and operated by the United States, to make sure that the United States could not escape the consequences . . . ' Finally, they had to be 'deployed in a vulnerable enough way that Washington would have to use them early in a conflict or lose them.' Thus both the Soviet Union *and the United States* would be deterred from limited war in Europe by the new deployment.

'Thus in their continuous quest to insure coupling as the United States becomes in their eyes increasingly unreliable, the West Europeans have turned the USSR into a coupling mechanism,' Canby and Dörfer wrote. 'Yet Bonn felt that this thinking had to be hidden from Western, particularly US, public scrutiny. The coupling forces were described as a response to an allegedly new threat, the SS-20, which was in fact a replacement for much older and unwieldy SS-4 and SS-5s.' Canby and Dörfer suggest that Schmidt and his strategists were out-foxed by the Americans in this manoeuvre. 'Because they concealed their true coupling rationale, however, West German officials were forced publicly to advocate the need for a number of theatre weapons too large to best achieve coupling.' For while 'a small number of missiles increases coupling, a large number, such as 572, decreases coupling by the prospect of a Eurostrategic balance and the limited nuclear war this balance would theoretically make possible.' (This secret coupling rationale, and failure to grasp the decoupling implications of a 'Eurostrategic balance', seems to underlie official French enthusiasm for the NATO Euromissile deployments.)

'For a generation West German leaders have used code words in the transatlantic dialogue to communicate to West European and American elites while shielding themselves from public scrutiny,' Canby and Dörfer wrote. 'With Schmidt's speech, this tactic backfired.' What happened was that, in the absence of any clear military use for the new missiles, the 'nuclear use theorists' (NUTS) rushed into the breach with their 'decapitation' and 'horizontal esclation' to transform the Pershing-2 from a deterrence trigger into a key piece in a global panoply developed to fight and 'prevail' in nuclear war against the Soviet Union. This redefinition was the downfall of the man who liked to boast that he 'knew how to handle the Americans.'

16. *Germany Debates Defense,*

17. Eckhard Lübkemeier, *PD-39 and LRTNF Modernization: Military, Strategic and Security Political Implications of Extended Deterrence for the Federal Republic of Germany,* Bonn 1981.

18. Rik Coolsaet, 'The "Conventionalization" of NATO's Military Strategy', discussion paper prepared for the Belgian Socialists, March 1984.

19. It is interesting that the Soviet member of the Palme Commission, Georgii Arbatov, favoured even more radical reductions up to a complete ban on medium-range and tactical nuclear weapons. See *Common Security: A Programme for Disarmament,* London 1982, p. 147.

20. Egon Bahr recounted the background of the Palme Commission conclusions at a hearing of the 2nd European Nuclear Disarmament Convention in Berlin on 10 May 1983.

21. Egon Bahr essay in *Der Spiegel,* 13 February 1984.

22. Oskar Lafontaine, *Angst vor den Freunden,* Spiegel, 1983.

3

France: La Nouvelle Realpolitique

Unpleasant Surprises

The election of a Socialist, François Mitterrand, as President of the French Republic on 10 May 1981 aroused hopes in a European left that by the end of the seventies had to console itself as best it could. Mitterrand himself was, indeed, a Fourth Republic war horse, a patriotic politician of the French radical republican stamp, who had been Interior Minister at the start of the war in Algeria. However, the French Socialist Party (PS), reorganized under Mitterrand's leadership in 1971, seemed a relatively fresh, bright and bold newcomer. Often critical of the compromises of 'social democracy', willing to govern in coalition with a particularly uningratiating Communist Party, the PS enjoyed an image to the left of its fellow-members of the Socialist International. Italian Communists hoped that the French Socialists could provide the bridge between themselves and the Social Democrats of Germany and northern Europe in the construction of a coordinated 'Euroleft'. After the Socialists' landslide victory in the legislative elections following Mitterrand's victory over Valéry Giscard d'Estaing, the French Socialist Party held an absolute majority in the National Assembly as well as a seven-year mandate to control the strongest state apparatus in the Western world, in the European nation traditionally most jealous of its independence from the 'Superpowers'. All this seemed certain to favour a coordinated European resistance to the Reagan administration's efforts to force Europe to live with its own reactionary policies in fiscal priorities, rearmament and the Third World.

These hopes were soon shattered as Mitterrand, his external affairs minister Claude Cheysson and other official spokesmen of the new Socialist government began to echo Reagan administration positions on NATO rearmament. Cheysson promptly scuttled France's long-standing role as Moscow's privileged Western contact.by announcing during a visit to Washington on 6 June 1981 that 'so long as Soviet troops are in Afghanistan, you can't expect there to be normal relations between France and the USSR.'

Germans discovered Mitterand's position on the Euromissiles in an interview in the 8 July 1981 issue of *Stern* magazine. 'The Soviet SS–20 and Backfire bomber,' said the French President, 'are upsetting the balance in Europe. I cannot accept this and I grant that there must be a rearmament to catch up and restore balance. From then on, there should be negotiations.' At that time, the Reagan administration itself did not dare say publicly that Pershing-2 and cruise missile deployment should *precede* negotiations aimed at achieving a balance of forces. The French Socialist was actually taking the lead (verbally) in championing the necessity of NATO Euromissile deployment.

'If I condemn neutralism, it's because I believe that peace is tied to a world balance of forces,' Mitterrand told *Stern*, thereby introducing German readers to two of his pet concepts, 'neutralism' (bad) and 'balance' (good), that they would hear repeated again and again in the months to come. In fact, 'balance' had been a continued refrain in Mitterrand's writings over the years. In his 25 September 1981 press conference he suggested that lack of balance could be enough to cause war: if he had 'sounded the alarm at the massive installation of SS-20s', this was because he did not want 'the simple relationship of forces to be so unbalanced that war results'. Nothing in Mitterrand's statements indicated any awareness that 'balance' was a highly abstract concept, that it was becoming ever more difficult to agree on a precise and concrete definition, and that the search for 'balance' played a key role in fuelling the arms race.

As for 'neutralism', this was the new danger which French officials and media discovered lurking in Federal Germany and condemned with increasing vigour as a large German peace movement emerged in 1981 and 1982. The French know remarkably little about Germany, considering its proximity and primary importance as a trading partner. Post-war Franco–German economic relations have been fruitfully developed by technocrats, but the only popular emotional input has tended to be negative — witness the scenes of angry French farmers dumping their produce on the roads, as experts work it all out in Brussels. As in Britain, for similar reasons of colonialist heritage, popular imagination and intellectual inquiry tend to be turned toward more distant regions, dominated areas or rival empires, rather than toward neighbours who are different but essentially equal. Centuries of complex Franco–German rivalry, in which material interests intertwined dangerously with philosophical pretensions, seemed definitively settled by two world wars that left Germany in the wrong and France justified. There remained precious little curiosity about the real trends in Germany, except when they seemed dangerous to France.

The French Left, in particular, has retained an image of Germany as an essentially and fundamentally right-wing nation, whose police are more repressive, whose unions and socialists are more conservative, whose citizens are more conformist than their French counterparts. German competence does not extend to politics, where history is widely believed to have established French superiority. French Socialists were scarcely motivated to pay attention to the problems of German Social Democrats. The PS was 'to the left' of the SPD, and Schmidt was Giscard's friend. Despite membership in the same International, relations between the two parties were minimal. French Socialists had not had the opportunity to study the Euromissiles problem thoroughly or to become acquainted with German feelings about it, much less to work out a joint position with the SPD.

If any German could overcome French suspicions and develop an internationalist understanding with the French Left, it ought to be Willy Brandt. On 20 August 1981, he went to see François Mitterrand on vacation in the French countryside. According to Brandt's version of the conversation, recounted by *Der Spiegel* on 24 August, the SPD leader complained that by speaking out in favour of Pershing-2 and cruise missiles, Mitterrand was helping the German right. Brandt explained that the SPD wanted to prevent deployment through negotiations. The desirable outcome would be the 'zero option': NATO would give up US missiles in return for removal of Soviet SS-20s.

Mitterrand disagreed, and insisted that the United States must first arm and then negotiate from a position of strength. According to the *Spiegel* report, the gist of his reasoning was that France needed an even balance between the blocs in order to remain as free as possible of responsibility for defending Germany and thus able to concentrate on last-resort nuclear deterrent defence of its own territory. The French president could appreciate the distress of a nation piled high with nuclear weapons controlled by others; but when Brandt told him that Germans were becoming 'fed up with being treated like a colony by the Americans', Mitterrand shrugged and observed: 'That's a result of the war.'

When Mitterrand kept trying to turn the conversation to the subject of relations between East and West Germany, Brandt retorted that German reunification was today essentially 'a French question' which was not even discussed in West Germany. The conclusion from the meeting was that politically, nothing could be expected from Mitterrand.

The German Left's resentment of the French Left reached a climax with President Mitterrand's speech to the Bundestag on 20 January 1983, on the occasion of the twentieth anniversary of the Franco–German friendship treaty concluded between Adenauer and de Gaulle. SPD deputies sat stonily while the right side of the Bundestag applauded France's Socialist president, well aware that his support for NATO missile deployment would help the German right parties in the midst of a crucial election campaign. Far more offensive than the simple statement of an unwelcome position, however, was the innuendo of certain sentences, and especially this one: 'Anyone who would wager on decoupling the European continent from the American continent would challenge the balance of forces and thus the maintenance of peace.' This was the point when the right applauded most and the left least, because it sounded as if Mitterrand were accusing the German Left of responsibility for that dread 'decoupling'. The German Social Democrats, who were used to being accused by French Socialists of excessive loyalty to the United States, must have been taken aback by the sheer nerve of Mitterrand's pronouncement, all the more ironical in that it was delivered on the anniversary of a treaty which had been conceived by de Gaulle precisely in an effort to 'decouple' Germany from the United States. (The effort inspired John Kennedy to rush to West Berlin to proclaim, 'Ich bin ein Berliner', and the decoupling did not take place, to de Gaulle's annoyance.) The irony was further enhanced by the fact that Mitterrand himself, as a deputy in the French National Assembly twenty years before, had abstained on the vote ratifying the treaty, complaining to the government: 'You are making Germany the leader, and, at the very moment you assert that role for us, you have just given it away.'

In his speech to the Bundestag, Mitterrand attributed thirty-eight years of peace in Europe to nuclear deterrence and insisted that the French nuclear force could not be included in the Geneva negotiations. 'One can only compare what is comparable', he said, and between the two superpowers and France there was a 'difference in nature'. The French nuclear force was and would remain independent, under sole responsibility of the French president, and this increased 'the uncertainty for an eventual aggressor, and only for him'. For these 'precise and serious' reasons, 'the French forces cannot be taken into account in the Geneva negotiations by the two

overarmed superpowers . . . . Any arrangement based on a calcula-
tion of that sort would be resolutely rejected by my country.'

The conclusions Germans might draw from this speech are rather
limited: on the one hand, that France enjoys a special privilege
bestowed by history which Germany must admire but not challenge;
or, on the other, that any nation wishing to be taken seriously must
possess a nuclear deterrent of its own. Neither conclusion was satisfactory to the German Left. Other of Mitterrand's hints and rhetorical flourishes seemed to point to the second conclusion. The
French president declared his belief that there was 'no fatality' dicta-
ting 'Europe's decadence', and called for 'will' and a 'strong'
Germany, France and Europe.

A man of sixty-six years, his youth deeply marked by Nazism and
the French Resistance, Mitterrand seemed to feel he was making an
important gesture of reconciliation by paying tribute to German
'greatness' and 'strength'. Coming from a nation which has emerged
on the victorious and righteous side of recent European wars and has
thus been able to maintain its patriotic good conscience intact, he
apparently had no idea how unpleasant his tranquil assertions of
national self-interest sounded to Germans whose personal penance
for the crimes of Hitlerism has involved radical rejection of
nationalism in all its forms.

Novelist Günther Grass, for instance, said he 'took Mitterrand's
speech to the Bundestag as an affront. The military part of that
military speech could just as well have been given by Franz-Josef
Strauss. That sort of Gaullist socialism is most highly distasteful to
me. The French, and the French Left in particular, would do well to
show a little more awareness that it is not a sign of good neighbour-
liness to treat Germany as a glacis meant to take blows in your stead.'[1]
Philosopher Jürgen Habermas said of the speech: 'I disliked it
heartily. Mitterrand is the best Gaullist president France has ever
had.'

A complaint to be heard among Germans irritated by 'French
arrogance' is that 'we are paying for French nuclear weapons aimed
at our country.' This refers to the fact that Germany, like a number of
other countries, in effect subsidizes the French nuclear industry by
paying the centre in La Hague, Normandy to store and, theoretically,
to 'recycle' radioactive waste from German nuclear power plants.
This revenue may help finance French nuclear weapons such as the
short-range Pluton missiles which, if fired from their bases in France,
would explode in the Federal Republic.

Three days before Mitterrand's speech, Saarbrücken mayor Oskar

Lafontaine, SPD Bundestag member Gert Weisskirchen and French Resistance leader Claude Bourdet issued a statement at a press conference in Bonn which described the French Socialist–Communist government's support for American nuclear arms 'modernization' on European soil as 'a slap in the face to all progressive and peaceful forces in Europe'. The statement noted that the planned modernization of French tactical nuclear weapons — the Hades short-range missile earmarked to succeed the Pluton, and the neutron, or enhanced radiation, bomb—would be further steps in the 'nuclearization of the "French" battlefield in the Federal Republic of Germany'. The targeting of nuclear missiles on German territory was 'incompatible with Franco–German friendship'.

At the same time, SPD Bundestag member Hermann Scheer wrote in *Der Spiegel* that France's 'self-reliance' had always been 'built on the backs of others: the German glacis is the military buffer, the protective shield for France's atomic autonomy.' Scheer observed that both Paris and Bonn seemed to be rejecting Moscow's latest offers at the Geneva negotiations precisely because they could make it possible to forego deployment of Pershing-2 and cruise. But the French and German motives were different. 'For the French government, it would be a matter of assuring their autonomous role, for which we must pay with deployment and ever greater dependence on the United States.' The Kohl government, on the other hand, hoped that modernization would bind Germany closer to US military planning. In an accompanying editorial, *Der Spiegel*'s editor-in-chief Rudolf Augstein commented caustically: 'France as the cradle of humanity can have no claim made on it for arms control negotiations; it has given humanity too much for that . . . '

For some time, the left wing of the French Socialist Party associated with Jean-Pierre Chevènement's Centre for Socialist Study, Research and Education (CERES) preferred to say, hope and perhaps even believe that Mitterrand's ostentatiously ·pro-NATO stance was temporary and tactical—a way of calming American apprehension over his inclusion of Communists in the government and other domestic audacities. Not only CERES but also much of the central current of the PS, the 'Mitterrandistes', were taken by surprise by the close alignment with Washington on East–West security issues. Yet scarcely any debate developed among Socialists. Electoral victory had left the rather small party somewhat overextended with the new responsibilities of office, absorbed in domestic problems and in no way prepared to challenge Mitterrand's conduct of foreign affairs. Such challenge would be useless, anyway, in the Fifth Republic designed by General de Gaulle to give the President unfettered control of international policy.

Foreign policy by its nature is the most secretive part of public affairs. Governments may deceive their own population in the course of deceiving foreign adversaries, and the elaborately created illusions may be dispelled only much later, by historians, if ever. Acutely aware of this reality, many politicized people on the French Left were slow to pass judgement on a government they basically supported, in relation to such a seemingly obscure and complicated issue as the Euromissiles controversy.

How the French Left Learned to Love the Bomb

Mitterrand's ten years as leader of a new Socialist Party, with a rhetorically daring left wing and a programme for governing in coalition with the Communists, tended to make people forget that his whole past showed him to be a convinced *Atlantiste*—that is, a firm believer in the necessary primacy of France's ties to the English-speaking democracies. This did not prevent him, before he became president, from expressing certain doubts about Alliance strategy. In a 31 July 1980 interview with Michel Tatu of *Le Monde*, Mitterrand said that 'the Alliance rests on a fiction: American intervention in Europe in the event of Soviet aggression.' 'The American theory of graduated response,' he added, 'does not in my view make sense.' Those who chose to do so could read into these remarks a promising independence from American strategic thinking, although in fact neither of those criticisms would come as a surprise to American strategic thinkers.

Atlantiste or Gaullist? Or both? The contradiction vanishes with the dawning realization that (1) the American 'nuclear umbrella' is indeed unreliable, as de Gaulle was first to declare; and (2) a separate national nuclear force does not seriously impair American domination, but may give 'the West' another card to play. American leaders themselves have gradually come around to favouring a sort of 'Gaullism' for Europe. Thus Mitterrand's own evolution from opposition to the *force de frappe* to grudging and finally ardent defence of it ran parallel to a similar evolution in American thinking.

'Hurrah for France!' shouted de Gaulle over French radio on 13 February 1960. France had just exploded its first atomic bomb. The *force de frappe* was born. It was denounced throughout the sixties by the whole French Left: socialists, communists and radical republicans of all stripes. Campaigning against de Gaulle in 1965, Mitterrand opposed nuclear armament, and Socialist Gaston Defferre toured the country calling the *force de frappe* a 'ruinous and absurd waste of men and resources' which diverted France from economic development and European construction toward a 'mirage of false grandeur'.

But by 1969, Mitterrand, still sharply critical of nuclear armament, forecast that it would soon be 'irreversible' and could not be 'drowned like puppies'. 'I said during my 1965 presidential campaign that I would ban the *force de frappe*. I will no longer be able to say that tomorrow . . . '[2] It was still being said, however, in the Common Programme for government signed in June 1972 by the French Socialist and Communist Parties that sealed the 'Union of the Left'. 'General, universal and controlled disarmament will be the government's principal objective,' stated the programme; and defence policy would be based on 'renunciation of the strategic nuclear strike force in any form', reconversion of the military nuclear industry to peaceful uses, an immediate halt to nuclear testing, and adherence to the test ban and non-proliferation treaties.[3]

In 1977 the Union of the Left fell apart in wrangling over efforts to update the Common Programme for the March 1978 legislative elections. It was in the course of this revision that the two major parties of the French Left rallied to nuclear armament, separately and each in its own distinctive fashion. Some basic motivations may have been the same. Claude Bourdet[4] explains that they 'wanted to secure the support of the non-reactionary part of the officer corps' and believed that this could be achieved by supporting the French deterrent. Bourdet also argues that both Socialists and Communists had been 'infected by the Gaullist theory' of *défense du faible au fort* (the weak's defence against the strong) — to wit, that even a very small nuclear force like that of France could inflict enough damage to deter a potential aggressor. This 'infection' was able to spread because there was never any debate on strategic issues in French political circles. Christian Mellon has summed up the evolution:

> Within the old socialist party, opposition to the nuclear strike force went without saying. That may be a cause of its subsequent weakness. Where arguments were needed, opposition was expressed in sentiments, ideals; instead of openly raising the question of French socialist defence policy, there was facile criticism of the Gaullist 'bombinette'. The result: when the *bombinette* had grown into a veritable operational arsenal, there was no choice left but to rally to the *fait accompli*. Without wishing to exaggerate the paradox, one may say that the socialist party's rallying to nuclear

armament is less the fruit of pro-nuclear efforts than of the poverty of reflection on defence questions within a political tradition which has too often confused the aspiration for peace with disinterest in defence problems.[5]

As the Left, after twenty years in opposition, faced the prospect of actually exercising government responsibility, it had to come up with a serious defence policy. To do so, it had to borrow from the right. It was the Communist Party leadership that took the plunge first, springing the new line on its unwary membership on 11 May 1977, when the Central Committee unanimously approved a report by Jean Kanapa. Communists, it said, remained fundamentally hostile to nuclear weapons and would continue to strive for their worldwide prohibition. But like it or not, 'today, as far as France is concerned, nuclear armament is a fact. Today, it represents the only means of real deterrence available ... to meet a threat of aggression, to neutralize any possible imperialist nuclear blackmail.'

In reality, de Gaulle's nuclear deterrent was never put to the test of actually having to deter an aggressor. But that does not mean it was useless. It helped to turn the attention of the disgruntled (and dangerously rebellious) French officer corps away from their colonial losses, notably in Algeria, and to focus their pride on an ultra-modern and *thoroughly French* weapons system. It provided a technological and psychological stimulus to de Gaulle's programme of modernizing both French industry and the French empire. The explosion of the *bombinette* occurred in the 'year of Africa', 1960, when de Gaulle rapidly granted formal independence to France's African colonies, while binding them close to the *métropole* by a series of 'cooperation' agreements. The theoretical keystone to this neo-colonial order was the independent nuclear force which, by making France a 'sanctuary' against attack by other roving world powers, allowed it to play its own game in the Third World.

'One of the postulates of the existing world political system,' Admiral Antoine Sanguinetti has explained, 'is that the nuclear nations whose territory is now kept safe from any armed attack by the balance of terror are thus enabled to practise an indirect strategy in the rest of the world, going as far as armed action without risk to themselves. Unfortunately, these capacities for indirect strategy in the nuclear age have let loose all sorts of greed in a new reign of force. In practice, nuclear nations help themselves to the right to intervene as they wish by armed might in the affairs of others.'[6]

De Gaulle took up the challenge of the post-war American anti-colonialism that reached a symbolic climax in Washington's disavowal of the Franco–British Suez expedition in 1956. The Suez misadventure became the justification, the founding myth, of the independent national nuclear force: Britain and France had had to withdraw because they were opposed by the two nuclear powers, the USA and the USSR. But armed with his *force de frappe*, de Gaulle would be able to defend French national interests in the Third World against all comers, including the Americans. He could even resort to ringing anti-imperialist rhetoric on occasion. De Gaulle's verbal clashes with Washington and his withdrawal from NATO's unified military command in 1966 struck sympathetic chords in sectors of the French Left, which otherwise had little to rejoice about. The *force de frappe* thus served, paradoxically enough, to forge a certain national consensus between right and left.

The 1977 Kanapa Report made official a longstanding wishful interpretation of Gaullist nuclear deterrence: that it could be *tous azimuts*, pointed in all directions, thus assuring French independence from both superpowers. The Kanapa Report actually called for the intermediate-range nuclear missiles stationed on the Albion Plateau in south–eastern France, and currently aimed eastward, to be given a 'multi-directional capacity of 360 degrees', so that they could be fired at any point on the globe. In reality, this modification (never again mentioned) might have given France the capacity to blast away at the mid-Atlantic, or perhaps the Azores; but the bold words served the more immediate purpose of suggesting to the Party rank and file that France might be able to advance toward socialism under its own little nuclear umbrella. Whether Communist leaders really believed this is open to very serious doubt. But it provided an ultra-left sugar coating to the bitter pill of the endorsement of nuclear weapons.

More seriously, the Kanapa Report was a defence of classic deterrence against President Valéry Giscard d'Estaing's *Atlantiste* deviation — that is, his move back toward integration of French forces and strategy into NATO. In his close working partnership with Chancellor Schmidt, Giscard had taken steps toward the participation of French tactical nuclear weapons in the 'forward battle' in Germany. Communist leaders had grounds to suspect that the Socialists harboured a similar heretical intention of flexible respone, and their early adoption of the *force de frappe* constituted an attempt to pull the Socialist Party toward a more Gaullist position. Many rank-and-file Communists, however, oblivious to strategic niceties, welcomed the Kanapa Report as a sign that the PCF was defining its own independent 'Eurocommunist' position on defence questions, in defiance of Moscow.

It took Socialist leaders several months longer to secure their party's endorsement of the nuclear force. Meanwhile, Mitterrand had suggested that the troublesome question might be settled by popular referendum, while the rival factions in the Socialist Party cast the issue — and drowned it — in terms of their habitual ideological infighting. A key role in winning the PS over to nuclear weapons was played by Chevènement's CERES, which embraced the same left-Gaullist interpretation of nuclear national independence as the PCF, apparently with less scepticism. For the CERES it was unthinkable that the Left could carry out 'its ambitious project under American nuclear protection'.[7] Chevènement's group at the time was championing the 'ambitious project' of a 'rupture with the capitalist system', and it seemed evident that the only way to succeed with such audacity — which would surely be fought by powerful American and German interests — was to be 'sanctuarized' by a weapons system assumed to have the last word. Such debate as there was in the PS tended to be reduced to confrontation between the nationalist left around Chevènement and the pro-American conservative wing led by Robert Pontillon, who still put his faith in the American nuclear umbrella.

However, the CERES support for nuclear weapons was scrupulously selective. Chevènement opposed development of the neutron bomb, because it was a tactical weapon that could draw France into America's NATO strategy of 'flexible response' and thereby weaken the strategic deterrent.

By this time, the anti-nuclear movements of the sixties seemed to have vanished almost without a trace. In the mid-seventies, on the margins of the PS and around the small Unified Socialist Party (PSU), a new critique of nuclear weapons was beginning to focus on the undemocratic social model that they implied and indeed imposed. This critique appealed to the social value system expressed by the term *autogestion*, or self-management, at that time the rallying cry of the left intelligentsia. In May 1977, a number of prominent left intellectuals[8] addressed a series of questions on nuclear defence to the Socialist and Communist parties, observing that 'the atomic weapon is not socializable', that heavy techniques 'by their concentratin of power, rigid functioning and unity of command, facilitate the domination of an "elite" over the "mass" and of the state apparatus over society, but exclude democracy, *autogestion* and socialism.' The intellectuals warned that 'nuclearization of society is a means of strengthening the most authoritarian forms of power.'

Christian Mellon has noted the striking and almost total absence, in the French nuclear debate, 'of two types of argument which are used massively by the new European movements: fear and ethics.' It is a significant commentary on the French political mood that appeals to emotion or ethical considerations are generally eschewed on the left as intellectually feeble, dishonest or, in any case, ineffective. In practice, however, the purely political appeal to democratic values has aroused very little popular response.

At the end of the 1977–78 policy debate in the PS, the anti-nuclear minority accepted a compromise calling for the 'maintenance' of the third leg of the nuclear strategic force, nuclear submarines, during a transition period in which the government would search for an alternative form of defence. As a gesture toward disarmament, the other two legs of the nuclear triad, the land-based missiles on the Albion Plateau and the Mirage-4 nuclear strategic bombers, could be sacrificed.

These sacrifices were forgotten in the party's new programme, the 'Socialist Project' written by Jean-Pierre Chevènement and published in 1980.[9] Strongly marked by the ideology of its author, the Project laid out policy guidelines based on a view of France as a potential 'hinge between North and South', ideally situated to approach a 'transition toward socialism in the heart of the developed world' and a 'rupture with the international capitalist order'. To this end, France would have to promote 'independence from the two superpowers' and 'disengagement from blocs'.

All this seemed a far cry from the *Atlantisme* of the old Socialist party, the SFIO. The Project argued that the traditional defence orientation, directed solely against a threat from the Eastern bloc had to be broadened out, since 'the logic of blocs' bore in itself 'infinitely greater threats'. The SALT negotiations had created two 'sanctuaries', American and Soviet territory, which left Europe as potential battleground between the two. NATO risked being reduced to a 'satellite European sub-system' of the American defence system. Thus France must refuse to get dragged back into NATO's integrated operational command, as Giscard seemed to be doing by agreeing to take part in the 'forward battle'. France would maintain its obligations to the Atlantic Alliance, but must at the same time retain fully autonomous control of its deterrent force. In the Socialist Project, the French nuclear force was no longer tolerated as a *fait accompli*, it was presented as crucially important to Europe. 'Because it is in a position to spoil the prospects of a battle in Europe, the French deterrent is henceforth a factor of stability for the whole continent. It constitutes a key element in negotiating a collective security agreement in Europe.'

The Socialist Project laid out the verbal compromise between Mitterrand's favourite old-fashioned concept of 'balance' and CERES's radical-sounding rejection of 'blocs' which was to become a standard feature of French Socialist defence rhetoric. To allow European security to depend on a permanent balance between the two superpowers 'would mean resigning oneself to maintenance of the political and social status quo,' the Project noted, adding that it was impossible to 'endorse the maintenance of existing military blocs without undermining in advance the very possibility of an original socialist experience in France.' On the other hand, no autonomous European defence could be envisaged if there was not even the prospect of a common European political authority 'capable of exercising deterrence.'

The only 'practicable' course was thus to keep the 'independent French deterrent force, an element of collective security conceived on the European scale'. It was no longer to be scrapped (as the Communists had wanted in 1972), nor merely 'kept as is', as the Left had decided in 1977, while waiting for disarmament. The task now was to improve it. Its 'modernization' would not cost as much as people thought, since deterrence *du faible au fort*, of the strong by the weak, does not require the huge arsenals of the superpowers. Besides, the Project said optimistically, 'a modernized French deterrent would see its effectiveness multiplied by the present balance between the two superpowers, neither of which can allow the part of Europe it dominates to fall into the other's sphere.'

An implicit belief in France's unique revolutionary role in world history is a crucial, if unavowed, factor in the political culture of the French Left. It helped condition French socialists to accept nuclear nationalism as the necessary defence of world revolution and progress.

Many, perhaps most Socialists, however, never actually agreed with the CERES position. In the January 1978 defence debate, Jean-Pierre Cot attacked its 'narrow nationalism', its 'militarist spirit' and its 'exaltation of the *force de frappe*'.[10] But the Socialist Party's declaratory policy on this as on most issues was above all the product of Mitterrand's own personal 'balance of forces' between warring factions. His talent at finding ambiguous formulations to hold them together and come out on top had been necessary to get him to the Elysée Palace. Once he was there, his policies would necessarily be formulated by a somewhat different process.

But how? The institutional power of the French presidency is perhaps at its strongest when it comes to keeping secrets from the public. After their electoral victory, the Socialist cabinet ministers, their four Communist colleagues and their immediate personal staff found themselves a thin layer poured over the inalterable, impenetrable and for the most part invincibly hostile corps of civil servants. Ministers soon discovered that they were largely prisoners of their ministries, of their statutorily irremovable senior personnel whose cooperation was necessary to find out the contents of the files or to implement the slightest directive. Many of the Socialist ministers had been to the elite École Nationale d'Administration and were similar in background and competence to their predecessors, but the ideological prejudice of the French right against socialists and communists is not so easily overcome.

The *sens de l'état* means a lot in France. The new Socialist cabinet ministers wanted to prove they had it. So they did not go running to the media to complain that their efforts to govern were being sabotaged from the very start by recalcitrant subordinates, and the French media have such a *sens de l'état*, except for a couple of renegades, that they did not seek to disclose such unseemly goings on. In a country used to strong government, where the government is referred to as *le pouvoir*, a high-priority task of Mitterrand's team was to create the image of being serenely in control. To the extent that they succeeded, they set themselves up to be blamed for much that was not really their fault.

The left government's dependence on unsympathetic civil servants was particularly pronounced in the formulation of military and foreign policy, where the establishment is small and secretive, closely linked to a ruling class accustomed to using the state to defend its interests. The French left had no think tank of its own, no independent research institute, such as exist in Germany and northern Europe; and Mitterrand's government had little leeway to do more than follow the existing policy-making establishment, while trying to add a 'socialist' coloration in explanatory speeches.

Only a few months after Mitterrand's election, massive protest demonstrations against Euromissile deployment were being held all over Europe — except in France. French Socialists were joining the chorus against the dangers of 'pacifism' and 'neutralism'. In October 1981 Véronique Neiertz, then in charge of international relations for the French Socialist Party, explained naively that 'since coming to power, the Socialists have access to information they didn't have when they were in opposition and which confirms the existence of an imbalance of forces to the detriment of the Western camp.' This new information, she said, 'fully justifies the decision taken by NATO.' It would not be fair to hold negotiations on the basis of the present imbalance. 'On the subject, it is accurate to say that we totally agree with the American analysis,' she said. 'For us, in fact, the key point is the notion of imbalance in favour of the Soviets.'

What was this information that caused the French Socialists to change their position? Neiertz did not say, and it is characteristic of the French press that no newspaper tried to find out and tell its readers. Such prying would be irresponsible, the sign of a faulty *sens de l'état*. It is done only by clownish publications like *Le Canard Enchainé* and, occasionally, *Libération*.

Nuclear Bluff

Deterrence is psychological, and the French nuclear deterrent in particular is based on bluff. If you stalk around looking fierce and saying, 'Don't anybody touch me or I'll blow everything up', others may believe you. And then again, they may not. A time may come when even the most convincingly *acted* bluff just doesn't work any more. As President, Mitterand has played his role as keeper of the doomsday button as convincingly, and indeed more emphatically than his last two predecessors, Giscard and Pompidou. But does he or anybody else believe in it? Almost certainly not. Surveys show that even French citizens who support the *force de frappe* are over-whelmingly opposed to its use. It is probably supported precisely because of the certainty that it will never be used. Indeed, who can imagine a French president launching nuclear missiles at Leningrad and Kiev, knowing what he could expect in return? This conviction that no one, least of all the French, would ever use nuclear weapons certainly goes a long way toward explaining the absence of anti-nuclear protests in France. Why protest against a harmless fiction that seems to work better than the Maginot Line in keeping the peace? Many French people are sincerely and spontaneously frightened by anti-nuclear protests that threaten to take away their protective fiction and bring them face to face with real conflicts, real wars.

However, the small elite of specialists realize that the French deterrent is being fatally undermined, not only by the inherent lack of credibility of such a suicidal 'defence', but also by technological exhaustion. Mitterrand himself was aware of this in 1969 when he wrote:[11] 'I know the Gaullist argument: the balance of terror prevents war. It is enough for the weak, ten thousand times weaker than the strong, to reach the threshold of terror to be preserved. France reaches the threshold with its *force de frappe* . . . . I see that threshold ever moving away and France running after it, exhausted . . . . Today one has the bomb one has manufactured. Tomorrow one will buy it.'

There is always a possibility that the qualitative, technological arms race will outstrip the capacities of any medium-sized industrial nation. Thus State Department official John H. Kelly has pointed out 'how dependent the French are on the ABM Treaty signed by the United States and the Soviet Union in 1972. Without that American negotiating initiative, the French nuclear forces would be unable to strike the Soviet Union in a meaningful way. Under the treaty's limitations, the French can envision overwhelming the 64 missiles in the Moscow ABM belt or even the 100 missiles permitted by the treaty, but French missiles could not penetrate a nationwide ABM net and reach critical targets. If the ABM Treaty is abrogated or terminated and the Soviets deploy an extensive anti-missile system, the French will confront a choice: either to abandon their deterrent completely, or to concentrate on battlefield systems in the hope that the US strategic umbrella will continue to deter the Soviets.'[12] This is why the French, otherwise so enthusiastically supportive of Reagan administration arms policy, let out cries of alarm and indignation when Reagan's 'star wars' speech suggested that the United States might abandon the anti-ballistic missile agreement with the USSR to build a defensive net protecting American territory. The Russians would then obviously do the same, and the French would no longer be able to threaten them with nuclear retaliation.

A second technological threat to the French force comes from the progress in nuclear submarine detection: it is just as devastating but more subtle and goes to the heart of the *real*, as opposed to the declaratory, strategy behind the *force de frappe*. According to France's former ambassador to NATO François de Rose:[13]

> In effect, the question is whether NATO would use its nuclear weapons in case of aggression. If the answer is yes, it is obvious that it would not be necessary for France to make use of its nuclear arms as long as it was not directly involved in the conflict, because the exchange would be taking place between two powers much stronger than France. If, on the other hand, a threat was posed to either France or its vital interests without NATO availing itself of its atomic weapons, France would interpret this to mean that the Allies had acquiesced in their own defeat, leaving France perfectly free to put its own strategy of deterrence into operation to ensure its own security.

What sense is one to make of this? That if Soviet tanks were rolling across Germany toward France, and the United States declined to use its strategic nuclear forces against the USSR, France would thereupon fire its own nuclear missiles at the Russians? But the Russians could be expected to respond by wiping France off the map. Unless . . . they could not tell who fired at them. If a nuclear shot is fired at the USSR from a nuclear submarine somewhere in international waters, who's to know who did it? The Russians would be likely to think it was the Americans, fire back at them, and thereby force them into nuclear defence of Europe.

There are names for both the declaratory and the less avowable strategy in specialized circles:

> First, France would be able to deter attack by the Soviet Union because the French nuclear force, though limited, could inflict damage on an aggressor that would be out of proportion to any benefit the aggressor could gain from launching the attack. This was sometimes called the 'tear off an arm' theory. Second, and less openly argued, was the proposition that the Soviet Union would not risk even a conventional attack on France for fear that nuclear war, once begun by an inevitable French nuclear response to any attack, would set off a chain of events that would be likely to end with a nuclear exchange between the superpowers. This was the 'trigger' theory.[14]

It might also be called the 'let's you and him fight' theory. In terms of deterrence, the French force theoretically could strengthen the credibility of the American deterrent since both Russians and Americans know that in case of crisis, the French 'trigger' or 'spark' might drag them into nuclear war. This is the real element of 'uncertainty' which, it is often said proudly, the French nuclear strike force contributes to NATO defences.

Now, nuclear bombs fired from the Albion Plateau in France or dropped from Mirage bombers could be too easily traced to France to serve to trigger or spark a Soviet–American exchange. Their main function is thus probably to give the French Army and Air Force a piece of the action. The sea-based missiles are on five nuclear submarines, with a sixth on the way. This is not a lot of submarines to keep track of, even if all were out at sea at once, which is not ever the case. Advances in submarine-tracking could cancel out the 'trigger' strategy, once the Russians, the Americans or both could tell who fired the shot.

This is certainly not the sort of problem most French Socialists were ready to tackle. Yet is is crucial in regulating France's relations with the rest of the world — unless Mitterrand were to lead a real social revolution, including an upheaval at the Quai d'Orsay, which he never had either the intention or the mandate to do.

In late 1981, Véronique Neiertz was relieved of her responsibility for PS international relations and replaced by Jacques Huntzinger, who had worked with the United Nations Disarmament Commission and was one of the few people in the Party familiar with nuclear strategy and arms control. His appointment signified that diplomatic protection of French strategic policy was to take priority over everything else in PS relations with foreign parties, and in particular the Socialist International.

Huntzinger was both aware of the fragility of the French nuclear deterrent and eager to defend it. In an article published a year before Mitterrand's election,[15] Huntzinger acknowledged that doubts were being raised about not only the American but also the French deterrent. Both partisans and sceptics, he said, were concluding that 'the future of a national deterrent is uncertain because France will have more and more trouble persisting, by its own financial and technological means, with a strategic arsenal that is called on to meet nearly insurmountable challenges, such as constant progress in submarine detection, growing precision of warheads, the development of counterforce capacities on the other side, the inadequacy of an anti-cities strategy in limited war scenarios, and the increased possibility of surprise nuclear aggression.' The French nuclear strategic force was being 'put into question by experts and politicians of every outlook'. 'Some do not say so but think that the big powers are really too big for it to be possible to think seriously in the future of proportional deterrence, even if France must continue to pretend to believe in it for political and diplomatic reasons.'

More traditional doubters are those whom Huntzinger calls the French 'hawks', hostile to the USSR, détente, SALT and Soviet influence in the Third World, and openly supportive of NATO modernization. This school, according to Huntzinger, 'expresses the resurgence in France of Western attitudes traditionally distrustful of détente, sceptical about the credibility of the French nuclear force, and favourable to a new balancing of forces in favour of the Atlantic Alliance.'

A certain pessimism seems to provide the common ground where Huntzinger can meet the hawks. 'For more than thirty years we have been watching an intense militarization of international society which is without equivalent in all human history,' he wrote. 'International society is less than ever ready to disarm, for never have there been so many states, large and not so large, disposed to practice a policy of influence or power.' This is simply the way things are, and the only choice is between an 'unchecked and irrational arms race and a controlled race, that is, arms control'. One has to recognize the 'irreversible' nature of the nuclear revolution and to formulate 'very strict rules' of deterrence and balance. Intead of a 'chimeric and dangerous neutralization of Europe', it is necessary to 'take into account Third World demands and to anticipate nuclear proliferation, while seeking agreement among the interested parties for moderation.'

Huntzinger recommended that the French triad of submarines, land-based missiles and Mirage-4 bombers should be replaced in fifteen to twenty years by about ten new submarines. As for arms control, its purpose was to define the rules of the game in such a way as to save deterrence from technological progress.

Some other French Socialists, aware of the technological and above all financial threats to the French nuclear force, have looked hopefully in the direction of the Federal Republic of Germany. In January 1983 Jean-Yves Le Drian, Socialist mayor of Lorient and defence budget rapporteur on the finance commission of the National Assembly, suggested the 'hypothesis' of a 'Franco–German defence agreement in which Germany would invest essentially in its classical forces while putting itself under the protection of the French nuclear umbrella that it would help finance'.[16] This came to mind because the 'American doctrine of "decoupling" has been underway ever since US strategic superiority has no longer been obvious . . . The American umbrella is closed, gone away . . . '

The Germans, however, showed not the slightest interest in buying a small, unreliable French umbrella to replace the big American one. And Jacques Huntzinger squelched the idea immediately by saying that the 'idea of a Western Europe dominated by French nuclear deterrence strikes me as very dangerous. It would arouse resentment and distrust.'[17] Huntzinger ruled out disarmament. He wanted SALT negotiations between the USA and the USSR to save deterrence, but insisted that Europeans should stay out. He dismissed the possibility of extending the French nuclear umbrella to Germany. What prospects, then, are left for Europe?

In the Huntzinger view, everything starts with the French nuclear force, which must be saved from being counted into the strategic balance. He admits that from the Soviet viewpoint, it makes sense to count up together all warheads aimed at their territory. But it might be possible to circumvent this problem by a new approach.

Huntzinger observed[18] that 'the classic approach to arms control was to take into account existing and foreseeable types of weapons and to establish aggregates satisfactory to both parties in the form of ceilings . . . and equivalences . . . The balance of forces and the stability of deterrence were supposed to rest on numbers and precise quantities of weapons, just as nuclear imbalance was identified with numerical disparity of arsenals.' This made sense at first, in the race for delivery vehicles. 'It makes almost no sense today . . . the race . . . now has to do with improving warhead performance, miniaturizing them, replacing old vectors with new systems, such as mobile missiles . . . cruise missiles, satellites, anti-submarine warfare,' and so on. The balance of terror has been undermined, not by numbers, but by the 'risk of preventive use of the atom and the temptation of counterforce'.

Thus Huntzinger recommended negotiations that would concentrate, not on numerical ceilings, but on the 'coordination of strategic intentions', implying, apparently, agreement on the built-in strategic intentions of various systems in order to eliminate those susceptible of arousing first-strike temptations to knock out adversary forces. Huntzinger advocated the American doctrine of Programme Assured Restraint (PAR).

This line of reasoning emerged in the French Socialist Party statement of 25 May 1982, on 'Peace, Security and Disarmament', which stressed the need for negotiations to restore *deterrence*, and not, as Mitterand goes on saying, to restore *balance*.

> Contemporary competition has become a race for refined capacities of nuclear combat, and thus of limited nuclear exchanges. It will no longer be a matter of waiting for aggression from the other side but of preceding it by destroying vulnerable nuclear systems. The strategic arms race of the two big powers is indeed as follows: the new systems deployed should allow preventive nuclear war by counterforce strikes. The nuclear balance was already very fragile. It is giving way to an unstable and dangerous situation in which ideas of conflict and rational use of atomic weapons are threatening to spread.
>
> The primary objective of future strategic negotiations should thus be the restoration of deterrence.

The Socialist Party statement went on to propose an evolution from quantitative to qualitative arms control negotiations:

> The two major powers should open a new phase of SALT negotiations on a

different basis from the first two negotiations, while parallel to that, the five existing nuclear powers should meet regularly to debate their doctrine and their nuclear strategy.

Future SALT negotiations should not settle for defining numerical limitations, which would in no way guarantee a restoration of deterrence. What is needed is no longer to put ceilings on arsenals, but to ban or limit production of destabilizing weapons systems.

In SALT–III, the statement added, the two superpowers should find ways to prevent the development of defensive systems, such as anti-missile defence and anti-submarine combat, and to regulate the military use of new technologies.

This analysis is considerably more in harmony with the facts than are Mitterrand's strictures on 'balance'. It also serves to outline a framework in which there would be no reason to count French systems with anybody else's as part of a Western or European balance. The pitfall in Mitterrand's combination of 'balance' with loyalty to the Atlantic Alliance has been that it undermines the case for leaving French missiles out of superpower calculations. Huntzinger offers a way out of that difficulty. Françoise Sirjacques-Manfrass has noted that the emphasis on 'restoring deterrence' suggests that the problem is not so much Warsaw Pact superiority as a shortage of deterrence on the NATO side, connected with short-comings in the US safeguard of Europe. 'In this perspective, the French potential looks more like the beginning of an otherwise lacking nuclear safeguard for Europe than like a factor in Western super-iority.'[19]

One may wonder whether this emphasis on negotiations to save deterrence is not an elaborate apology for French nuclear weapons, contradicted by France's own current plans to develop tactical nuclear weapons for the European battlefield. France remains entirely dependent on NATO, on US 'flexible response' doctrine, on US intentions in strategic arms control negotiations; if French deterrence is to be saved, the Americans and Russians will have to save it. Ostensibly a guarantee of French national independence, the *force de frappe* is more and more a factor making France dependent on the United States. As its plausible independent deterrence strategies are wiped out by technological advance, it relies on the United States to save its credibility and to refrain from calling its bluff.

The Return of the Soviet Threat

In France, these strategic questions are discussed in public only in veiled terms, and usually in specialized reviews such as *Défense Nationale*, published by the Defence Ministry. Just as there is scarcely any peace movement in France, there is scarcely any public debate on nuclear armament. These two absences are obviously closely linked. To an outside observer, aware of the debates in other Western countries, it is obvious that a tacit consensus exists among those who control opinion through the media or positions of authority to prevent the development of any debate. It is easy to see why. The *force de frappe* has become, over the years, a factor of national consensus whose collapse would have unforeseeable consequences.

Above all, it is the domestic consensus that bolsters the French nuclear deterrent's otherwise fragile international credibility. No French government, Socialist or other, wants to lose the international influence, whether in Africa or in East–West relations, that comes from being a credible nuclear power. French leaders are able to boast at NATO meetings that they have no large movements of 'pacifists' and 'neutralists' to deal with. This boast is at once an advertisement for an independent national nuclear deterrent, a boost to its credibility, and an asset in dealing with other powers.

Peace movements in other European countries have been astonished and exasperated by French indifference to the Euromissiles, to the whole nuclear arms race, to the movements in neighbouring countries. Disappointment is bitter among many Europeans who cherished romantic images of France as the home of revolution and social progress, and who thought that the left victory in 1981 would bring the triumph of those most glorious traditions. Intead, they have discovered France as a bastion of anachronistic nationalism and the main obstacle to a unified European socialist approach to nuclear disarmament. However, the vast majority of French people, on the left as elsewhere, are completely oblivious to the resentment building against them in the rest of the European left.

This French peculiarity is a disturbing sign of the power of the media, in a period when masses of people have recently abandoned politicial activism. For activism, such as thrived in the period after May 1968, stimulates the need for independent information and analysis and keeps alive bulletins and publishing houses which provide critiques and alternatives to official versions of issues. This source has largely dried up in France in recent years. Membership in revolutionary groups and the politicized trade unions has fallen off drastically. Sales of political books have plummeted. More than ever before, government-controlled television and the mainstream press are in a position to mould and manipulate public opinion.

Blocking out of the picture the whole debate on nuclear strategy, the French media have focused on the Soviet threat and made the SS-20s responsible for the whole Euromissiles crisis. Worse still, they have played on latent anti-German prejudices to slander the peace movement as the latest manifestation of the errant and irrational German soul, always ready to plunge into some excess that threatens the tranquillity of sensible Frenchmen.

That the right-wing press, such as the string of newspapers including *Le Figaro* accumulated in violation of the law by former Vichy functionary Robert Hersant, should enthusiastically revive the Soviet threat was to be expected and would not have sufficed to create the new Cold War mood in France. Left-wing and intellectual circles were much more influenced by publications such as the weekly *Nouvel Observateur*, with a reputation for being mildly left-wing, and above all by the prestigious daily *Le Monde*. The entire French elite forms its opinions on the basis of what it reads in *Le Monde*. Thus one of the most crucial political events of 1981, following the election of Mitterrand, was the battle within the editorial staff of *Le Monde* to reverse the staff's democratic election the year before Claude Julien to succeed the editor-in-chief, Jacques Fauvet, at the end of 1982. Julien had been chosen by 62 per cent of the staff at a time when the newspaper was under attack from the Giscard government. Editor of *Le Monde Diplomatique*, whose concern for Third World problems places it on the left end of the French press, Claude Julien is a political moralist of rare integrity who could be counted on to defend the newspaper resolutely from government pressure of any kind. But with Giscard out and the left in office, the staff no longer felt the need for such a stalwart champion and began to fall prey to worries that a man of such integrity might be a tough task-master. His defeated rival Jacques Amalric, *Le Monde*'s foreign editor, was able to lead a counterattack suggesting that Julien would run the paper as Pol Pot ran Cambodia. Finally, Julien was repudiated and replaced by a weak editor-in-chief, André Laurens, who has left all power in the hands of service chiefs. Thus foreign coverage is in the hands of Almaric, whose unpleasant stint as Moscow correspondent seems to have left him convinced that the USSR is the root of all evil.

The French 'hawks' as Huntzinger called them, were able to make a strong comeback in the early eighties because their anti-Sovietism was a good rallying point for numerous minor intellectuals who, having clambered onto what looked like a revolutionary bandwagon in the late sixties, were anxious to alight when the political failures of Third World revolutionary movements and the growing weakness of European labour suggested that history might not be moving in that direction after all. The blame for failed revolutionary hopes could all be put on the Soviet Union, the great lumbering paranoid giant that suppressed Europe's best chance for a truly socialist democracy, and a truly democratic socialism, by invading Czechoslovakia in August 1968. In fashionable French intellectual circles around the *Nouvel Observateur*, criticism of the Soviet Union, which began with justifiable indignation against specific practices, was inflated into an ideology which enabled a large part of a generation to swing from the far left as far right as it cared to go. The adulation of Solzhenitsyn and obsession with the 'gulag' stemmed not from genuine astonishment at his revelations, but from a widespread desire among blossoming career-intellectuals to drop a tedious revolutionary role. Indeed, the generation of self-styled *nouveaux philosophes* who made Solzhenitsyn their cult hero were striking poses when they pretended to have their eyes opened about the Soviet Union, which they had never particularly admired (contrary to an older working-class generation) and which many of them had always hated as counter-revolutionary. This leftist, or ex-leftist anti-Sovietism revived the fifties Cold War ideology of totalitarianism, which assumes that a domestically repressive regime is *by its nature* militarily aggressive and expansionist, whereas a democratic regime (like the United States) must be peaceful and defensive.

France differed from the United States in that the Solzhenitsyn cult, at least initially, tended to crystallize around the centre-left of the political spectrum, close to the Socialist Party, rather than on the far right. The presence 'on the left' of these most vociferous enemies of 'the gulag' may have helped convince the 'hawks' that an all-out anti-Soviet policy orientation would be easier to achieve with a Socialist government than with Giscard's right-wing regime.

French hawkdom clusters around two related sets of interests: the military–industrial complex, and France's overseas interests, primarily in Africa. As regards European defence cooperation, it became clear that Giscard's partnership with Helmut Schmidt was an asset undergoing devaluation as Schmidt's own political position was undermined, and that a leadership less sensitive to German dilemmas could be more useful in weathering the brewing storm over Pershing and cruise. Giscard lacked the domestic political space for a perceptible rightward shift in foreign policy, since this threatened to provoke a surge of protest that could connect with movements in the rest of

Europe and destroy the domestic consensus. Far from mounting an anti-Soviet crusade after the invasion of Afghanistan, Giscard helped to 'cover' his friend Schmidt (and West German *Ostpolitik*) by meeting with Brezhnev.

Giscard had also made enemies on the right through his conduct of Africa policy. Giscard and his family had great interest, and interests, in Africa. But his agents were locked in complex feuds inherited from the Gaullist regimes. Partly as a result of these, Giscard was never able to master the Chad imbroglio, and in 1979 African governments meeting in Nigeria asked for and obtained France's departure from that former colony. For certain die-hards, this was surely an unforgivable defeat which could be reversed only through close alliance with the United States, where a new generation of right-wing leaders showed fresh appreciation for France's traditional role in Africa.

Central Africa provided an even more spectacular calamity. After compromising himself by indulging the *folies de grandeur* of the Empereur Bokassa, Giscard, embarrassed by the diamond scandal, turned around and used an Amnesty International report on child-killing as an excuse to unseat the dictator in 1979. Giscard's rightist enemies were furious that he had thus betrayed the feudal trust of France's 'friends'. Giscard was considered too soft to be able to withstand the Sahel revolutions being promoted by Kadhafi's Libya.

Although he had taken part in the Guadeloupe summit meeting that gave the green light to the missile deployment (whereas three deployment countries, Italy, Belgium and the Netherlands, were excluded), Giscard declined to endorse the NATO 'double decision' publicly. France, after all, did not take part in NATO's Nuclear Planning Group and formally had nothing to do with the decision. Giscard explained later that his silence was intended to prevent the Russians from including French nuclear forces in the Geneva INF balance. The hawk consensus, however, was that this was a faint-hearted interpretation of Gaullist independence, and that in this perilous time, when the United States was losing patience with its European connection, France had to give top priority to firmly anchoring the Federal Republic to the West. Moreover, right strategists were optimistic that the Pershing-2s would lock the United States back into strategic deterrence by providing a trigger for an American–Soviet nuclear exchange on German soil; and that their deployment would effect a partial abandonment of the flexible response 'sell-out'.

In the wake of Reagan's victory, his Cold War rearmament policy naturally found supporters in France, who also emulated American use of the media, primarily television, to influence public opinion without the intermediary of a political party.

When the minor candidates were lining up for the first round of the May 1981 presidential elections, a brave little woman came forward to announce that she was running for President. Most people had never heard of Marie-France Garaud. But this was soon remedied by the media: television turned her candidacy announcement into a major event, and for the first time the public learned that this well-groomed woman in her late forties had been the most trusted assistant and counsellor of the late President Georges Pompidou a decade earlier. There were hints of a grey eminence who was emerging from the shadows only to help save the *patrie* from dire peril. Her mission: to alert France to the threatening military expansion of Soviet totalitarianism.

With no party and no visible backing, Marie-France Garaud nevertheless won 1.33 per cent of the vote in the first round. Her campaign, which was mainly directed against Giscard's softness on Moscow, was a signal to part of the right that Mitterrand was preferable to Giscard. Her share of the vote — enough to swing a close election — showed what could be done by a talented unknown with that line of argument and only a few T.V. appearances.

In early 1983, Marie-France Garaud was back in the news at the head of her own *Institut International de Géopolitique* (IIG), whose co-founders included Zbigniew Brzezinski, William Buckley, Lord Chalfont, General Pierre Gallois, Samuel Huntington, Edward Luttwak, James Schlesinger and other prominent personalities, not all of them identified as 'hawks' in their own country.

Again, the media treated her with amazing reverence. In an hour-long prime-time television interview on 14 April 1983, journalists who rarely let a woman finish a sentence listened attentively as she weighed her words. As the Joan of Arc of the *force de frappe* and a smart woman in a man's world, Garaud knows how to turn her femininity to advantage in surprising ways. In her presidential campaign, for example, she suggested that it would make nuclear deterrence even more effective to have a woman's finger on the doomsday button, because there is something irrational about the 'all or nothing' threat that corresponds to female psychology. But generally, her sober, direct manner contrasts favourably with the condescending and hypocritical airs of most male stars of French politics. Her tone has made it possible to pull off lines like: 'Better red than dead is a meaningless slogan, because Communist totalitarianism is the same thing as death.'

Like Joan of Arc, Marie-France Garaud wants to influence the king — or rather, the president, which comes to the same thing in the Fifth Republic. Garaud, who knows it from the inside, calls it a 'monarchy with a time limit'. In her hour on television, she dismissed political parties as insignificant relics of the past, useful only for helping to elect a president once every seven years. The rest of the time, all that counts is the president — who 'can do anything he wants' — and 'public opinion'. After telling Mitterrand he needed to communicate with the public, she showed him how to do it.

Her message was this: Mitterrand's economic austerity policy is technically all right, but he is not selling it to the public. People will respond to appeals for 'blood, sweat and tears' if their children's freedom is at stake, but not to improve the balance of trade. The French are grumbling at the economic sacrifices required of them. But a mobilizing theme is at hand: the deadly menace to France's freedom from the East.

Garaud specified that she had washed her hands of Giscard when she heard him say that Germany could never have nuclear arms of its own because the Soviet Union would consider it a *casus belli*. To let Moscow decide what weapons a free Western country could have, she said indignantly, was the 'first step to Finlandization'. She insisted there could be no progress toward a unified Europe without raising the problem of Germany's 'non-classic' armament. She thus broke the long-standing taboo on public discussion of allowing West Germany to have its own nuclear weapons. French journalists feigned not to notice the trial balloon as it floated off. But although Garaud and her lobby repeated the hints throughout the year of the Euro-missiles, no favourable echoes could be heard from the other side of the Rhine.

Garaud's only criticism of Mitterrand was that he was wrong to keep Communists in the government. This was inconsistent with his foreign policy. Otherwise, she has carefully emphasized her independence, not to say scorn, in regard to all political parties — a stance which has enabled her to peddle her wares to Socialists.

In early June 1983, Madame Garaud was hostess to a private international colloquium on 'War and Peace' which, according to the *Nouvel Observateur*, she wanted to make 'the most *in* forum in the world on the three wars: the economic war, the political and ideological war, the military war'. Carefully selected guests included Jeane Kirkpatrick, Senator Henry Jackson and other leading cold warriors, along with plenty of Socialists and France's most fashionable journalists, François de Closets, Christine Ockrent and Serge July, editor of *Libération*. The *Nouvel Observateur* called the event a *fête de l'intelligence*. Garaud had set out, it said, to achieve what Solzhenitsyn had not been able to do: to convince the free world that it was on the wrong track. Soviet totalitarianism, she warned, is a 'slave society that threatens like a cancer to eat away all our freedoms, one after the other'.

Once the tone had been set, the media and prominent persons spent 1983 flailing the cowardly 'pacifism' and 'neutralism', the 'spirit of Munich' that seemed to be engulfing the rest of the West. On a visit to Washington, Defence Minister Charles Hernu complained that American Churchmen critical of nuclear weapons were perhaps even 'more demoralizing than the neutralist movements in West Germany'. Foreign Minister Claude Cheysson warned against 'Finlandization' at a Paris briefing of the Socialist International Disarmament and Arms Control Advisory Council, whose chairman was Finnish prime minister Kalevi Sorsa. 'Pacifism is Moscow's neutron bomb because it destroys persons without damaging buildings,' former army chief-of-staff General Jean Delaunay told a colloquium on 'pacifism and disinformation' held at the Sorbonne by the Association for Free Russia.

On 8 November 1983, at Lourdes (a site with connotations of the most anti-intellectual and socially retrograde strains in Catholicism), the French bishops rather hastily adopted their own pastoral letter on nuclear weapons entitled 'Gagner la Paix'. The letter designated 'Marxist-Leninist ideology' as the enemy that justified nuclear deterrence. ('Sainte Bombe protégez-nous!' headlined *Libération*.) Much of the text reflected the pessimism of a Church short of parishioners, vocations and money in a largely de-Christianized country. 'What force can practical Western materialism oppose to the theoretical materialism of the East?' Looking around the French landscape, the bishops could apparently see nothing better than the bomb. They did add that non-violence was worth exploring. But in an original and generous rendering unto Caesar, they stipulated that 'non-violence is a risk individuals can take', but not states.

The bishops made clear that their favourite nuclear deterrent was the French nuclear deterrent, since it could protect 'the weak from the strong'. Using nuclear weapons would of course be wrong, but 'threat is not use', they concluded, side-stepping contradictions that have troubled their American colleagues. In particular, the bishops evaded the question posed by the Vatican Council's condemnation of anti-city targeting, which takes civilian populations hostage. The French deterrent targets cities. Asked about this, the Bishop of Beauvais,

Jacques Jullien, a principal author of the text, replied: 'The United States has the means of its policy, whereas our country has only the policy of its means.'

The French bishops' statement was the product of a weak Church, frightened of Communism, with no grassroots peace movement strong enough to counter the persuasions of Army chaplains.

Over the months, the people whose job it is to do all the talking seemed to convince themselves. But what of the people who listen? Some slight clues to public thinking can be gathered from the few published opinion polls on relevant questions. In a February 1984 Louis Harris survey, a round fifty per cent said 'yes' to the very loaded question whether the United States was right to 'instal Pershings to restore balance with the SS-20s and ensure peace in Europe'; 35 per cent chose the other answer made available to them, that even if the USSR kept the SS-20s, the United States should give up the Pershings and negotiate. Asked how they felt about the prospect of a unified European defence implying German control of nuclear weapons, 44% were for and 40% against. A rather odd series of options produced these results: 40% for a military alliance between Western Europe and the United States; 19% for counting on French deterrent forces outside any alliance; 25% for reducing armament and adopting a position of strict neutrality; 2% for an alliance with the USSR; and 14% who did not answer. As a portrait of national enthusiasm for the Atlantic Alliance, that leaves much to be desired. At the same time, the survey respondents were not in favour of foreign military adventures: 58% were for the withdrawal of troops from Lebanon, while 47% disapproved and only 37% approved the presence of French forces in Chad. Only 24% were worried that nuclear war was a probability, whereas 69% thought it was not.

However, a major international Louis Harris poll in November 1983 showed that after the Italians (who on all counts came out as the most emphatically peace-loving of all Westerners), the French were the most worried about threats of war, with 44% concerned (compared with 55% among Italians, 31% among British and only 28% of the supposedly frightened West Germans). But more Germans were concerned about nuclear weapons: 38% compared with 49% in the Netherlands, 35% in Italy, 29% in Britain and 26% in France. To some questions regarding nuclear arms, French and British responses were remarkably similar, considering that there is a large popular nuclear disarmament movement in Britain and not in France. While 47% of Italians (and 58% of Japanese) said that nuclear weapons should 'never' be used, even in response to a nuclear attack, 27% of the French said 'never', rather more than the British 24%; 61% of British favoured nuclear retaliation to nuclear attack, compared with 52% of French, 42% of West Germans, 36% of Dutch and 28% of Italians. Unilateral nuclear disarmament won favour among 35% of Italians, 25% of Dutch, 23% of West Germans but only 17% of Britons, hardly better than the 16% of French. Even that lead was cancelled by the fact that only 12% of Britons and 13% of French were willing not to increase nuclear armament even if the USSR did. Sixty-two percent of Britons favoured 'restoring nuclear balance while waiting for an acceptable agreement', compared with 47% of French. But 18% of French were undecided, compared with 5% of Britons. It was this greater percentage of people who had not made up their minds which seemed the sharpest difference between French and British public opinion on nuclear weapons issues.

Poll results suggest that the heavy-handed campaign against 'pacifism' in France may have been a pre-emptive strike by controlling elites to head off the formation of a popular peace movement in a public that was potentially as receptive as others in Europe. Again, judging by poll results, the biggest success has been in arousing a somewhat greater fear of expanding Soviet influence than in other Western European countries.

The watershed event in forging the anti-Soviet consensus, at least at the visible level of the media, was the imposition of martial law in Poland on 13 December 1981. The first reaction of the French government, like most of the others in Western Europe, was disapproval tempered by the restraining thought that a Polish military coup was not as bad as a Russian invasion. However, the French media and a chorus of intellectuals rapidly pushed the government into a stronger position. While in Northern Europe, the tendency remained to hold back the strongest reactions, in France the Jaruzelski coup was treated as if it *were* a Russian invasion. For several days, television newscasts and special bulletins were devoted almost wholly to Polish events, and time was found for documentaries and panel discussions of Polish problems. For weeks, Poland was the lead story on the front pages of every newspaper, and day after day *Libération* devoted over ten full pages to news of Poland and of French gestures of 'solidarity with Solidarnosc'. Paris intellectuals were kept busy signing one another's protest statements to *Le Monde*, and there was little letup in the marches, rallies, vigils and galas on behalf of Poland. Throughout most of 1981 and 1982, while the question of nuclear disarmament held centre-stage in Germany and other European countries, in France the main issue was Solidarnosc and Poland. If it used to be that truth was different on the two sides of the Pyrenees, in the early eighties the news was different on the two sides of the Rhine.

Of course France has long seen itself, and believes the Poles see it, as martyred Poland's traditional guardian angel, its recourse against German and Russian enemies. This sentimental attachment is a by-product of French diplomacy's traditional exploitation of Polish nationalism to weaken its Austrian, German and Russian rivals. Over the centuries, France has taken in large numbers of Polish refugees and immigrants, from kings and artists to coal-miners. But the historic relationship is not enough to explain the extraordinary French reaction to events in Poland. The truth is that Poland was used as a mirror in which the anti-communist left could see itself in heroic and pathetic terms — robbed, this time perhaps for ever, of its dream of *autogestion* and democratic socialism by Communist Party hacks and Soviet stooges.

The enormous paradox of Mitterrand's election in May 1981 is that it came at a time when the French Left was already in the advanced stages of a deep decline. To a certain extent the Socialist Party grew, at least temporarily, through an influx of defectors from more radical currents, including the Communist Party. But as the militant grass-roots left of Communists and revolutionaries and, above all, trade unionists dries up, the Socialist Party risks losing its source of vitality and its essential constituency. The crowds that converged on the Place de la Bastille in Paris to celebrate Mitterrand's election on the evening of 10 May were aware of the Left's decline and hoped that the Socialist victory would bring fresh encouragement and a much-needed respite. But instead the decline has continued. It will be up to historians to judge whether the Left's visible decline was a necessary precondition for Mitterrand's election, since part of the anti-Giscard right could afford to take a chance on the Socialist candidate without the risk of radical social change.

The sense of a reprieve on the night of 10 May was particularly sharp among leaders of France's second-largest trade union con-federation, the CFDT (Confédération Française Démocratique du Travail), an heir to Catholic social thought which radicalized to explicit anti-capitalism in the sixties, and in the seventies became the leading proponent of *socialisme autogestionnaire*. The guiding spirit was closer to liberation theology than to Marxist class struggle, but this scarcely mattered to an unmanageable rank and file where variegated libertarians, Maoists and Trotskyists shared a common impulse to outflank Communists on their left. Leaders like Edmond Maire dis-tinguished the CFDT from the Communist-led CGT (Confédération

Générale du Travail) by a stress on decentralization and an openness to new movements such as feminism and ecology. For a number of years, despite an open shop system which fuels union competition for influence and members in every workplace, the CGT and the CFDT managed to cooperate in day-to-day matters. But then the French Communist Party's retreat back to sectarianism, after its split with the Socialist Party in 1977, had devastating effects on the labour movement. Although there was some initial resistance, the PCF succeeded in whipping the CGT into its own sectarian line, which in turn inspired a fresh wave of anti-communism in the CFDT.

By 1980, both the CGT and the CFDT were hanging on the ropes, as they continued to slug it out. The CGT was losing thousands and thousands of members, although it would not admit it publicly. (The CFDT was generally thought to have about one million members, while estimates for the CGT ranged from about two million down to fewer than thirteen hundred thousand.) Old methods of struggle, strikes and demonstrations, were powerless to stop factory shutdowns. At best, they obtained early retirement or payments for voluntary redundancy. As the organized working class continued to shrink, the unions fought each other for what was left. At the same time, the bosses used economic restructuring as a good occasion to eject the most militant unionists from the factories. The CFDT losses were not as large as the CGT's, but it had entered the recession with a lower membership.

The CFDT has no organizational links to the Socialist Party and is wary of strong government. However, feeling weak yet full of ideas, its leaders rejoiced that the Socialist victory might give their union a chance to grow and blossom. The first Socialist Labour Minister, Jean Auroux, did legislate some 'workers' rights' which were designed to attenuate class hostility at the workplace, the better to improve productivity. But in terms of membership and influence among employees, the CFDT continued to stagnate after 10 May. Bigger and more disciplined, the CGT was able to retain more of its organizational muscle.

The CFDT's sympathetic identification with Solidarnosc was quite natural: the very term 'solidarity' recalls the social Catholicism at the origins of the old CFDT. Solidarnosc seemed to want *socialisme autogestionnaire*, just like the CFDT. It also provided an obvious opportunity to compete with the CGT by championing a popular cause, workers' rights in Poland. And finally it offered, on an unconscious level, a way to evade all the problems that seemed to have no solution. How in fact does one go about creating *socialisme autogestionnaire* in a

Western industrialized country with a democratically elected Socialist government (that is, with a limited inter-class mandate)? If anyone had the answer, it was not apparent. But in 1981 and 1982, this thorny question was dropped, and the burning question became: Will the Russians allow Solidarnosc to create *socialisme autogestionnaire* in Poland? When they did not, then it was the Soviet Union that was solely responsible for the non-realization of *socialisme autogestionnaire*. There has been less and less talk of autogestion in France ever since.

French left intellectuals were fascinated by Solidarnosc's intellectual advisers, who were doing what they had so long wanted to do but had always been blocked from doing by the French Communist Party.[20] Seeking mirror images for their own secular, even de-Christianized society, they seemed to overlook the special role of the Church in mediating the encounter between workers and intellectuals in Poland.

In the aftermath of the declaration of martial law in Poland, a number of intellectuals mobilized by the CFDT, including Michel Foucault, met at the Sorbonne to discuss an economic boycott and other possible measures of retaliation against the Soviet Union — an approach which implied subjective identification with the government of France and even of the United States as the only instruments capable of carrying out such punishment. That was a serious contradiction for would-be libertarian currents.

French attitudes towards Eastern Europe are inextricably bound up with attitudes toward the French Communist Party. In this period, Georges Marchais and other PCF leaders continued to appear on television from time to time exuding imperturbable self-satisfaction, as more and more virulent waves of hatred washed all around them. They have contributed to this hatred by years of semi-lies and half-truths, by a style of collective behaviour that has left many who were closest to it feeling the most bitterly betrayed. This dangerous anti-communism is used in the PCF to close ranks. It can be interpreted as the old class hatred that massacred the Communards, that has torn France apart for two centuries, that gave the French working class its countless martyrs and deep sense of alienation from bourgeois society. Outside hostility helps Communists feel that they are 'the Party of the French working class', as French as baguettes and red wine, as ineradicable as the *peuple* in the nation. This comforting role-playing, with its compulsory demonstrations of unity, masks internal conflicts and dims realization that the Party is unable to define a coherent policy of strategy. So long as the Party is a way of life that can appeal to working people, it does not really need serious political prospects in order to survive. Too much political debate would threaten the unity necessary to preserve the way of life. It is a tacit inner consent, and not orders from Moscow, that preserves democratic centralism. Those who disagree can go away. The Party shrinks but does not split.

The PCF's paralysis and decline affect the whole working-class movement, the whole left, the whole French political culture. The PCF has been the only large grassroots party, and as it dwindles, nothing takes its place. The municipal elections of 1983 provided a warning sign that in working-class districts, the Communist Party's lost votes were no longer going to the Socialists or the far left but to far right candidates of the National Front, who turn feelings of insecurity against Arab immigrant workers. Without the PCF's missionary presence, many working-class neighbourhoods can become sullen jungles.

The PCF's general loss of credibility has affected French attitudes to the Euromissile controversy in a doubly distorting way. The Party has feigned a certain indifference, as if it did not want to commit itself very deeply to a cause that could be interpreted as pro-Soviet. But this has not prevented even the most cautiously even-handed protests against Pershings and SS-20s from being denounced as Moscow-directed propaganda.

The most accurate coverage of the European peace movement was in the PCF daily *L'Humanité*, whose influence is restricted to the heart of the Party ghetto. However, although the Communists are some-times almost alone in telling the truth, they generally refrain from telling too much of it. In the heat of the deployment controversy they organized a couple of large national demonstrations on very general themes, such as 'I Love Peace'. The main purpose seemed to be to show that if there were to be a real peace movement in France, they were the ones who would build it, or control it. This message was apparently addressed to François Mitterrand.

In June 1981, as a precondition for the participation of four Com-munists in Prime Minister Pierre Mauroy's government, a short agreement on policy was signed by Georges Marchais for the PCF and Socialist Party leader Lionel Jospin. The agreement said that the two parties would 'support France's international action, respecting its alliances, for peace and gradual disarmament with a view to the simultaneous dissolution of military blocs, while ensuring the balance of forces in Europe and in the world, and the security of each country. In that spirit, they favour the rapid holding of international negotia-tions on arms limitation and reduction in Europe. These should deal notably with the presence of Soviet SS-20 missiles and with the decision to instal American Pershing-2 and cruise missiles.'

The agreement was meant to keep the PCF on a short leash. So long as it stayed in the government, the PCF was likely to try to make itself useful, by keeping what there was of a peace movement under control, and at the same time occasionally flexing its organizational muscle by marching two hundred thousand people through the streets. It also sought to present arms negotiation formulae that might appeal to Mitterrand. In the summer of 1983, for example, Marchais proposed, as the best way of advancing toward the goals set out in the PCF–PS agreement, that the Geneva talks should be opened to all European governments. Nodding respectfully to Mitterrand's *idée fixe*, 'balance', Marchais went on:

> Now we observe that on this question of balance there are contrary opinions, and that the Geneva negotiations on limitation of nuclear armament in Europe between Soviets and Americans are not getting anywhere. This is why I have sent a letter to all heads of government, to all leaders of political parties of the continent. I have made a new proposal, capable of unblocking the situation: open the Geneva negotiations to all European governments. Isn't this logical, because it's about Europe? And since the negotiations are not getting anywhere with two, let's all try together![21]

Aside from the merits of the suggestion itself, which surely deserved more discussion than it got (exactly none), it was couched in Marchais's emphatically ingenuous style that instantly convinces a large part of the French population that he is up to no good.

Quite a different approach to the whole issue was taken by Serge July in an editorial in his newspaper *Libération* on 13 June 1983. July found Mitterrand terribly clever because he had used the Pershing deployment and anti-Soviet moves to 'make life unbearable' for the PCF. The 'deliberately anti-Soviet' expulsion of 47 Soviet diplomats in April (vaguely accused of economic espionage) 'literally knocked the PCF permanent apparatus for a loop.' As another turn of the screw, a new military programming law specifically designated 'Soviet expansionism' as the enemy (so much for *tous azimuts*). Defence Minister Charles Hernu and other Socialists turned out en masse for Marie-France Garaud's colloquium. Then there was the Williamsburg declaration endorsing 'global' security and the Euromissiles, and the NATO meeting held in Paris for the first time since de Gaulle . . . . After all that, concluded Serge July, 'the trap is closing' on the PCF. 'Any challenge to the government's economic policy will be interpreted as a Soviet initiative aimed at causing Mitterrand trouble. *A fortiori*, leaving the government would make the PCF look like a simple Soviet branch office in France.' Such Byzantine calculations occupy the minds of the brightest commentators on the French Left.

France Against the 'Superpowers' and Their 'Blocs'

The 'Socialist Project', the statement of 25 May 1982 on Peace, Security and Disarmament, and the oratory of various French Socialist leaders at home and abroad blame the dangers of war on the 'superpowers' and the 'logic of blocs'. Sometimes the danger is that the superpowers will conflict; at other times, that they may see eye to eye. Thus, the Socialist Project warns that the 'two superpowers, more and more, are arriving at a joint planetary vision of world security.' This could reduce Europe to a 'stake' and a 'battlefield' for their confrontations. 'One may wonder whether the real project of the Atlantic and Soviet chiefs of staff is not to wage the battle in Europe in case of East–West conflict.'

France, it is said again and again, is the champion of the liberation of peoples from the two superpower blocs. Such declarations have managed to annoy American leaders intensely and to arouse hopeful expectations in other parts of the world. But the vigorous French support for American nuclear missile deployment in Europe has left this rhetoric sounding hollow. It is not meaningless, but its meaning may be misunderstood.

More than in other Western countries, ideological reference plays an important role in social relations in France. Perhaps because of the dominant role of the centralized secular state, no political project can be taken seriously unless it is embedded in a global world view in which philosophically consistent underpinnings are at least implicit. Moralism and pragmatism are scorned. Thus France has a particularly large and visible intelligentsia engaged in defining social relations in ideological terms.

In the period following the Second World War, French intellectual horizons and political conflicts were defined by the two rival victorious ideologies — or more precisely, by each victorious power's ideological designation of the other. French publicists developed the rival concepts of 'totalitarianism' and 'imperialism' with considerable fervour, and attempted breakaways were often patched together from the most aggressive parts of the two dominant rival ideologies, in an effort to achieve national reconciliation through hostility to both superpowers. This stance was taken by de Gaulle in justifying the

French independent nuclear *force de frappe*. The double hostility was then reinforced from the left by French Maoism, which readily echoed Chinese hostility to both superpowers as the correct position of revolutionary nationalism. Indeed, the French 'Maoist' sensibility has made such a contribution to contemporary French ideology that its origins are worth tracing.

The French Communist Party was for many years totally responsive to Soviet dictates. This entailed abrupt policy reversals which greatly surprised and embarrassed party militants, especially those most committed to the abandoned lines. Some 'swallowed the snakes' and stayed on. Others left immediately or eventually, the most tenacious forming rival chapels devoted to orientations 'betrayed' by the PCF leadership. The most notoriously uncomfortable switch in line was occasioned by the Ribbentrop–Molotov pact of 23 August 1939. But that was the last time the PCF would offend French national sentiment so brutally for the sake of Moscow. The Nazi invasion of the USSR gave the PCF the opportunity to compensate for its confusion during the invasion of France by taking the lead in 'patriotic' resistance to Nazi occupation. Gone forever was the heroic (if misused) internationalism of French Communists of the twenties, who defended the German working class against French chauvinism.

The Resistance revived and glorified the tradition of French left patriotism, and the PCF did everything to exploit it in order to escape from its old ghetto and root itself in the nation. New recruits attracted to the Party at that time were often imbued with a freshly self-righteous populist patriotism and an approval of war as the necessary means of popular liberation. Internationalist pacifism was discredited.

As the Cold War got under way in the late 1940s, the fighting spirit inherited from the War proved to be compatible with Andrei Zhdanov's definition, in August 1947, of the 'two camps' confronting each other: the 'socialist camp' and the 'capitalist camp'. The Kominform line, although ambiguous, could initially be interpreted as a sharpening of class struggle in prospect of revolution, especially by the most enthusiastic Communists in the West, in France and Italy. However, it was evident that Stalin was merely trying, in a clumsy and unsuccessful manner, to pressure the West into accepting the Yalta division without rearmament.

In August 1948 at a Congress in Wroclaw, a Peace Movement was founded. The Kremlin had perceived that if the relationship of forces between the 'socialist' and 'capitalist' camps was drastically unfavourable, a better relationship of forces could be established between the 'camp of war and imperialism' (the most dangerous forces in the capitalist world) and a 'peace camp'. In 1950, the Stockholm Appeal to ban the atomic bomb launched by the World Peace Council was well-received. And at the first post-war congress of the Soviet Communist Party in August 1952, Malenkov's opening report suggested that the danger of war had receded.

'Since 1950,' writes Philippe Devillers,[22] 'Stalin had shown his interest in normal economic relations with all those in the West or elsewhere who accepted the game of peaceful coexistence. The idea was to offer industrialists an alternative to rearmament and to turn the selective blockade to which Atlantic leaders were subjecting the socialist camp. But playing this card also implied less emphasis on class struggle than on "the struggle for peace", and the task assigned to the CPs was less one of bringing their country to socialism than of converting their government to a more positive attitude toward the USSR, and of encouraging anti-American nationalism.' The 'struggle for peace' was tolerated for a while by some particularly militant Communists on the assumption that it was a temporary ruse. But after the death of Stalin on 5 March 1953, the ambiguity was dissipated with the official abandonment of the theory of 'inevitable war' and a whole-hearted commitment to peaceful coexistence by Nikita Khrushchev at the 20th Congress in February 1956. The Kominform was dissolved in April 1956 and the Western CPs given a new degree of independence.

This was felt as a betrayal of revolutionary duty by some of the most dogmatic Communists. They felt (perhaps wrongly) that good old Stalin would never have done a thing like that. They nursed a bitter hatred of 'peace movements' as inter-class fronts which subordinate class struggle to the leadership of bourgeois elements and sacrifice revolutionary struggle to the Soviet state's selfish desire for peace.

On 4 October 1957 the first Sputnik went up. Later that month at a Moscow conference of sixty–four Communist Parties, Mao Tse-tung argued that this made it possible for the socialist camp to carry the offensive against the American 'paper tiger' into the planet's 'tempest zones' in the Third World. Socialism, said Mao, would rise triumphant on the ruins of nuclear war. Khrushchev rejected this invitation, stressing that with its technological breakthrough the USSR had acquired the ability to 'prevent war'. However, he tried to combat some of the criticism by publicly proclaiming loyal support to anti-imperialist struggles in the Third World. The newly elected President John Kennedy took this seriously and promptly moved into war in Laos. But when Khrushchev, at the United Nations on 18 September 1959, proposed general and complete disarmament over four years under strict international control, the West paid no attention.

The Sino–Soviet split that followed Khrushchev's refusal to give atom bombs to the Chinese gave a new ideological home to revolutionaries with a 'national liberation struggle' sensibility. The Maoists could claim that Khrushchev had betrayed the revolution defended by Stalin — which in reality was not so much the Bolshevik revolution as the 'great patriotic war' in Russia and its allied partisan struggles which brought communist regimes to Eastern Europe, China, North Korea and Vietnam.

This brief historical survey helps to explain the presence in France of a strong current of sceptical hostility toward 'peace movements', as *both* instruments of Moscow *and* a betrayal of *genuine* revolutionary movements. Denunciation of 'pacifism' has thus proved to be the slippery terrain on which some have felt able to execute a 180-degree turn from left to right without actually having to change labels. (The champion in this exercise is one-time Maoist 'new philosopher' André Glucksmann, who has made himself the most impassioned advocate of The Bomb and 'better-dead-than-red' without ever publicly burning his leftist credentials.) On the other hand, denunciation of blocs and superpowers is felt by less bellicose sectors of the independent left to be the safest way to criticize the nuclear arms race without falling into pro-Soviet apologies. The trouble is that demonization of superpower rivalry is so overworked that it tends to become an ideology, a schematic pattern used to plaster across reality, more useful in labelling and covering up than in analysing and penetrating below the surface.

Maoist and Gaullist ideological strains, despite obviously discrepent origins, are able to converge in anti-superpower rhetoric because both have been used to advance the national aims of second-rank powers. Mitterrand has spoken of France's role of 'moral leadership for medium and small countries' — a constant presumption that goes along with the denunciation of 'blocs' and 'superpowers'. This denunciation itself, however, as practised by French Socialists, tends to blur crucial differences between the two. The Soviet 'bloc' is compact, heavily policed, held tightly together but basically defensive. In most of the rest of the world, the United States, an extremely mobile power, also exercises control over its interests, but in a quite different and much looser fashion. The rhetorical equation of the two superpowers masks a further crucial distinction: for although the French Socialists accuse them both of wanting to make Europe their long-distance battlefield, the fact is that Russia, unlike the United

States, is itself a European power, and would not be spared by a war confined to Europe.

In the 1961 Berlin Crisis, de Gaulle was mot supportive of US projects to escalate to nuclear war. The question really must be asked whether the perpetual French strategy of 'let's you and him fight', accompanied by a suspicious hostility toward both superpowers that can do nothing to diminish their suspicious hostility of each other, is appropriate to the present world situation. Theoretically, the advantage of French Socialist policy directed against blocs and superpowers should lie in the 'moral leadership' it gives France vis-à-vis smaller powers. But the test of this policy is to be found in France's relations with its European neighbours, and with the Third World.

The hope for a relatively independent European approach to East–West relations and North–South problems depended in the first instance on cooperation between France and Germany, along the lines advocated by the Socialist International under the leadership of Willy Brandt. Yet the first two years of French Socialist rule were marked by a sharp deterioration of the already lukewarm relations between the French and the German left. In the Socialist International, Jacques Huntzinger did his best to block disarmament initiatives with 'anti-superpower' arguments — for example, that disarmament was no help to oppressed third world peoples fighting for their liberation, and that France was proud of having sent arms to Sandinista Nicaragua and would do so again.[23]

However, the main occasion, or excuse, for the souring of relations was Poland. Four days after General Jaruzelski's coup, the Socialist International secretariat issued a statement signed by chairman Willy Brandt and general-secretary Bernt Carlsson which reflected northern European concern to prevent something much worse — that is, a Warsaw Pact invasion by Russian and East German troops that could end in a new, de facto partition of Poland. The Brandt–Carlsson statement expressed hope that 'the Polish people will be able to solve their problems without outside interference and without bloodshed.' It reminded 'all states concerned that they are bound by the principle of non-interference as laid down in the Helsinki Final Act' and added: 'The Socialist International is aware that unwanted advice or strongly worded declarations will not help the people of Poland: only the restraint and the will for cooperation of those wanting peace constitute effective assistance.' The statement was tactful to the point of exaggerated optimism in expressing its political demands: 'The Socialist International takes note of the intention of the Polish leadership not to interrupt and reverse but to continue the process of reforms and renewal of their country. It is to be expected that the people arrested will be released and that trade union rights will be restored.'

This statement was a bad mistake. Such extreme caution could be justified in terms of German history, but it certainly did not express a consensus within the Socialist International and least of all the passionate Polophile reactions of the French. An uproar ensued, and a special meeting was held in Paris on 29 December 1981 to draft a new statement, which this time *demanded* 'the immediate release of all imprisoned and detained people, the possibility for the free trade union Solidarity to exercise freely its activities, and the end of repression and martial law'. 'The Socialist International', it declared, 'considers that the democratic process which took place in Poland gave rise to great hope for Poland and the world as a whole . . . . We cannot accept that this popular movement is crushed by force.'

That was, of course, the sort of 'unwanted advice or strongly worded declaration' that Brandt, who did not attend the Paris meeting, was convinced would 'not help the people of Poland'. German prudence was reflected in the Paris statement's appeal 'to all concerned not to use the Polish crisis as a pretext to slow down the efforts for détente and arms control, nor to use it as an alibi for any intervention in other parts of the world.' It also called for 'concrete' help to the Polish people in the form of food and medicine, which in fact was provided in large quantities by West German donors. Germans felt that they were giving the Poles real material help, while the French were mainly contributing floods of words.

Brandt's commanding position in the Socialist International could no longer go unchallenged once the French Socialists were in office in their own country. In the French Left, the Polish events spontaneously awakened deep suspicion against Germans and their *Ostpolitik*. German 'indifference to the fate of Polish workers' became the reason, cropping up in almost any conversation about the peace movement, for the profound distrust of German protests against missile deployment.

This feeling was too unanimous ever to be debated in France, but some of the French attitude spilled over into Germany in a debate that developed between Rudolf Bahro and André Gorz in 1982, after Gorz gave an interview to *Der Spiegel* attacking the German peace movement for its alleged 'indifference to freedom'. Gorz made it clear that what he disapproved was not 'the peace movement's emphasis on the national question' but its acceptance of 'the present division of Europe and the oppression of Poland'. 'In my opinion,' he continued, 'a pacifist ecological movement should reject the whole ideology of détente. That ideology comes from the sixties when people figured that an economic–technological rapprochement was going to bring about a political rapprochement between the capitalist and Soviet systems. There was talk of a convergence of consumption models, life styles, types of society. People were convinced that industrialism and productivism, because common to the two blocs, would impose similar political systems on them. In Western countries people dreamed of achieving this result through the export of technology and Western products, which was also supposed to overcome the crisis of capitalism. Total failure.'[24]

Gorz summarized as follows the alleged attitude of the German peace (always called 'pacifist') movement: 'If the Russians are in Poland, if Poland is oppressed, it is ultimately our fault historically — therefore, let's not get mixed up in that business.' He added that 'one has no right to reason like that' and called the attitude worthy of condemnation 'politically and morally'.

Gorz's attack overlooked the very mixed character of the German peace movement, the variety of viewpoints within it, and the complexity of the German attitude toward Poland. His suggestion that the USSR had 'Finlandized' West Germany, by frightening Germans with its SS-20s, was a dangerous confusion that was extremely hard for those accused to answer. In Gorz's view, the dissolution of blocs was the only way to get the USSR to relax its pressure on central Europe. 'But for such a policy of dissolving blocs to succeed, there has to be a kind of "spirit of resistance" in Western and central Europe. Such as exists . . . in little countries that all accomplished their bourgeois revolution and where the small peasantry played a decisive role in the struggle against feudalism.' This spirit is of course lacking in Germany, whose historic original sin is not to have accomplished its bourgeois revolution correctly.

If I am well-informed — which is not certain — French foreign policy is inspired by the strong need to rebuild a classic, integrated European defence, which in the long term would make it possible to liberate Europe completely from American protection. But there is also a doubt as to the attitude of the German people, who do not necessarily want this type of purely defensive conventional defence, with its risks particularly of material destruction. So we come back, as in the time of Charles de Gaulle, to a purely national deterrent based on existing nuclear warheads.

It is out of the question to give up French nuclear deterrence: the *force de frappe* could be the subject of negotiation only if there existed a very great certainty that the other European nations are animated by that spirit of resistance to all Soviet pressure about which I was talking earlier.[25]

Gorz conceded that the atom bomb was 'a totalitarian arm by its essence, the arm of the total State'. However, 'inter-state relations have their own ethics. If one tried to submit foreign policy to moral standards, that could produce the worst results.'

In his response Bahro argued that 'freedom', as defined by the French Revolution, had provided the perfect rationalization for Europe to continue with its 'Conquistador' colonialization of the world that started with the Crusades. Gorz's anti-Soviet policy was the surest method of perpetuating the dominance of the military in the USSR.

While concern about Poland enabled French commentators to condemn the German peace movement on the basis of high principle, it was not long before more selfish concerns gradually began to emerge. Pierre Lellouche, director for European security questions at the semi-official French International Relations Institute (IFRI), offered an unusually frank explanation of French policy in a letter to *Le Monde* on 22 January 1983:

> The new and fundamental factor in Germany is that the nationalism which used to be right-wing has today moved to the left and expresses itself by anti-Americanism and the neutralist temptation. The danger for France is thus not that of a vengeful Germany with nuclear power provided by Washington, but rather of a Germany rendered insecure, neutralist and denuclearized under the double pressure of military and political black-mail from the USSR and the nationalist dream of certain German ecolo-socialists.
>
> This is what is really at stake with the Euromissiles. Beyond the military relationship of forces, the key question in Europe is that of divided Germany which Moscow is trying by all means to tear from its Western 'anchor', at the same time obtaining the final breakup, so greatly desired, of NATO . . . .
>
> What would become of our defence concept, 'weak against strong', so comfortably resting on the German glacis, protected by the American nuclear guarantee, if that glacis should collapse in an accommodation with Moscow? . . .

Lellouche raises the veil on the French foreign policy establishment's criticism of Giscard, explaining why Mitterrand may be preferred:

> If the former president had had the courage to take a position right at the

start of the Euromissiles affair, five years ago, instead of feigning a touchy indifference, no doubt we would have been able to hold back — if not totally avoid — the neutralist drift among our neighbours. In France's absence, the latter, and notably West Germany, have had no choice but to put themselves totally in the hands of the more and more incoherent leadership of the United States.

In this French establishment view, a snubbing of the German Left (as in Mitterrand's Bundestag speech) is part of the necessary task of *strengthening ties* with Germany to prevent its 'neutralist drift'.

Mitterrand has promised closer military cooperation with Germany. The land-based French tactical nuclear weapon Pluton, which if fired from its positions in France would explode within the Federal Republic, is to be replaced by the longer-range Hades, which could be fired all the way to East Germany. The Hades should be ready by 1992, and will be the first French delivery vehicle equipped with enhanced radiation, or neutron bomb, warheads. Defence Minister Charles Hernu observed the first test firing of a French neturon bomb on Mururao Atoll in the Pacific in August 1981.[26]

Mitterrand's government has clearly and firmly rejected either a nuclear-free zone in central Europe or an extension of the French nuclear umbrella to cover Federal Germany. Instead, it is strengthening its capacity to contribute to the tactical nuclear defence of West Germany in cooperation with the German Bundeswehr. 'Mitterrand's basic concept seems to be "appropriate response" — which gets away from nuclear "all or nothing",' notes Françoise Sirjacques-Manfrass.[27] 'As it is not limited to French territory but includes the forward field, France is enabled, through a sort of division of labour with NATO, to concentrate on the strategic portion of this European flexible response.' Moreover, 'for the French government close Franco–German cooperation up to the tactical nuclear level also has the advantage of anchoring the Federal Republic more firmly in the community of Western interests.' NATO rearmament and cooperation with West Germany are complementary aspects which allow the maximum advantage to be drawn from France's geopolitical situation and its status as a non-integrated NATO member with a 'NATO-covered' forward field. Nevertheless, there is a latent contradiction in this view. 'The idea that with such missiles, "decoupling" — that is, the lack of a US nuclear safeguard — could be countered, does not hold up. It recalls an idea that grew up at the beginning of French nuclear armament, the so-called "spark theory", implying that the use of French nuclear weapons would serve to force the United States to use theirs — an idea discarded as erroneous by all

French theorists. Nothing can force the United States into using strategic nuclear weapons — and certainly not medium-range missiles whose purpose is to prevent just that.'

When taken in conjunction with Caspar Weinberger's strategy of 'horizontal escalation' of a conflict in the Gulf to, say, Poland, the French government's preparations for nuclear war-fighting in central Europe and Mitterrand's declamations against 'Yalta' cannot be designed to have a soothing effect on Russian nerves.[28] Moscow can be expected to respond by clamping down on East Germany and helping to revive tension between East and West, so that any potential drift from détente toward German reunification may be halted. For there is an iron consensus in the French foreign-policy establishment that 'maintenance of a divided Germany is the cornerstone of the European system, to such an extent that a reunified Germany, on the Western or the Eastern side, would sooner or later involve the risk of breaking the present balance.'[29]

If reunified Germany could not be either East or West, could it perhaps be neutral? Certainly not. 'If Germany one day chose neutrality — it has the right, after all — there would be a grave crisis in Europe,' Jacques Huntzinger warns. 'A country like Germany, placed in the heart of the European continent, with multiple links both East and West, cannot be neutral. Any desire for neutrality would signify an aspiration to control the balance in Europe (*jouer un rôle de balancier de l'Europe*). I do not believe that would be desirable.'[30]

Claude Bourdet has explained that opposition to German independence has deep roots. 'One word, in French diplomatic and political circles still calls forth a reaction of dismay: Rapallo.'[31] Despite the speeches against 'Yalta' (which gave France an occupation zone of Germany it did not disdain to accept), French Socialist policy in Europe is firmly devoted to keeping the bloc system tightly clamped on Germany.

Global Strategy

In the Third World, the advent of a Socialist government in France raised hopes of European support for a democratic alternative to American-backed military dictatorships. French leaders made speeches defending human rights in Central America and, as we have noted, for a brief period even sold some military equipment to Nicaragua. But from the start, there was no effort to coordinate this approach with the Socialist International, which under Brandt's leadership had first attempted to encourage a democratic 'third course' in the Third World, notably in Latin America. The French Socialist government chose Mexico as a partner for its statement of principle, remaining aloof from fellow-Europeans. No attempt was made to promote a coordinated European initiative that might have carried some weight. What was really accomplished? The arms sale was a business deal, the speeches were public relations for France Inc.

The joint European initiative to seek a peaceful solution in the Middle East, begun by Giscard, was abandoned. Instead, France agreed to follow the Americans into Lebanon as part of a peace-keeping force whose role was to shore up the joint Israeli–Phalange occupation, while the Palestinian presence was eliminated and the Lebanese Popular Socialist Party, a member of the Socialist International, suppressed and broken.

The return to Lebanon with the Americans had a political and historic significance that was discreetly played down. It marked, in fact, the triumph of a certain right-wing 'Gaullist' conception not limited to France. Here, for example, is the view of Ferdinand Otto Miksche, de Gaulle's old companion in exile, speaking at a colloquium organized by himself in Hamburg in 1980: 'The Franco–British expedition to Suez in 1956 was, had it succeeded, the last chance to channel the evolution of the Third World and especially of Africa into a path favourable to the West. In obliging Paris and London to withdraw their expeditionary corps, the United States committed one of its most catastrophic blunders. Since that dramatic scuttling, Western prestige has fallen into the *oubliettes* of history. The Third World has escaped all control.'[32] The Reagan administration's strategists surely would not disagree with that. The American ruling class seems to have repented of its earlier impetuous anti-colonialism; or perhaps it is more accurate to say that reverses in the Third World have convinced a new, openly imperialist section of the American right to seek reconciliation and alliance with the old imperialist forces in Europe.

As the over-exploited third world sinks into ruin, the problems caused by neo-colonialist corruption of rulers and dislocation of societies run beyond the left's capacity to chronicle and analyse. Simple old-fashioned explanations are easier to grasp. Listen again to Miksche:

To be sure, the white man could not preserve his hegemony forever and everywhere. However, didn't he act frivolously by abandoning . . . the control of economic and strategic positions of vital importance? By suddenly bringing into the world a number of economically unviable states devoid of any political maturity, decolonization created more sources of conflict than it resolved antagonisms . . . . Tribal and racial rivalries, nepotism, corruption of new masters threaten to destroy what colonialism had built. Other dramatic upheavals are in the offing: struggles underway for ever scarcer energy sources, quarrels for a new distribution of world income, famines provoked by the demographic explosion as well as the inevitable proliferation of nuclear weapons will occupy centre-stage of world politics before the end of the twentieth century. Not counsels of wisdom but raving mad passions will guide humanity.[33]

It was no doubt the sight of the Iranian revolution that served to clinch this argument in Western power circles. Up until then, the main threat to unconditional Western access to Third World resources and economies seemed to be more or less rational revolutionaries, usually communist-inspired. Techniques were perfected to eliminate such dangers, in Uruguay, Argentina and Central America. Also in Iran; but instead of rational revolutionaries, a new danger appeared. Another way for a country to opt out of the world capitalist system is to *go crazy*, in its traditional way. The white man must take up his burden again, especially at a time when most of the world is sliding into hopeless bankruptcy and will be almost obliged to try opting out of the world capitalist system.

In 1960, de Gaulle explained that a point on which the North Atlantic Treaty had to be revised was 'the limitation of the alliance to the zone of Europe. We consider that at least among the world powers of the West, there must be a certain organization, from the standpoint of the alliance, with respect to their political and eventually their strategic behaviour outside Europe. Particularly in the Middle East and in Africa, where the three powers are constantly involved.'[34]

American strategists have been converted to 'Gaullism', in the sense of a coordinated Western condominium over the Third World, and the joint American–French–Italian–British peace-keeping force in Lebanon was an early concretization of the new strategy. As Ferdinand Otto Miksche put it: 'The survival of Western Europe presupposes a global strategic concept and, from there, solidarity on the part of the Atlantic world. What must be defended . . . is not just the lines of defence between the Baltic and the Alps, but strategic and economic positions mostly located outside the zone covered at present by the North Atlantic Treaty.' This was made official at Williamsburg, Virginia, on 29 May 1983, when the leading economic powers of Western Europe and North America, plus Japan, signed a surprise statement that 'the security of our countries is indivisible and must be approached on a global basis.' The same statement endorsed American Euromissile deployment. It also expressed opposition, in oddly self-contradictory terms, to Soviet demands to count French and British nuclear missiles at the Geneva INF talks: 'Attempts to divide the West by proposing inclusion of forces of third countries, including those of France and the United Kingdom, are doomed to fail.' Inclusion is division?

The 'global' approach to security was soon put to the test, in Chad. Under heavy American pressure, Mitterrand sent French forces in to back the government of Hissène Habré, who with CIA support had overthrown the government of Goukouni Oueddei, shortly after Mitterrand had successfully persuaded Oueddei to order Libyan forces out of Chad. Not surprisingly, Oueddei and his 'national unity transition government' had run back to Libya for help. The whole scenario was scarcely designed to enhance Mitterrand's credibility as the scourge of the 'superpowers' and the 'blocs'.

Ambitions and Options

'Today,' according to Jacques Huntzinger, 'French Socialists say clearly that strict respect for Atlantic Alliance obligations is tightly linked to struggle for the dissolution of blocs.' Does that sound contradictory? 'Life is not linear, it is dialectic,' Huntzinger explains.[35]

The apparent contradiction in French defence policy seems to be justified by its advocates as the mere contrast between different moments of a phased policy. The final phase, considered historically inevitable, will be large-scale United States military withdrawal from Western Europe: this may be interpreted in terms of the 'dissolution of blocs' if one likes. Meanwhile, every effort must be made to ensure that the eventual American withdrawal occurs in the most favourable conditions. The problem for French policy is to retain France's privileged status as a nuclear power while promoting closer military cooperation with a non-nuclear Federal Republic of Germany. The key to this appears to be the fostering of industrial cooperation with Germany in arms manufacture, while putting off the strictly military questions. However, it is difficult to see how the military questions can be answered. The French have their own financial reasons for clinging to nuclear weapons: the cost of switching at this stage to conventional defence would be ruinous. But this argument is of little interest to the Germans. How, then, can the French present their nuclear force as of value to the defence of the West as a whole, and of West Germany in particular? ·

To tackle such thorny problems, the French prefer restrained forums where the nuclear powers, France and Britain, carry particular weight — in particular the Western European Union, a phantom grouping of core NATO countries (Britain, France, Italy, Benelux and West Germany) which in 1954 undertook to monitor West German rearmament. At that time, Adenauer pledged that there would be no production on German soil of atomic, biological or chemical weapons, long-range missiles, strategic bombers, heavy ships or submarines or non-conventional motors. Lauded as a forum where the 'serious' NATO powers can get down to business without being distracted by peripheral Greco–Turkish quarrels or Scandinavian pacifism, the WEU might be used for industrial horse-trading.

The WEU was relaunched at a four-day assembly in Paris in late November 1982 whose first order of business was 'problems for European security arising from pacifism and neutralism'. Defence Minister Charles Hernu reserved his harshest criticism for the four former officials — Robert McNamara, George Kennan, McGeorge Bundy, Gerard Smith — whose *Foreign Affairs* article initiated the 'no first use' campaign. 'The very same men who presided over the impressive American arms buildup of the sixties,' he complained, 'the same men who poured over Vietnam a quantity of explosives exceeding that of the last World War; these men now tell us that the European states should in practice do without the American security guarantee.'

The WEU moved on to practical business at a Paris meeting in June 1984, when it agreed to lift the post-war ban on German manufacture of certain arms, in particular, strategic bombers and long-range surface-to-surface missiles. This seems to authorize German production of cruise missiles. The WEU could link NATO to the European community or spearhead the transformation of the EEC into a European superpower.

In contrast to the Socialist approach of trying to pose industrial problems first, some attempts have been made on the French right to start with the military end of the dilemma. But here logic led straight in a direction that not all were ready to take, at least not publicly, not yet.

According to orthodox Gaullist doctrine, the *force de frappe* must be reserved to 'sanctuarize' French national territory. The father of the doctrine himself, 72-year-old retired General Pierre Gallois, made the point in brutal terms in an October 1983 interview with a Spanish newspaper that was widely quoted in the German press.[36] Asked what France should do in case the Russians invaded West Germany, General Gallois replied: 'Not lift a finger. Hold still. Let time go by so the Soviets can solve the German problem while we protect France. I prefer to have the Soviet Army on France's border than to allow France to be destroyed.' There would be 'no other choice' but to 'leave Germany to the Soviets'. Moreover, the Gaullist General was 'sure' that the Soviet Union would invade West Germany some time in the next twenty years.

This was merely the most bluntly provocative of a series of French statements that seemed designed to excite German envy of a nuclear force able to 'sanctuarize' national territory and even protect it from movements of 'pacifists'. In the long run, Gallois seemed to be saying, will there not have to be a German nuclear force to replace the American 'umbrella' and to stand between the Soviet and French nuclear arsenals? For if Germany were to accept a sort of neutralization (like Austria or Sweden) that would hasten the orientation of the German economy toward the East, where would that leave France?

Just as General Gallois was airing his dire predictions, the Mayor of Paris and leader of the neo-Gaullist Rally for the Republic (RPR) Jacques Chirac, arrived in the Federal Republic for private talks with CDU leaders. Chirac had already pointed to the 'sanctuarization of Europe' as the problem of the day.[37] In Germany, he hinted at an eventual three-power arrangement between Britain, France and the Federal Republic. 'In less than five years,' Chirac told a select audience at the Konrad Adenauer Foundation in Bonn, 'with the system of multiple warheads, the British nuclear force and the French nuclear force will have increased considerably. They will represent a force and a deterrent capacity which will be truly important, decisive.' In a follow-up interview in *Le Monde*, Chirac said: 'It must not be forgotten that France's and Britain's strategic nuclear deterrent means are growing rapidly, which is one of the reasons for their categorical refusal to see their forces counted in the American–Soviet relationship.' Thus Chirac suggested that the French missiles should be left out of the Geneva calculations not because they were 'not comparable' (as Mitterrand insisted), but precisely because they *were* comparable. France simply wanted to make even more of them without anyone comparing, or counting, or paying too much attention.

Chirac's main point, however, was the need for a European nuclear force in which Germany would share responsibility. Once the French and British nuclear forces have been expanded, he said, 'one can envisage in the foreseeable future a European–American deterrent guaranteeing the security of Western Europe. But one cannot imagine it without Germany participating directly at the level of responsibility.' In Germany, Chirac argued that 'the impression felt by public opinion in our countries that the fate of Europe is, in the last analysis, only a stake in the rivalry between the two superpowers offers a favourable terrain for pacifist propaganda.' In West Berlin, he also stressed that he was in favour of German reunification.

The Gaullist approach, then, has been to follow up condemnations of the 'nationalist' peace movement with incitements to a nationalism that would find its expression in nuclear arms. The logic of this position is that the nuclear 'sanctuarization' of France can be perpetuated only if Germany is allowed a similar national sanctuarization. On the other hand, Chirac's proposals were publicly rejected in January 1984 by Bordeaux mayor Jacques Chaban-Delmas, leader of the centrist current of Gaullism, who said that a 'full and entire European defence' would 'not be possible to achieve'.

As Euromissile deployment commenced, there was growing concern in French ruling circles to limit the damage to Franco–Soviet relations. These had already sunk to their lowest point for years, expressed most eloquently in an unfavourable trade balance which the Russians were making no effort to improve. French suggestions of 'double key' arrangements to share nuclear weapons with Germany could arouse an unpredictable degree of Soviet hostility, and in any case the feelers to Bonn had failed to strike the expected chord among German 'nationalists'.[38]

On 7 February 1984, in a speech in The Hague, Mitterrand himself clearly rejected 'extended sanctuary' and 'double key' arrangements. 'The Atlantic Alliance,' he said, 'is not about to be supplanted by a European alliance. This stems from the fact that no military force is in a position to substitute for the American arsenal. France in any case will not use its nuclear capacity other than for its own deterrence policy, and Europe as a whole will not take the risk of being found uncovered . . . . France has not hidden from its allies that outside the protection of its national sanctuary and the vital interests attached to it, she would not be able to take responsibility for Europe's security. But for strategic reasons and for reasons of international politics resulting from the last war, the decision whether or not to use French nuclear weapons cannot be shared.'

Thus insistence on an independent national nuclear deterrent leads right back to dependence on the American strategic deterrent. French nuclear weapons, until further notice, remain an obstacle to a fully integrated European system — and yet, such integration is increasingly perceived as necessary to meet the staggering costs of advanced military technology.

Traditional champions of the Atlantic Alliance such as Jean Lecanuet, president of Giscard's UDF (Union Pour la Démocratie Française) and chairman of the Senate foreign affairs and defence committee, hope for greater Franco–British nuclear cooperation, as proposed by Edward Heath back in 1970. Noting, however, that Britain's choice of the American Trident makes cooperation difficult, the UDF document points to the 'difficult problem of lifting the American veto which still prohibits the British from discussing nuclear matters with third parties', although it expresses its conviction that military cooperation was 'the deep underlying motivation' behind Britain's decision to join the European Community, and that joint Franco–British persuasion could obtain at least a loosening of the American veto on British nuclear sharing with France. In order to strengthen the 'European pillar' of the Atlantic Alliance, the UDF proposes the establishment of a 'European Security Council', with a leading role for Britain, France and West Germany.[39]

Underlying these proposals, and the proposals of all parties, is a frantic and secretive search for viable industrial combinations. On the top, as frosting for public consumption, are more or less Gaullist appeals for greater national and European independence from the United States. Even the *Atlantiste* UDF approvingly cites Britain's war in the Falklands as 'striking proof of independence' in the face of American displeasure.

'European defence' is largely a code term for the financial, technological and industrial wherewithal for new Falklands wars. Former defence minister Yvon Bourges has pointed out that arms policy depends on the conception of 'France's role in the world'. 'Specific means are required' for the protection of overseas territories, 'a French presence in various parts of the world, military assistance stemming from our commitments toward certain countries, and the possibility of pinpoint actions to preserve vital interests. According to whether such missions are recognized for France or whether one prefers to fall back on Europe, our forces should or should not have appropriate means at their disposal.'[40]

In the last analysis, France must retain nuclear weapons in order to continue its imperial role. The fact that the left is in office has made the consensus complete, because the left is convinced that a strengthened French role in the world can only be beneficial. The manifest errors of American policy in Central America and Lebanon reinforce this conviction. Yet, precisely in order to assure the 'coupling' protection provided by the United States, France refrains from any initiative against even the blindest alleys of American policy. Rather than correct Washington's vagaries in the Third World, European powers are quite capable of inflicting additional errors of their own. The French left is unlikely to be in office forever, and Suez and the Falklands suggest doubts as to the enlightened and progressive use of European power projection.

Mitterrand's mediating talent, proved in holding together the Socialist Party, has served to forge a consensus around a new version of Gaullism subservient to American 'global security' concepts. This consensus, which has prevented any real debate on alternative, left-wing approaches, weighs heavily in the all-European context and constitutes a major obstacle to a unified European left.

Notes

1. *Libération*, 28 March 1983.
2. *François Mitterrand: L'Homme, les Idées, le Programme*, Paris 1981.
3. *Programme Commun de Gouvernement*, Paris 1972.
4. *END Bulletin* number 6, autumn 1981. Claude Bourdet is a former French Resistance leader and founder of the Mouvement Pour le Désarmement, la Paix et la Liberté (MDPL).
5. Christian Mellon, 'Histoire du ralliement', in 'La Gauche Nucléaire', *Alternatives Non-Violentes*, December 1982. Contains key documents.
6. Admiral Antoine Sanguinetti, 'Les Interventions militaires françaises', in *Tricontinental 1, La France Contre l'Afrique*, Paris 1981.
7. Pierre-Luc Séguillon, 'Défendre le Socialisme français', in *La Gauche Nucléaire*.
8. At least one of them, André Gorz (Michel Bosquet), has since changed his mind. Others included Simone de Beauvoir, General Jacques de Bollardière, Claude Boudet, René Dumont, Alain Joxe, Henri Laborit, Brice Lalonde, Alexandre Minkowski, Théodore Monod, Jean-Paul Sartre, and the farmers of Larzac.
9. *Projet Socialiste*, Club Socialiste du Livre, 1980.
10. *La Gauche Nucléaire*, p. 22.
11. *François Mitterrand* . . .
12. John H. Kelly, 'French Defense: An American Appreciation', in 'French Security Issues, A Symposium', *AIE Foreign Policy and Defense Review*, Vol. 4, Number 1, 1983, American Enterprise Institute for Public Policy Research.
13. François de Rose, 'The Relationship of France with NATO', ibid.
14. Anton W. DePorte and Hugh De Santis, 'The Politics of French Security Policy', ibid.
15. Jacques Huntzinger, 'La France et SALT-II', *Défense Nationale*, April 1980.
16. Interviewed by Carlos de Sa Rego, *Libération*, 22 January 1983.

17. Interviewed by Carlos de Sa Rego, *Libération*, 1 February 1983.

18. 'La France et SALT-III'

19. Françoise Sirjacques-Manfrass, 'Grundzüge der französischen Sicherheitspolitik in der Ära Mitterrand', *Die Neue Gesellschaft* (theoretical review of the German Social Democratic Party), Bonn, February 1983.

20. Two caustic critics suggested that French intellectuals saw coming in Poland 'the fantasy that had always plagued them: the intelligentsia's encounter with a popular movement which accepts self-limitation of its demands in order to pave the way for the intelligentsia to advance upwards to new "responsibilities".' See Jean-Louis Garnier and Louis Janover, 'L'Ordre Règne à Paris', *Le Monde*, 15 June 1983.

21. Interview in *Le Matin*, 21 June 1983.

22. Philippe Devillers, *Guerre ou Paix?*, Paris 1979.

23. This, it should be remembered, was at the Socialist International Congress in Portugal in April 1983, when the shipment of French military equipment had already stopped.

24. Interviewed by Claus Leggewie, *Zeitung zum Frankfurter Friedenskongress*, 17–20 June 1982.

25. Ibid.

26. *Le Monde*, 28 June 1983.

27. F. Sirjacques-Manfrass, 'Grundzüge . . .'

28. How this may look to the Russians may be surmised from a glance back to 1966 when, just as President Lyndon Johnson was escalating the bombing of North Vietnam and trying to set up a NATO multinational nuclear force including West Germany, General de Gaulle 'robbed the alliance of much of its offensive potential' by withdrawing from the NATO military command. The decision was announced on 7 March 1966. 'Deprived of the use of French territory, NATO would hardly be able any more to adopt an offensive posture and constitute a grave threat to Warsaw Pact countries. It was in a way neutralized as an offensive organization, for the FRG and the US could no longer envisage coming to blows with the East with an uncertain France to their rear. This reinforced the sense of security of the Slavic countries.' Devillers, *Guerre ou Paix?*

29. Jacques Vernant, editor of *Politique Internationale*, in a review of Anton de Porte's *Europe Between the Super-Powers: The Enduring Balance*, in *Défense Nationale*, April 1980.

30. Interview with Carlos de Sa Rego, *Libération*, 1 February 1983.

31. 'The Treaty of Rapallo (a trade treaty signed in 1922) heralded an era of friendly coexistence between the Weimar Republic and the Soviet Union . . .

'Although militarily the France of 1922 was a "superpower", French people remained terrified both of Germany and, for other reasons, of Russia. There was a discrepancy between the French view of the balance of forces and the view which prevailed elsewhere. French opinion then, as now, was wrong . . .

'This underlies current French hostility towards German "national pacifism". The same reaction has greeted all efforts, however limited and isolated, to make the Federal Republic a little more independent of the West and a little less anti-Soviet.

'Moves towards European unification, including the aborted European defence community (1952–54) were "sold" to the French as a means of fastening Germany to the West lest she should again be tempted by a flirtation with Moscow.

'French opinion later greeted with loathing Nikita Khrushchev's short-lived attempts to establish coexistence and confederation of "three Germanies": the middle one being a neutral unified Berlin.

Even Willy Brandt's "Ostpolitik" was not viewed as completely safe or satisfying. French politicians, statesmen and diplomats would often say privately that France and the USSR had a common interest in keeping Germany divided.' Claude Bourdet,

'Overcoming the Fear of Breaking the Blocs', *END Journal* number 3, April–May 1983.

32. Ferdinand Otto Miksche, 'La Sécurité de l'Europe Occidentale', *Défense Nationale*, February 1981.

33. Ibid.

34. Quoted by George H. Wittman, 'Political and Military Background for France's Intervention Capability', AIE Review, Vol 4, Number 1, 1983.

35. Interview with Carlos de Sa Rego, *Libération*, 1 February 1983.

36. *La Vanguardia*, 17 October 1983.

37. Interview in *Le Point*, 6 June 1983.

38. Speaking to French industrial executives, Bonn defence ministry state secretary Lothar Ruehl, the CDU's leading defence theoretician, stressed that the Federal Republic could be a Western 'glacis' only in diplomatic terms. The narrowness of its densely populated territory made it an unsuitable military barrier. It would be an illusion, he warned, to imagine the Federal Republic of Germany as some sort of protective wall for the West. Ruehl added that while Paris–Bonn understanding was essential, Britain and Italy should not be left out. West Germany would always need the United States to ensure adequate defence. The European Community could not achieve a balance of forces on the continent, but if strengthened, it could provide a means to influence American policy. (See the report in *Pariser Kurier*, November 1983.)

39. See *Défendre l'Europe*, UDF pamphlet, 1 March 1984.

40. See *Le Monde*, 2 November 1982.

4
Italy: Missiles, Mafia and Militarization

In Italy the Euromissiles were given a special welcome as a continuation of politics by other means. For the governing coalition parties, the American wish to deploy nuclear missiles in Italy was a godsend providing them with a fresh excuse to ostracize their main rival, the Italian Communist Party (PCI), just when the old pretexts were wearing out.

In late 1979, the period of 'national unity' was coming to an end, and the Communists were being pushed back into the opposition after three years of supporting the government from the outside. The profound cause of that interlude had been the extraordinary upsurge of the working-class movement in Italy in the late sixties and early seventies. The ruling Christian Democrats hoped to blunt this upsurge, and the PCI hoped to channel it into institutional forms, and the two parties agreed on the same device for these conflicting aims: an association of the Communists with the government. In retrospect it is clear that this ambiguous arrangement, known as the 'historic compromise', helped to confuse and divide the Left. The experiment, regarded with suspicious hostility by both the Italian far left and United States governing circles, was brought to a brutal end in early 1978 when the Red Brigades kidnapped and murdered Aldo Moro, the Christian Democrat negotiator of the 'historic compromise'. By that time, under the leadership of general secretary Enrico Berlinguer, the PCI had endorsed NATO, asserted its independence from Moscow, and one by one met all the conditions of compromise set by the ruling parties. The PCI's moderation throughout this period was discredited more than it was rewarded, while the popular movement that had brought it to the threshold of government was weakened and demoralized by the disintegrating effects of economic recession and terrorism.

The Christian Democrats and their partners have had good

reasons of their own to maintain undivided control of the country's rich spoils system, and to keep at bay a party with the best record of honest local government whose third of the electorate probably includes a majority of the most productive and culturally active part of the population. Nevertheless, it is doubtful whether they could have succeeded so well for some forty years without the automatic horror and revulsion of their great ally, the United States, for anything bearing the name 'communist'. The Americans' distrust of Communists has not only entailed that the PCI must be kept out of national government, on the pretext of defending NATO; it has also involved close cooperation between the two countries' counterintelligence services to protect security, to check up on Communists. In the fifties the unions were split and an attack was mounted on the Italian General Confederation of Labour (CGIL), on the grounds that factories with strong Communist-led unions would not be eligible for US offshore procurement contracts. In the mid seventies, American attention seemed to wander. But the decision to strengthen its military bases in Europe in the eighties was a sign of renewed interest, vigilance and control.

The Italian government was the first to give its consent to the missile deployment. The main reason for this haste was probably the rivalry between the government parties, especially the Christian Democrats and the Socialist Party led by Bettino Craxi, for the favours of Washington. This rivalry peaked in early 1981, as Socialists and Christian Democrats jostled each other in hopes of anointment by the newly installed Reagan administration.

Because of his smaller share of the Italian vote and his party's socialist label, Craxi had to try harder. The result, said FIAT chairman Giovanni Agnelli in an interview with *Le Monde* in June 1983, was that 'Washington appreciates him because without the Italian Socialist Party the missiles would not have gone through.'

Italian Parties Seek Friends Abroad

Italian national pride does not take the form of imagining that the country is fully independent. Italian politics is very openly conditioned by international relations.

The kidnapping and assassination of Aldo Moro in the spring of 1978 was a heavy blow to the discreetly autonomous foreign policy that had been developing during the 'national unity' period. Northern Italian industrialists looking for new markets and investment areas welcomed the opportunity to take advantage of the PCI's long-standing international contacts with the Arab world and the new leftist African regimes, as well as with Eastern Europe. The ambiguities of the Carter foreign policy left room for European initiatives in the world outside Europe. But the reaction quickly built up in the United States itself: Europe had to be called to order as a 'regional power' that could not run off making deals for itself under protection of the American global umbrella. Europe would have to pay its military dues; to 'share the burden'. The Italian role in the Arab world in particular was surely always less than fully independent, hinging in part on Italians' willingness to cooperate with the CIA in countries where the United States was politically hampered by its alliance with Israel. The Moro killing came as a reminder that this was a dangerous world for compromisers seeking a 'third way' between the superpowers and their ideological orthodoxies.

In the months following, Craxi launched a rather half-baked ideological offensive against the PCI, pretending to situate the rivalry in the ethereal realms of philosophy. Within a year, Christian Democrat party chairman Benigno Zaccagnini was returning from Washington with the word that 'a realistic evaluation of the internal and international situation' ruled out direct Communist Party participation in an Italian government.

In December 1978 Prime Minister Giulio Andreotti ostentatiously ignored Communist demands that Italy should negotiate favourable terms for membership in the European Monetary System and demand a *quid pro quo* from the Germans in return for tying the lira to the mark. On 26 January 1979, faced with the brutal realities, Berlinguer took note of his party's growing isolation and withdrew support from Andreotti's government. However, although this officially ended the 'historic compromise', the weight of the PCI's responsibilities for local and regional government, including Italy's major cities and the prosperous centre of the country, has kept it firmly engaged in the day-to-day practice of compromise and the search for accommodation with the other parties. Coalition seems to come more easily than opposition.

The main theme of the Italian Communist Party congress held in Rome the following April was the search for new friends abroad. 'Communist internationalism', after half a century of betrayals, had just been given the *coup de grâce* by the war between Communist states in Southeast Asia. Berlinguer called for a 'new internationalism', in which acceptance of diversity between parties and nations would be the basis for peace and development. Berlinguer noted that foreign policy was no longer a divisive factor among Italian parties, and that substantial agreement existed in relation to events in Indochina and support for African liberation movements. The implication was that the PCI's rich international experience and contacts (visibly displayed in the well-attended foreign delegates gallery) could be an asset not only to Italy but to Europe as a whole. Two months before the first European Parliamentary elections, the Italian Communists were issuing a tacit invitation to Willy Brandt's Socialist International in particular, and European progressive forces in general, to work together in tackling major international problems, especially relations with the Third World.

At this point the Euromissiles came along to shatter prospects of an independent European approach to world affairs, if only by reorienting foreign policy debate around the pros and cons of somebody else's weaponry. In the autumn of 1979, the West German government signalled its willingness to comply with the NATO long-range theatre nuclear force modernization, on condition that it was not the only European country to do so. Britain, as a nuclear power, was not in a comparable position, and Belgium and the Netherlands were both holding back. Full pressure was thus brought to bear on Italy, in the weeks preceding the NATO decision in Brussels. If Italy said yes, then Germany would agree and the deployment could go ahead. If Italy said no, the whole plan was in doubt.

Of course there was never any realistic prospect that Italy would say no to NATO. At most, it might have found the nerve to say 'maybe', like the little Benelux countries. This was, in fact, what Berlinguer proposed in the parliamentary debate on 4 December 1979. The PCI called on the Italian government to ask NATO to postpone the decision to build and deploy Pershing-2 and cruise missiles for at least six months, and to use the time to sound out the Soviet Union on mutual arms reduction in the European theatre. A PCI motion also called for an invitation to the USSR to suspend construction and deployment of SS-20 missiles, and for an immediate opening of negotiations to achieve a military balance in Europe 'at a lower level'. It noted the 'deterioration of the international situation' and warned that introduction of the new weapons 'would start a process which would be extremely difficult to stop' and would 'inevitably create an atmosphere of distrust, division and sharper tensions in international relations'.

The government majority parties, Christian Democrats, Social Democrats, Republicans and Liberals, argued on the contrary that, by 'restoring the balance of forces', the decision would consolidate détente, persuade Moscow to negotiate, and provide the necessary 'reassurances' for the US Senate to ratify SALT–II.

The two small left parties in the Italian parliament, the Radical Party and the Democratic Party of Proletarian Unity (PDUP), rejected the NATO missile deployment more categorically than the PCI. The Italian Socialist Party, however, was in a delicate position. Craxi wanted to please the Americans, but in the last months of the Carter administration the way to do so was perhaps not totally clear. He also wanted to please the German Social Democrats. But which ones? While not approaching the high level of inner contradiction and outward ambiguity of the SPD, the Italian Socialists were neither united nor clear. The PSI's aging 'historic' leaders, veterans of anti-fascist unity with the PCI, would have liked to wait and try for negotiations. The PCI proposal seemed reasonable to many Socialists, and to independent observers such as Eugenio Scalfari, director of the influential daily *La Repubblica* and spokesman for the Northern Italian 'enlightened bourgeoisie' that backed the 'historic compromise'. 'Coming from the largest Western Communist party, the proposal amounts to a decision of exceptional importance, which dissociates the PCI from flatly pro-Soviet positions . . . and offers all Italian and European democratic forces a reasonable platform, for agreement', *La Repubblica* stated in an editorial. A group of prominent Italian intellectuals appealed to the whole left to move together to stop both sides from installing more missiles.

Claudio Signorile, at the time the second-ranking PSI leader with aspirations to rival Craxi from the left, came up with the idea of a 'dissolving clause' to be tacked onto Italy's agreement, such that the whole NATO decision would be 'dissolved' in the event of successful arms negotiations. This was in line with the Belgian government position and with the thinking of many northern European Socialists. But Craxi decided to dissolve the dissolving clause into a mere 'wish' and instructed his party to vote for the Christian Democrat resolution accepting the missiles unconditionally.

At the end of the month, Soviet forces moved into Afghanistan. PCI leaders condemned the invasion, and held lively explanatory sessions in all eleven thousand local party branches throughout the country. In Strasbourg, Italian Communist representatives helped draft the resolution introduced by the Socialist caucus in the European Parliament condemning the Soviet invasion of Afghanistan, but, as French Socialist Claude Estier disclosed, the PCI name was taken off at the demand of the German SPD and the PSI. Italian Socialists and

Christian Democrats both called in their German counterparts to help isolate the PCI.

The Italian Christian Democratic Party congress in February 1980 ended in a crushing comeback for the anti-PCI ultras. Afghanistan had just provided proof of PCI independence from Moscow, and the outgoing Christian Democrat general secretary, Benigno Zaccagnini, opened the congress with a suggestion that the PCI should no longer be blackballed for ideological reasons. CDU chairman Helmut Kohl changed the mood of the gathering. 'In our view,' the German party leader told the congress, 'it seems more unthinkable today than ever before that a party whose spiritual sources are the same as the brutal invaders of Afghanistan, as the oppressors of Eastern Europe and a part of my own country, should participate with a Christian Democratic party in a European government.' This wasn't exactly the way things looked from their own vantage point, but the Italian Christian Democrats were more than willing to accommodate their foreign friends. With Kohl's tacit blessing, old warhorse Amintore Fanfani won a majority on a hardline anti-communist position.

As the PCI could no longer credibly be accused of alignment with Moscow, it began to be condemned for its *non*-alignment. Christian Democrats demanded that the PCI reject the idea of a 'third force' European approach to the Third World that could weaken Western solidarity.

When the election of Ronald Reagan confirmed America's swing to the right, Craxi's Socialists held a trump card in their pro-NATO contest with the Christian Democrats: namely, their control of the Defence Ministry in the coalition government. Socialist Defence Minister Lelio Lagorio gave full satisfaction to Pentagon planners, submitting an enormously increased defence budget[1] and agreeing to raise the level of Italian involvement in the Mediterranean. In August 1981, Lagorio announced that Comiso in Sicily had been chosen for the US base that would be home to 112 cruise missiles with nuclear warheads.

Craxi had to quell one final revolt in his own ranks. In October, several Socialist members of parliament objected to Craxi's order to the PSI caucus that it should vote for unconditional acceptance of cruise missiles in Sicily, as part of a motion approving government foreign policy. They said Craxi should have consulted the party's policy-making bodies — which, when last heard from, had preferred to link the missile decision to arms negotiations, along the lines of other European socialist parties. In protest, six Socialist deputies abstained. As they were leaving the chamber, PSI administrator Giorgio Gangi loudly insulted one of them, Rome university professor Franco Bassanini, and slapped him in the face. The next day seventeen Socialists, including several respected veterans of the anti-fascist resistance, issued an 'appeal to Socialists' complaining that Craxi had abolished internal party democracy and lowered the party's standards of morality. A few days later Bassanini and six others were expelled in an arbitrary procedure which, some old Socialists said, was more Stalinist than the PCI had ever been at its worst.

Was this fracas meant to impress Washington? Gangi, the slapper, was one of a series of personal envoys sent by Craxi to Washington in an attempt to organize a meeting with Reagan. However, the Christian Demorats were not content to sit back and let the Socialists upstage them indefinitely. Having lost points to the Socialists in the area of defence, they soon sought to recuperate on economic issues, by advocating austerity policies of the Reagan and Thatcher type.

The PCI and the Peace Movement

Meanwhile, on the sidelines of this competition, the Italian Communists hesitated a long time on the edge of the emerging peace movement. Before taking the plunge, they were searching for allies both abroad and at home. Abroad, their preference went to socialist parties of northern Europe — which, however, did not agree among or even within themselves. At home, they had to smooth out their own inner contradictions. The PCI leadership succeeded in stifling attempts to revive a fifties-style pro-Soviet peace movement, and did its best to allow left Christians to take the lead in a new disarmament movement. With regard to the Euromissiles, the PCI has argued that the principle of 'balance' is more conducive to negotiations between the two superpowers than unilateral initiatives might be — a position which puts it at variance with British unilateralism and with much of the independent European peace movement. Without attempting to ascribe any precise objective meaning to 'balance', the Italian Communists have persistently criticized the Russians for overdoing their SS-20 deployment and thus *appearing* to upset the balance. The PCI insists that the USSR should scrap some SS-20s as a step toward a 'balance on a lower level.'

PCI foreign policy spokesman Romano Ledda explained in March 1981 that his party's primary concern was 'the way the two superpowers look at each other, their perceptions of each other', the way

Reagan sees a Soviet threat in El Salvador and Soviet leaders see Western agents at work in Poland. 'On the contrary, we are facing autonomous movements that have nothing to do with superpower games', Ledda said. 'So we are very attentive to trying to dissipate these suspicions. We want the great powers to take a more realistic view of the world, which is much more diverse than they imagine. For that reason we are a little cautious at this time about making any move that might feed suspicions.'

This caution, this resolutely restrained and constructive approach has long been characteristic of the Italian Communist Party. It is dissatisfying both to many activists who would like to see the PCI commit its mighty organizational forces to a vigorous popular movement against the missiles, and to intellectuals pursuing an analysis that delves beneath the perceptions, or perceived perceptions, of political leaders. Thus while the PCI hesitated, the intellectual centre of the Italian peace movement developed independently around the Rome weekly *Pace e Guerra*, whose editors included prominent members of the Independent Left such as Stefano Rodotà, expelled Socialist Bassanini and European Parliamentarian Luciana Castellina. However, *Pace e Guerra* shut down in September 1983 after its backer, Castellina's small Democratic Party of Proletarian Unity (PDUP), lost its financial autonomy by running its candidates (and saving their seats) as independents on the PCI list.

The rise of a peace movement in Italy raises problems of political culture. The type of individual moral witness practised in northern European countries with a strong Protestant tradition seems pointless to most Italians. To be taken seriously, a movement needs to be part of a more global project and a more complete political analysis than is provided by a single-issue demand such as the abolition of nuclear weapons. The Italian left, in recent decades, developed a culture of struggle, with a minority tendency toward mimicry of the wartime Partisan struggles and post-war liberation movements which culminated in the disastrous 'armed struggle' adventures of the seventies. The terrorist experience no doubt created a certain receptivity toward pacifist and anti-militarist themes in part of the left, but it also helped to foster disillusion and disengagement from all forms of political commitment. In the early eighties, the Italian Communist Party officially adopted the approach long advocated by its 'left' theoriest, Pietro Ingrao, of alliance with the new social movements, notably the women's, ecology and peace movements. The PCI seems to be hoping that these will contribute to a congenial new political culture.

At the same time, in order to survive and grow in Italy, a peace movement must revive and incorporate the anti-militarist and internationalist traditions of the Italian working-class movement. There is awareness of this in the Italian General Confederation of Labour (CGIL), which has nevertheless been cautious in its involvement in the nuclear disarmament movement in order to avoid friction between Communists and Socialists in its own ranks and to influence over time the two other trade union federations, the Christian Democratic CISL and the Social Democratic UIL. This caution is necessary in view of the obvious attempt to use the revival of the Cold War and the NATO buildup to undo the whole laborious progress achieved during the sixties in healing the divisions in the Italian labour movement.

The PCI has serious reasons for sincerely welcoming the growth of an independent peace movement. But this friendly attitude does not change the fact that Italian civil society remains largely organized in political parties. In this situation, the PCI is bound to be blamed either for neglecting the peace movement, or for taking it over. (The other side of this dilemma is illustrated by the Radical Party, which has rather surprisingly abandoned the peace movement to devote itself to complaints about *partitocrazia*, the rule of the parties.)

The Italian protest movement first flared up in response to Defence Minister Lagorio's announcement in mid-August 1981 that Comiso had been chosen as missile base site. A traditional non-violent march from Perugia to Assisi drew an unusually large number of people, estimated at eighty-thousand, in September. (The province of Umbria is unique in Italy for its deep-rooted non-violent movement.) Then on 24 October 1981, half a million people unexpectedly participated in the first big peace demonstration in Rome —encouraged, probably, by the massive turn-out in Bonn a fortnight earlier. Other large demonstrations followed, and a petition drive against work on the Comiso base collected twelve hundred thousand signatures in Sicily alone in less than two months in 1982.

In January 1983, about seven hundred delegates from 150 local peace committees held their first national coordination assembly in Rome to define the organizational form and political platform of the peace movement. A concluding motion stated that the 'bloc' system had become the main cause of conflict and pledged to campaign to overcome the division of the world into military, political and economic blocs. 'The need for freedom and independence of oppressed peoples, the general social, cultural and economic crisis of the two huge systems which have governed the world, and the extraordinary diffusion of atomic and conventional arms every day provide new opportunities for war and dangerous military conflicts,' the motion declared. 'The campaign for peace and disarmament is the struggle against the use of force to resolve conflicts in various parts of the world, against armed intervention which violates the sovereignty of states, the freedom and rights of peoples.' The motion encouraged opposition to all forms of militarism — in particular conscientious objection to military service — attacked the high level of military spending, and called for projects to reconvert the arms industry to peaceful production. The Italian movement could thus be said to be focused against militarism, and not just against nuclear weapons.

Since the Italian constitution does not allow defence questions to be submitted to popular referendum, the peace movement decided to organize an unofficial mass referendum around two questions: (1) Do you agree with the deployment of nuclear missiles in Italy? (2) Do you agree that the supreme decision on this issue should be taken by the Italian people through a special referendum called by the Italian parliament?

As to the form of the movement itself, it was decided that the local peace groups would no longer be umbrella structures to coordinate affiliated organizations, but would be based on individual participation. This important decision could enable the peace movement to develop a more autonomous life and political culture of its own. But that is easier said than done; although eight hundred thousand people turned out for the demonstration in Rome on 22 October 1983, the Italian peace movement has continued to be relatively feeble in its day-to-day life.

A Peninsula Pointing Toward the Middle East

The uniqueness of the Italian political situation should not mask the fact that it is exemplary in many ways. All the main political implications of the Euromissile affair are present in Italy in especially strong form. The missiles are the spearhead of an aggressive attempt to inflict a historic defeat on the European working-class movement in a moment of weakness and confusion. This function is clearest in Italy, precisely because it is the country where the working-class movement was the strongest and most revolutionary.

In international terms, the very eagerness of Italy's governing politicians to please the strategists in Washington has meant that the real strategic purpose of the base in Comiso has scarcely needed to be concealed. Nobody imagines for a minute that it has anything to do with the defence of Western Europe from Warsaw Pact aggression. Instead, it clearly has everything to do with the establishment of a *de facto* protectorate over the Middle East and northern Africa, and eventually the Balkans as well. In the early eighties, Italians were told over and over again by their newspapers and magazines that they were greatly appreciated — not only by Ronald Reagan but also by greyer eminences such as American Enterprise Institute study director Robert Pranger, Johns Hopkins University professor Michael Harrison and House Foreign Affairs Committee member Peter Abruzzese — for their exemplary fidelity to the alliance and their readiness to follow American leadership into the Mediterranean and beyond.

Italy was the first country to join the eleven-nation observation force hired by the United States, Israel and Egypt to enforce the Camp David accords after Israel's withdrawal from the Sinai on 25 April 1982. Italy sent three mine-sweepers and eighty–four men to patrol the Straits of Tiran and to help assure free navigation in the Gulf of Aqaba — the main reason why Israeli had seized the Sinai in 1967. With its rear protected, Israel was free to launch its invasion of Lebanon shortly thereafter. Speeches and articles celebrated the glory of the Italian Navy in being chosen for this crucial task. Egypt reportedly preferred the Italians to the Americans or French for historic and political reasons. But whereas French or American ships could sail to Indian Ocean bases in the event of a Suez Canal closure, the Italian vessels would find themselves more than a year from home ports.

The left opposition (PCI, PDUP, Radicals and some Socialists) in parliament objected strenuously that the naval contingent had been sent on its mission in flagrant violation of the Italian Constitution, which requires a vote of parliament in such cases; that the force was not covered by any international authority, whether the United Nations or the European Community; that the token Norwegian, Italian, Uruguayan, Fiji and other contingents were in the region simply to provide political cover for the presence of twelve hundred Fort Bragg Rangers of the US Rapid Deployment Force, not too far from their eventual field of action in the Persian–Arabian Gulf; and that Italian participation constituted a *de facto* abandonment of the official government policy of seeking an independent European contribution to a peaceful settlement in the Middle East.

In August 1982, Italy joined France and the United States in sending a contingent to police the Palestinian evacuation of Beirut. Whatever else may be said of them, both those ventures helped to bury the very idea of peace-keeping efforts under some sort of legal international control, thereby placing 'international security' directly under the control of the United States and its chosen allies.

Italy has accepted its new role as Mediterranean fireman both in practice and in theory. Asked about controversial 'out-of-area' NATO operations by the monthly *Italia Internazionale* in February 1983, Defence Minister Lagorio replied: 'Italy has always maintained that NATO is a defensive and geographically delimited alliance and that therefore NATO cannot get involved outside the area covered by the 1949 Treaty . . . . But our countries taken singly have vital interests at stake even outside NATO territory. It's enough to think of the Middle East and the Horn of Africa. That is why I said in parliament, when presenting the 1983 military budget, that the Atlantic Pact does not totally guarantee the defence of Italian interests.'

In another interview, given to *Panorama Difesa* at about the same time, Lagorio said that Italy had recently concluded that it had an interest and responsibility in intervening in the Horn of Africa ('a geographical area which, because of particular historical traditions, has conserved important relations with Italy'), in order to assure a 'greater balance between the parties in conflict' and to assist the region's development toward peace and stability 'outside the logic of blocs'.

The New American Strategic Order

The smoothness of the partnership brings into sharp relief some central features of the new American strategic order.

1. *Bilateralism.* Although the authority of NATO is invoked in relation to the Comiso missile base, what is most striking in the Italian 'modernization' is the overwhelming preponderance of the purely bilateral relationship with the United States. In the Mediterranean much more than in northern Europe, the political foundation of NATO appears to be, rather than some community of nations, a simple series of bilateral alliances with the United States. Multilateralism serves as an ideological facade to justify the fact that decision-making power is out of the hands of each secondary power. Bilateral relations between Washington and Rome tend to be coloured by a certain revival of the Italo–American community, or rather the Italo–American lobby of businessmen claiming to speak for some twenty million Americans of Italian origin who have recently discovered that they are one of the most prosperous ethnic groups in

the United States. This lobby, ignorantly and passionately anti-communist, a source of financial backing to the Italian right, notably the neo-fascist Italian Social Movement (MSI), helps to distort perceptions of Italy in the United States. The Reagan administration has been lavish with speeches designed to flatter Italians' presumably fragile egos and, perhaps, to help all Italians evolve into Italo–Americans.

2. *Rapid Deployment Forces*. Lagorio's Ministry has decided to shift Italy's military forces from the northeast, where they have waited in vain for over thirty years to repulse a Soviet attack, to the southern part of the country. There are also plans to reorganize the services and train rapid intervention units along the lines of American task forces.

3. *The Threat of International Terrorism*. In his Annual Report to Congress for fiscal 1983, Defence Secretary Weinberger acknowledged 'other threats' to peace and security than Soviet-armed totalitarian forces. 'For example, we and our allies have come to depend heavily for important resources on some parts of the world which are either hostile or turbulent, or both, and which may possess powerful modern weapons.' There are also dangers from proliferation of nuclear weapons. 'Moreover, the United States, together with its allies and friends, has to deter and contain terrorist threats by entities that act independently of the Soviet Union.'

The fight against international terrorism has been the leitmotif in celebrations of the reinvigorated Italian–American security partnership. On 17 December 1981 the Red Brigades captured, in Verona, US Army General James Lee Dozier, a deputy commander of regional NATO forces. The purpose of the operation was not very clear — least of all to the kidnappers themselves, who did not even interrogate their prisoner. Somebody had the bright idea of trying to sell their NATO General to Bulgaria in return for firearms, but a Bulgarian diplomat failed to keep the cinema appointment at which the captors intended to raise the deal. They could find nothing to do with their prisoner but feed him big American breakfasts until, on 28 January 1982, ten agents of the Special Security Operations liberated General Dozier and captured his kidnappers in Padua in what the ecstatic media called a 'blitz'. It was the occasion for a vast glorification of the anti-terrorist struggle, its specialized soldiers and the Italian–American alliance against 'international terrorism'. The Italian press was filled for days with General Dozier's praise for the 'fantastic' rescue by Italian agents of matchless 'professionalism'. (There was much suspicion among Italians that the rescuers were Americans; and some suspicion that the secret commanders of the kidnappers were also Americans.) It was also reported that President Reagan, awakened from his sleep for the good news, had said Americans would be 'eternally grateful to Italians' for saving the good General.

Regardless of who the terrorists may really be or what they think they are doing, 'international terrorism' has an important ideological function in the period of America's strategic overhaul. Through the identification of Red Brigade terrorists with Palestinians, Bulgarians, and all the inevitable rebels in those 'parts of the world which are either hostile or turbulent, or both', the ground is laid for the transformation of a military defence alliance, supposed to protect Western Europe from Soviet aggression, into quite a different sort of arrangement: a military system without any precise geographical confines or political control, technologically advanced, secretive, mobile, ready to strike at any moment anywhere in the world against the enemies of a certain social, political and economic order.

4. *Island Bases*. It was in 1935, when Libya to the south was Italian and Mussolini was beginning his conquest of Abyssinia, that the Magliocco military airport was built near Comiso, because of its position in southern Sicily across from Malta. Pentagon strategists are now following in Mussolini's footsteps by planning to use the small islands of Pantelleria and Lampedusa, off Sicily's southern coast, for radar surveillance of the Mediterranean.

Island bases are obviously of key importance in the new strategy of offensive mobility, of air and naval 'power projection', of hit-and-run rapid deployment. There are also important political implications to this military strategy. Communication with islands is difficult: what goes on there may never be known on the mainland. Comiso is, moreover, only one item in the ambitious plans for militarizing the island of Sicily. Already in the years just after the Second World War, General William 'Wild Bill' Donovan, head of the OSS, saw Sicily as the 'Malta of the future', the military base that would dominate the Mediterranean, the solid American fortress for the coming war against communism (which would presumably engulf mainland Italy). Such ideas about Sicily's role seem to have been revived since Britain gave up Malta. Greece and Turkey remain absorbed in their own quarrel, and the United States could use a convenient halt for its Rapid Deployment Force on the way to the Middle East.

The New Social Order

In 1947, an outlaw named Salvatore Giuliano wrote to US President

Harry Truman proclaiming his love for America and his dream of separating Sicily from Italy and 'annexing' it to the United States of America. Giuliano was encouraged in his fantasies by an American officer named Michael Stern. On May Day 1947, Sicilians were celebrating the left's first electoral victory in the island's history. Giuliano brutally interrupted the festivities in Portella della Ginestra, mowing down the townsfolk with machine-gun fire. Later, he further proved his love for America by unprovoked armed attacks on PCI offices.

The Portella della Ginestra massacre marked the end of the post-war political truce between the parties that had been united in opposition to fascism. It signalled the start of the right-wing campaign that drove the left out of the coalition government in Rome in 1948 and into semi-ostracism. The Sicilian bandit Giuliano fired the first shots in the Cold War in Italy.[2]

Almost exactly thirty-five years later, on the eve of May Day 1982, a crime was committed that reminded Sicilians of Portella della Ginestra. The head of the Communist Party in Sicily, Pio La Torre, was assassinated with his driver in Palermo in typical Mafia style. It was the first time the Mafia had assassinated a member of the Italian parliament—and not just any member: Pio La Torre, 54, who had fought the Mafia since it helped landlords intimidate peasants struggling for land reform in the 1950s, was the leading member of the Italian parliamentary commission investigating the Mafia. La Torre was also the first to call attention to the dangerous link between the missile base and the Mafia. When Comiso was chosen for the NATO base, he returned to Sicily to build the peace movement. The day after his assassination, he was scheduled to lead a big May Day demonstration against the missile base.

In the weeks before his death, La Torre had been warning that the Comiso base would make Sicily a crossroads for Mafia dealing, espionage and crime. That is already part of Sicily's image in the outside world, which is generally unaware of the long political and class struggles in the island, or of the role of the United States in restoring the power of the Mafia after the Second World War, particularly in northwestern Sicily, around Palermo and Trapani.[3] But the Mafia was not everywhere. It never penetrated Ragusa province in the south–east, with the most prosperous farms in the island and Communist mayors in towns like Vittoria and Comiso. In Sicily as in mainland Italy, the Communist Party thrives in the richest, not the poorest, regions. Its essential social base, in Ragusa as in the northern Italian 'red' province of Emilia–Romagna, is the cooperative movement, made up of independent-minded farmers and artisans who work hard and reject exploitation by middle-men.

The decision to site a NATO base in Comiso was an attack on the political and social foundations of the left in Ragusa province. Not long before, the Socialist Party had abandoned its longstanding support for the PCI (Comiso's largest party, polling close to half the vote) and gone into coalition with the centrist parties. As a result, the Communist mayor for a quarter of a century, Giacomo Cagnes, was replaced by a Socialist of the pragmatic Craxi school, Salvatore Catalano. The nuclear missile base looked like Defence Minister Lagorio's patronage gift to the Socialist mayor of Comiso.

To oppose the base, a Unitary Committee for Disarmament and Peace (CUDIP) was immediately formed under the leadership of Giacomo Cagnes. Its first headquarters in Comiso were provided by *Costruzione Sud*, a thriving building cooperative which had grown over the years from twenty five to two hundred and fifty worker partners. From the start *Costruzione Sud* — whose president, lifelong Socialist Giovanni Giurdanella, says he founded a cooperative rather than a private firm for reasons of 'class consciousness' — resolved not to accept contracts to build a base for weapons of mass destruction. A number of old Socialists indignantly resigned from their party in protest. The first reaction of Comiso people was so hostile that the missile base's local defenders lay low for a while, waiting for economic erosion to do its work.

Meanwhile, Catalano left unspent development funds which had been acquired by the previous municipal council. From 1981 to 1982, the number of building starts dropped precipitously from 253 to 63. Comiso was reclassified as a riskier seismic zone, requiring altered building plans and more time-consuming red tape. A town contract for a new hospital was taken away from *Costruzione Sud*. Comiso, which had enjoyed full employment, soon counted three thousand job-seekers out of its population of twenty seven thousand.

Suddenly, *Costruzione Sud* found itself in trouble. Indeed, the whole cooperative movement feels under attack from economic policies designed to diminish workers' share of revenue. The open structures and social policies of cooperatives make them especially vulnerable. A trucking cooperative which refused on principle to work on the base has already been forced out of business. But even if they had not opposed the base, the cooperatives could scarcely have hoped to obtain contracts from the American military authorities, who have circumvented Italian regulations to set up their own employment offices, 'for security reasons'. Before the June 1983 elections, job application forms were circulated, to create the impression that the base was providing jobs. But since applicants were asked to list five character witnesses, everyone knew that their only chance was to have known anti-communist notables vouch for them. This system was a boon to the Christian Democrats and the Catholic clergy in the 1950s. Today, it may swell the influence of the neo-fascists of the Italian Social Movement (MSI), which has been ostracized by all other political parties since the establishment of the Republic. The Americans see nothing wrong with it: MSI leader Giorgio Almirante has many friends among prominent American political figures, who praise him as a fine anti-communist patriot.[4]

After the June 1983 elections in Comiso, the PCI had as many municipal councillors as Catalano's centrist coalition. But the deadlock was broken on 5 September when one of the PCI councillors abruptly joined the conservative coalition and re-elected Catalano mayor. This surprise switch was attributed by CUDIP observers to threats and bribery. Meanwhile, the contracts for work on the base have been awarded to out-of-town firms, which have sub-contracted and spread the money among middle-men. This is the Mafia style of doing business, although the contractors are not necessarily *mafiosi*. Recently it has been officially confirmed that the Palermo Mafia has bought almost all the prosperous farmland around the town of Acate, just the other side of Vittoria. The Mafia has at last come to Ragusa province, if only because the international heroin trade has raked in so much money that it is rushing to buy real estate. In 'red' Vittoria, which in 1982 was the first of some seventy Italian towns to declare itself 'nuclear-free', heroin addiction has spread alarmingly in the early eighties.

Umberto Santino, who heads the Sicilian Documentation Centre[5] in Palermo, believes that the Mafia's interest in the Comiso base goes beyond the simple trio: speculation, drugs, prostitution. He suggests a 'more profound convergence of interests' between Pentagon projects and the Mafia. As at the time of the Allied landing in 1943, the United States needs a 'social and political subject' able to control Sicilian society. Comiso is the starting point for 'involving Italy in the revival of American hegemony', a project which has singled out the Mediterranean as 'strategically decisive'. For this, 'the Americans need an island as much as possible *under control*. And who better than the Mafia can ensure that control?"[6]

Italy has been roughly divided into three parts: big private industry dominates the north; medium and small businesses predominate in central Italy; and in the south, thanks to the policy of 'reparations' to a *Mezzogiorno* considered the historic victim of the unification of Italy, the state-subsidized public sector and the 'spoils system' have prevailed. In the seventies, a reorganization of the Italian power system was long anticipated but never achieved. Instead, Italy has been falling apart. According to Santino, 'within this framework, illegal accumulation has intensified and conferred on southern bourgeois strata an economic potential that has freed them from their old dependence.'[7]

The Mafia supported Reagan. No wonder, says Santino: Sicily has an important role to play within Reagan administration policy, and *mafioso* control of the economy and society could be 'guarantee that the project for occupying the island is carried out, in the sense that *mafioso* interests and violence already are, and will seek to be even more, an "effective deterrent" to prevent and hinder the growth of a mass movement able to block that overall project.' Santino defines the present-day Mafia as a 'bourgeoisie that accumulates wealth and exercises domination by a mixture of illegal and legal methods'. The Mafia organizational model has thrived 'because it has proved to be a winning model, because Italian reality has more and more become a sort of Byzantium, in which intrigue, plots, blackmail, violence in all its forms are becoming the normal way to carry on political struggle. That is: the Italian *grande bourgeoisie*, which up to now had a hegemonic role, have made their own some of the methods and ways of behaving that were and are proper to the Mafia bourgeoisie.'[8] This general civic demoralization coincides with a period when the income of productive labour has been increasingly squeezed.

A final detail may be added to this sombre tableau: in southern Italy, collaboration has been revealed between gangsters and terrorists in kidnappings for ransom. Terrorists of the Red Brigades or Prima Linea end up linked to the Mafia through drug and arms dealing. The circle is complete: terrorism justifies militarization which profits the Mafia which helps terrorists. And all of these secret organizations may be infiltrated and manipulated by the secret services of various powers, starting with the United States. The effort to carry on an open, healthy, democratic political life becomes increasingly difficult, even heroic.

At a higher level of social determination, the NATO modernization decision has helped to shift the political relationship of forces in favour of what may be called Italy's 'military-industrial complex' — in favour of those, that is, who advocate arms production as a remedy for economic stagnation, and 'military values' as a salvation from moral crisis. America sets the tone, and the whole panoply of 'security' arguments trotted out to justify the NATO nuclear forces modernization has managed in a remarkably short time to rehabilitate military production, military priorities, military concerns.

As an indication of the shift, Eugenio Scalfari's newspaper *La Repubblica*, which in December 1979 suggested that the PCI position could be a reasonable basis for a European stand against the nuclear arms race, was singing a very different tune by the summer of 1983. On July 8, the former chief political officer of the armed forces central staff, Luigi Caligaris, came aboard with a column entitled 'The Myth of the Euromissiles'. This argued that there had been much ado about nothing, that the superpowers took great precautions to avoid nuclear war. The real danger to Europe was rather that it would remain 'paralysed' by the Euromissile controversy. 'A Europe that has remained at the infantile stage in the strategic field will not be allowed into the debate between the Great Powers,' the new editorialist warned. Obsession with strategy has become the only way to be taken seriously.

A further factor in Rome's consent to the Comiso missile base must surely be the desire, on the part of leading industrial and financial circles, to protect Italy's share of the highly profitable and increasingly competitive world arms market. This could not be done on a collision course with the United States. In 1983, Italy was rated the world's fourth arms exporter — a very distant fourth, indeed, with from three to four per cent of the market, far behind the United States, the Soviet Union or even France.[9] Arms sales accounted for only four to five per cent of total exports. But in times of economic stagnation, this relatively small sector becomes a strong political lobby, bringing heavy pressure on government precisely because, in this field, government aid is decisive.

A perfect example of this: the complaints of Enrico Bocchini, president of the shipbuilders association, to *La Repubblica* at the Genoa naval show in May 1982. 'Ten years ago', he said, 'we had zero on the international market, and our exports are not over five hundred thousand dollars.' Noting that Italy had won 40% of contracts for frigates in the two-to-three ton class and 50% of contracts in the 500-to-1000 ton corvette class, as well as selling helicopters and electronic equipment to navies of fifty countries, he explained that the desire of Third World countries to patrol their 200-mile offshore 'economic zone' had created this booming market for light warships. 'But the trouble is, if we don't build at least one first for the Italian Navy, we won't sell any abroad,' the shipbuilder pointed out, complaining about recent defence budget cuts. 'Because one thing is

certain and goes for arms too: furnishing our own armed forces is a
guarantee to the buyer. One ship built for Italy sells five abroad.'

The ratios given about the same time by Defence Minister Lagorio
were four to one for naval vessels, and three to one for helicopters. But
the argument was the same: defence spending provides important
help to Italian industry, for financial stability, technological progress,
and competitiveness on the world market.[10]

Bocchini's complaint is a perfect illustration of what Fabrizio
Battistelli calls the 'vicious circle of the procurement-production-
export cycle'. Battistelli observes that the soaring cost of arms has
presented the European arms industry (and others) with the choice
between two types of solutions, 'restrictive' and 'expansionary'. The
'restrictive' approach involves specialization in individual weapons
systems and European collaboration on specific projects, in the realization that national arms industries lack the technological and above
all the financial resources to produce independently a whole range of
modern weapons. But European industry almost always prefers the
'expansionary' path of safer promotion. 'The strongest pressure',
Battistelli maintains, 'is that on the government, personified by the
Minister for Defence. (One should bear in mind that ever more often
in European governments the Minister's role is to express the
demands of the military and the arms industry within the cabinet
rather than to express the governments' requirements . . .) The aim
is to increase sales both domestically (through national procurement)
and abroad (through procurement by foreign armed forces). The two
sales outlets are closely tied. What emerges is a 'procurement–
production–export' cycle. Given the feed-back involved, it seems
perfectly correct to talk in terms of a vicious circle. A national arms
industry produces a specific weapon so that this can be adopted by its
own country's armed forces. For production to be worthwhile,
however, it has to be on a larger scale than that required to meet
national demand. A surplus is thus created for sale to foreign armed
forces. First, however, the weapon in question has to be adopted by
national armed forces. At times the cycle works in the opposite
direction. National armed forces have to adopt a specific weapons
system so that it can be exported, so that it can be produced, so that it
can be adopted.'[11]

The vicious cycle applies to all major industrialized countries. But
the Italian arms industry, of which some sixty per cent is publicly
owned, has some complicating features. Not only is it controlled by
the big state monopolies answerable to the Ministry of State Participation; but it is very heavily dependent on the United States, both

technologically and politically. These two peculiarities are in fact linked. For, ever since the end of the Second World War, the American-approved politicians in charge of the Ministry of State Participation have been able to enrich their patronage resources through profitable licensing and subcontracting deals with American industry.

One of Italy's big exporters is Agusta, which makes helicopters at Varese, or rather puts them together from US-made kits containing some eighty per cent of the parts. In the early fifties, Agusta obtained licences to produce and sell helicopters of American design, mostly Bell, but also Sikorsky and Hughes. Although State Participation left him with only a 20 per cent stake in 1972, the present boss is still Count Corrado Agusta — a man close to the heir of the house of Savoy, Prince Vittorio Emanuele (who caused a bit of a scandal a while back by fatally shooting a German tourist); a member of the jet society whose connections with the late monarchs of Iran and Ethiopia helped sales to those countries.

Other big exporters, such as Oto Melara which specializes in naval equipment and Selenia which makes both military and civilian airport control systems and other electronics, are also partly dependent on American technology, although not to the extent of Agusta.

The Italians specialize in medium-technology systems, often in a complete package including training, which have enjoyed a good market in Arab and other third world countries in the years of high oil prices. However, Italy's share of this market is now threatened by several factors. Many client countries may soon be too destitute even to buy arms; and the Italian government is also short of funds to subsidize the exporting industries through defence contracts. Besides, strenuous competition is expected in the eighties from the Germans and the Japanese, once they are pushed by the Americans back into a field where they still enjoy a high reputation from the war years. Finally, the sharpest competition in Third World markets is likely to come from the more industrialized Third World countries themselves: Brazil, India, not to mention Israel and South Africa, as well as Argentina, Taiwan and others.

In the face of such mounting adversity, industry is demanding an 'Italian Pentagon' to finance research and development and select projects.[12] But the original Pentagon would be even better. Already in September 1978, Defence Minister Attilio Ruffini signed a memorandum on arms cooperation with US Defense Secretary Harold Brown in which the Italians deepened their subservience to the United States in the hope that something profitable would come of it.

But Lagorio complained that when he took office in 1980, Italy bought from the USA seven times more than it sold. Three years later he said he had improved the ratio to four to one and had agreed with Caspar Weinberger on a target of 2.5 to one.

Nor is that all. Lagorio reported in early 1983 that he was trying to win Weinberger to the idea of a 'tripolar' accord between Italy, the USA and third countries like Egypt, Saudi Arabia, Somalia and Sudan to provide them with complete security. 'The United States and Italy', he said, 'have very advanced industries and can therefore furnish everything that can guarantee security to countries committed to a socio-economic policy of development and a foreign policy of international stabilization and refusal of what is called the "hegemonism" of the great powers.'[13] Lagorio was obviously ready to include a heavy dose of ideology in his security packages for worthy Third World governments.

Because of the very special relationship between Italy's governing politicians and the United States, the country's nationalized industries have been rather more dependent than the private sector on American business links. Thus in the late sixties, Italy's most important private industrial concern, FIAT, which had been part of a NATO consortium producing the Lockheed F-104 Starfighter, began to move away from the US connection toward Europe. FIAT chairman Giovanni Agnelli led the corporation into an Italo–British–German consortium for joint production of the first major European project, the multipurpose Tornado jet fighter. At the same time, FIAT and State Participation formed a mixed public–private company, Aeritalia, to handle the Italian side.

Lockheed seems to have taken badly this potential competition and, according to information divulged in court after the famous scandal in 1976, it persuaded certain journalists to write denigrating articles about the Tornado. That year, however, FIAT withdrew from Aeritalia after pro-American executives of the state holding company had drained its capital to finance a Boeing project.[14]

What has come to light of this fierce undercover industrial war between the American aviation industry and its first real multinational European competitor is enough to suggest that the whole 'radical chic' period of Italian politics, when the enlightened northern bourgeoisie was flirting with the PCI, could well be related to the conflict between FIAT in its 'European' period and the pro-American Christian Democrats in the Ministry of State Participation. All that is certain is that political life is often heavily conditioned by such industrial battles waged unbeknownst to the general public. This is true of industry in general, but the phenomenon is particularly damaging to democratic political life in the case of military industry, because of the heavy cloak of secrecy (justified by national security), the large public funds and the inevitable ideological smokescreen.

'In Italy, without anyone paying attention, a reconversion is already underway: from civilian to military production,' Battistelli has observed.[15] This reconversion follows in the wake of the American rearmament programme — for some of the same reasons (arms can be sold), and also because the United States can pull others after it in whichever direction it chooses. But the arms race quickly brings Italy face to face with formidable contradictions.

First there is the problem, in hard times, of the military budget. Italy, unlike the United States, cannot use high interest-rates to lure investment capital to feed on enormous debt that can be reduced in some subsequent period of conveniently arranged inflation. Where, then, is the extra money to come from? Nobody has an answer.

European countries have been able to modernize their arms systems only by shifting appropriations from manpower costs to arms purchases. The result is more and more fancy equipment for fewer and fewer soldiers[16] — a trend which is particularly alarming to officers in a shrinking army. In the United States, too, fears are being voiced that high-technology equipment is becoming too sophisticated for human soldiers to operate in a real battle. But whereas the Americans can at least console themselves with the knowledge of their technological predominance, no such comfort is available in a country the size of Italy. Present trends threaten to leave it with neither an advanced technology nor a viable army of its own.

Agnelli, recently branching back into the arms business, argued at the Atlantic Alliance's annual 'Shapex' closed gathering in Brussels, on 6 May 1983, that European industry should devote more resources to weapons manufacture, preferably neither nuclear nor ultra-sophisticated. He proposed the formation of 'families of companies' to rationalize production and minimize costs.

The Italian Army chief-of-staff, General Umberto Cappuzzo, has repeatedly called attention to the enormous problems being created by the technology race. Technology, he said in a speech in May 1982, is a means by which the superpowers maintain their superiority within their respective blocs. 'Only the superpowers can permit themselves the present pace of the technological race. Their "partners" on the level below cannot keep it up, even with co-production and cooperation in Western Europe. A real and proper technological polarization is being established, and not only in the nuclear field.'[17]

Noting that the previous thirty years had seen constant 'qualitative progress' in weapons at the expense of quantity, the Army man argued for a major reversal in priorities. After a period of indifference, he detected a growing public interest in military 'values', which he attributed to 'the widespread disorientation and latent malaise characterizing our society'. This in turn was the result of the 'total failure of the ideological myth', which pitilessly destroyed cultural behavioural forms without managing to put forth even the bases for valid modern alternatives.' Cappuzzo suggested that military values such as organization, professionalism, serious commitment, and 'high moral and spiritual tone' could contribute to the badly needed 'refoundation' of social solidarity. A vigorous effort was necessary to restore those moral values in order to create a 'conscious, generous spirit of collaboration' capable of overcoming particularisms and achieving 'that social peace to which all aspire'.

In other words, if advanced technology is depriving the army of its traditional role in fighting off foreign enemies, it can perhaps fall back on the function of restoring and preserving the internal social order. This argument is not without appeal in the confusion and demoralization of the early eighties, coming after a *riflusso* of revolutionary hopes and a return to private concerns. However, it is not clear what General Cappuzzo's moral militarization would entail. A 1978 law reformed Italian military discipline to allow a certain measure of democratization, and General Cappuzzo himself, in the winter of 1981–82, resisted efforts to involve the Army in the battle against terrorism. All that is certain is that as military problems and production take up more and more social space, they bring their own inner conflicts and contradictions. There is no unanimity within the 'military–industrial complex', which is constantly rent with bitter battles for available resources.

Even less is there any subjective accord between the soldiers and airmen who will man the new military installations and the *mafiosi* who will profit from them to invest their earnings from the heroin trade. As for terrorists, they are avowed enemies. Yet all these human possibilities — soldier, drug trafficker, terrorist — are part of one and the same social system that has been squeezing out the culture of productive work (the culture of industrial soceity, both bourgeois and working-class) with a new culture of security. As this fills the social space, its inner conflicts (cops and robbers, commandos and terrorists) absorb the attention of the media and mould the imaginations of the impressionable. But the more profound contradiction is between this whole system, this whole culture of security, and another which is still struggling to find expression.

A Way Out Of the Trap?

On 9 August 1983, Bettino Craxi got his reward. He took office as the post-war Italian Republic's first Socialist prime minister, flanked by two politically powerful former premiers, Christian Democrat Giulio Andreotti in the foreign ministry and Republican Giovanni Spadolini in the defence ministry. (The next day, oddly enough, Italy's mysterious master power-broker Licio Gelli escaped from his Swiss prison cell, with consummate ease, thus avoiding extradition.) In November, the government listlessly but relentlessly pushed final approval of cruise missiles through the Italian parliament.

But if social reality is everywhere a dialectical phenomenon, it is especially so in Italy. The total victory of the pro-American project could be the prologue to its collapse. All that is needed is a credible alternative.

The three-day debate in the Italian Chamber of Deputies, which preceded the Euromissile vote on 16 November was marked by massive absenteeism on the government benches. The greatest vigour in defending NATO modernization was displayed by police on the Piazza Montecitorio in front of parliament, who brutally charged non-violent protesters and even beat opposition deputies who went to speak to them. The anti-missile opposition easily dominated the debate, interrupted occasionally by cries of: 'The police are beating deputies!' or: 'Where are the Christian Democrats?' The absence was ambiguous; the missing deputies could always claim that they did not have to, or did not have the heart to, exert themselves for a foregone conclusion.

A few days before the Chamber gave its official approval, the United States had announced that even though the Comiso base construction was behind schedule, the cruise missiles would be brought in 'on time' — that is, right away — to the nearby Sigonella NATO base. Italians were thus shown that their permission was unnecessary for Americans to move nuclear weapons onto Italian territory.

There were signs of growing misgivings among NATO's champions. In a hasty interview obtained by retired General Caligaris for *La Repubblica* on 28 September, Caspar Weinberger welcomed all further Italian contribution to 'regional defence', notably a capacity to intervene in favour of 'Western interests, even outside NATO'. But he offered precious little in return. Caligaris then reminded the American Defense Secretary of Italy's contributions in Sinai, in Lebanon, and in the NATO missile decision. 'The doubt is arising, however,' said Caligaris, 'that this increased commitment has not brought Italy a real influence in the conduct of international affairs.' What did Weinberger think about that? Not much, judging from his noncommittal reply. Caligaris pressed onward: Italy's economic situation made more defence spending impossible. There was a need to balance payments and to improve the position of the Italian defence industry. Italy was known to spend much more in the United States than the other way around. What about the famous 'two-way street'? Weinberger replied vaguely about improved standardization, and possible co-production of the Maverick air-to-surface 'smart' missile and of the Italian-US Lerici minesweeper for the US Navy. But of course, said Weinberger, no one could pretend this would lead to parity. Finally, Reagan's Pentagon chief swiftly brushed aside Caligaris's insistent question about possible 'double key' control of the cruise missiles stationed on Italian soil.

In the Assembly debate, Radical deputy Gianluigi Melega stressed the sense of helplessness and hypocrisy at Italy's 'limited sovereignty'. It was 'absurd' to argue that the missiles needed to be based in European countries when they could perfectly well be sea-based. 'It is obviously a political operation aimed at involving other peoples in a global war operation: one of the two great empires is summoning under its own arms — literally — peoples who might run away, who might not want to get into the bipolar global contest.'

The left opposition introduced motions to suspend work on the Comiso base and prolong the Geneva negotiations for a year, and also to involve other countries belonging to NATO and the Warsaw Pact in the Soviet–American arms control talks. While speakers for the smaller left parties and the independent left exhausted the substantial arguments against cruise missile deployment, leading PCI speakers characteristically sought common ground with Socialists, in Europe and even at home, in the search for practical compromise. Antonio Rubbi, who has been given special responsibilities on the issue by his party, stressed that 'a great and prestigious party like German Social Democracy' had come around to the same position as the Italian Communist Party. He also noted the radical change in policy on the part of 'People's China, which four years ago called for a militarily strong Europe to oppose Soviet hegemonism.' Today, he pointed out, 'it advocates an autonomous Europe united for a constructive dialogue on East–West relations', supports disarmament and emphasizes the value of the peace movement. Italy could not be proud of having acquired the title of 'most faithful ally' at the price of 'limited sovereignty.'

'The value of the Euromissiles is more political than military,' said Rubbi. 'It is an attempt to subordinate fully Western Europe to the designs of American policy. Surrender to this policy has meant sacrificing the few spaces for autonomous initiative that Europe was conquering for itself, in the Middle East and Palestinian questions, or in the fruitful emergent dialogue of cooperation between North and South, between Europe, Africa and the Arab countries. In fact, Europe's role has regressed in these years as an autonomous force, and the process of greater political unity is harder. With the missiles, all of us, East and West, will be more dependent and more squeezed by a policy aimed at stiffening the opposition between the blocs.'

Toward the end of the debate on 16 November, PCI general-secretary Enrico Berlinguer made an extremely 'modest' and 'minimal' proposal. He had agreed with other left speakers, and with the recommendations of the Socialist Parties of Northern Europe, of the Greek and Swedish governments. But now he was suggesting something 'more immediate' and 'more modest' than any of them: 'We are proposing a path which, in our view, can be taken by our government if it will, even taking into account external factors conditioning it, conditioning our country.' The proposal had two parts: On the NATO side, 'the time should be dragged out' before the new missiles came into operational readiness in the countries concerned. Time could be gained for negotiations by stretching out the complex and difficult technological process, the transport and other arrangements requiring 'the most scrupulous security checks'. 'This would be a *de facto* postponement, politically significant in itself,' Berlinguer said. Meanwhile, the Soviet Union should not only freeze but, as a significant gesture, begin dismantling the SS-20s.

Berlinguer concluded that together, these moves would amount to 'important reciprocal signals' which could help avoid a break in the negotiation process. In reality, however, the explicit break came a week later, when the Geneva talks on intermediate-range nuclear forces were suspended. Berlinguer's proposal, in line with the PCI policy of seeking an eventual 'democratic alternative' coalition with the Socialists, constituted an offer to be useful to Craxi within the recognized bounds of Italy's 'limited sovereignty'. A few weeks later, Berlinguer and Antonio Rubbi set out on a private diplomatic mission to Bucharest, East Berlin and Belgrade, followed with sympathetic interest by government circles in Rome.

A major source of preoccupation in Italy was the new strategic alliance concluded between the Reagan administration and Israeli prime minister Yitzhak Shamir in early December. The two thousand or more Italian soldiers in Beirut were hostages to an American policy in the Middle East that, insofar as it could be discerned, could not be approved by Italians. On Christmas Eve, Italian President Sandro Pertini expressed the popular, and probably the government, sentiment by calling for withdrawal of the Italian contingent in Beirut.

Comiso could drag Italy further into unpredictable Middle East war. In early December, a week after the United States had unloaded the first cruise missiles at the huge Sigonella base outside Catania, American aircraft normally based there were sent to bomb Syrian positions in Lebanon. This is the sort of operation that could theoretically be taken over by the cruise missiles at Comiso.

National modesty makes Italians the most obedient of allies but also the most skilled in making friends on the other side. Or so it seemed in Lebanon. While the French and American contingents were the target of massive bomb attacks, the Italians, undisturbed, went about their humanitarian tasks looking after people in the Palestinian camps of Sabra and Chatila. The natural ease of the Italian soldiers in befriending children, their readiness to understand and sympathize with the problems of local people created a stock of good will that enterprising Italian businessmen would doubtless know how to exploit, if ever the shooting should end in Beirut. Dragged, like the French, into Lebanon by the Americans, the Italians nevertheless managed to keep their political wits about them and avoid being dragged into the Americans' military support of Gemayel.

Amidst tears and kisses, the Italian soldiers left Beirut in late February 1984. Defence Minister Giovanni Spadolini declared that they had raised Italy's prestige among peoples of the Middle East and the Arab world, as well as the national feeling and respect for the armed forces at home. At this rate, Italy's natural aptitude for 'peace culture' was on the way to being recuperated by the Army.

American-led militarization is not a form of order, but the ability to use force with mobility. Chaos is a favourable environment. There is an atmosphere in Italy of collapse, of unmanageable chaos, a wide-spread feeling that no systematic approach to social problems can be made to work. In this climate, political leaders may not so much define clear programmes or projects as try their best to preserve the ambiguity that passes for freedom of choice.

Notes

1. For the best study of Italy's increased defence spending, see Roberto Cicciomessere, *L'Italia armata*, Rome 1982.

2. See documentation compiled by Umberto Santino of the Centro Siciliano di Documentazione.

3. The United States secret services used Sicilian–American gangsters to combat the left and also to give credibility to the threat of a Sicilian separatist movement should a left government ever take office in Rome. See Roberto Faenza and Marco Fini, *Gli Americani in Italia*, Milan 1976.

4. An ominous precedent can be found in the village of Motta Sant' Anastasia, which houses two thousand American personnel from the huge Sigonella base near Catania (earmarked, incidentally, to replace Naples as NATO's southern command centre). Workers' efforts to organize in the CGIL have been repressed, and the MSI takes part in the centre-right coalition running the town.

5. Centro Siciliano di Documentazione 'Guiseppe Impastato', Via Agrigento 5, 90141 Palermo, Italy.

6. *Affare Comiso*, CSD, Palermo, 1983.

7. Umberto Santino, 'La conquista di Bisanzio. Borghesia mafiosa e Stato dopo il delitto Dalla Chiesa', *Segno* 34–35, 1982.

8. Ibid.

9. SIPRI gives Italy 4.3%, the USSR 36.5%, the USA 33.6%, France 9.7%, Britain 3.6%, and the Federal Republic of Germany 3%.

10. *Il Messaggero*, 4 March 1982.

11. Fabrizio Battistelli, 'Arms Production in Europe', *Bulletin of Peace Proposals*, Vol. 13, No. 4, International Peace Research Institute, Oslo 1982.

12. 'Business delle Armi', *Mondo Economico*, 16 June 1982.

13. *Avanti!* 27 February 1983.

14. See Fabrizio Battistelli, *Armi: Nuovo Modello di Sviluppo?* Turin 1982.

15. F. Battistelli, 'Le Armi dell 'Avvocato', *Pace e Geurra*, 26 May 1983.

16. F. Battistelli, 'Sociologia della corsa agli armamenti', *Il Mulino*, March–April 1983.

17. Lecture delivered on 21 May 1982 to the 33rd session of the Centro Alti Studi Difesa. See the substantial extracts in *Lotta Continua*, 3–4 June 1982.

5

Fragmented Europe

If the major difference revealed by the Euromissile controversy was between German and French attitudes, it is also true that Italy and every other country had its own way of perceiving the problem, of approving or opposing the NATO decision. In composition and rationale, the peace movements also differed markedly from one country to the next.

The NATO decision itself created differences in the rhythm of deployment and hence of opposition. Deployment began in December 1983 in three countries, with the Pershing-2 installation in Germany and the first deliveries of cruise to Britain and Italy. The schedule would then take in Belgium in 1985–86 and only afterwards Holland, allowing for greater procrastination by political decision-makers and longer uncertainty as to the final outcome.

British Particularism

Protest against cruise missile deployment in Britain revived an old movement, the Campaign for Nuclear Disarmament (CND), and gave birth to two new ones, the European Nuclear Disarmament (END) movement of intellectuals and the direct non-violent action of women at the Greenham Common missile base. END and the Greenham Common women also played influential roles in the Western peace movement as a whole.

Campaigning for unilateral British nuclear disarmament, the CND never had much in common with other European peace movments, which, except for the French, had no indigenous nuclear forces to protest against. The NATO double decision gave the British movement a common grievance to share with continental Europeans. There was still a difference, however. Britain already had nuclear missiles of its own, able to strike targets in Soviet territory, whereas the other deployment countries did not. Thus the British protest against cruise inevitably focused more sharply on the factor of purely *American* control.

END set out to use this common factor to pull the British movement out of its 'unilateralist' insularity and link it up with a broader European movement challenging the 'superpowers' and calling for a nuclear-free Europe 'from Poland to Portugal'. The British movement was most outspoken in promoting a sort of European patriotism — a welcome gesture from a British left until then regarded on the continent as fundamentally hostile to European unity on any grounds. E. P. Thompson's eloquent essays against 'exterminism' stimulated growing rejection of the arms race, which was perceived as a sort of inertial momentum of the species toward suicide.

In 1982, however, the Falklands war cast a harsh light on a couple of characteristic weaknesses of the British peace movement. Firstly, because of its single-issue focus and lack of a more general perspective or philosophy, it seemed unable to adapt to events by mounting effective opposition to a *real* war, in contrast to imaginary ones. Secondly, its concentration on East–West perils tended to make it oblivious to the more present danger of North–South conflicts.

Part of the trouble was that although the Falklands War *fitted perfectly* into the American global strategy of which Pershing-2 and cruise were a part, this relationship was not perceived in the movement itself. Instead, the prevailing vision was one of two equally irrational superpowers, foisting more and more mass destruction weapons on their hapless 'allies' out of sheer mad habit. Overlooked in their analysis was the American aim of involving its main European allies in Third World police tasks. True, the Falklands war engaged Britain against a nation, Argentina, firmly attached to the Western capitalist world, and for this reason United States diplomacy was obliged to maintain a certain ostensible neutrality. Washington, however, provided Britain with unstinting and decisive behind-the-scenes military support. No wonder: although pointless in itself, the Falklands war accomplished the political task of involving British forces in precisely the sort of global policing on which the United States insisted so strongly. Thus it was essential that the experience be successful and encouraging. As an extra bonus, there was the chance for the Pentagon to see how various weapons worked. Thanks to American diplomatic duplicity, the British could be persuaded they were heroically fighting for their sacred British principles even against American wishes.

The 'anti-superpower' line is perhaps not the best key to the truth in a country whose ruling establishment helped invent the Cold War. Resentment of superpowers is unlikely to do more for British workers than distract them from their misfortunes. At least, it has not been proven that the United States has forced British capital to abandon British industry and invest massively around the world. Both de-industrialization, which seems to be ruining Britain — but above all working-class Britain — and militarization are part of the same planetary restructuring which is, in effect, deporting the class struggle to Southern regions of the globe, while the North becomes primarily a command and control centre. The British ruling class may not always approve of the way the Americans see fit to defend their joint interests around the world, but that is merely an incentive for it to raise its own level of involvement.

The Falklands frenzy showed that the British peace movement was pitted against the bellicose attitudes of a deeply rooted imperialist culture. After Margaret Thatcher's triumph, it was hard for peace activists to feel like the spokespersons for a growing popular majority. The next phase of protest was dominated by the Greenham Common women, whose radical non-violent action directly tackled the funda-mental problem of the need to transform the culture. But this pointed up a dilemma: to grow, the peace movement needs to change cultural attitudes, but any attempt to do so risks marginalizing activists as eccentrics. Unless supported by a culturally rich and growing move-ment, Greenham Common women, attacked by institutions and the mass media, risk becoming a sort of Hyde Park Corner.

Holland: NATO's Pacifist Pet

Holland is probably the most pro-American and the most anti-missile country in NATO. This apparent paradox merits reflection by those who either hope or fear that opposition to the Euromissiles could be the basis for an anti-American European patriotism.

The reason for such massive Dutch opposition to nuclear weapons is not hard to comprehend. A ride through the countryside should suffice. The inhabitants of this most densely populated and fragile land would have to be completely unconscious to agree to serve as a nuclear battlefield. Nevertheless, Dutch authorities have long accepted the presence of thousands of nuclear warheads connected to the six 'dual key' responsibilities of the Dutch armed forces: the Lance rocket system, nuclear artillery, Hike Hercules surface-to-air missiles, nuclear depth charges, nuclear weapons to be fired from F-16 fighter-bombers, and, craziest of all, nuclear demolition mines. Obviously, it must have been confidently assumed that none of this arsenal would ever be used.

It can be argued that the scale of the Dutch anti-missile movement results primarily from two factors: the strength of the Churches, and the Netherlands' subjective proximity to the United States. The Churches are rich and confident enough to support an Interchurch Peace Council (Interkerkelijk Vredesberaad, IKV) that operates independently and on a large scale, initiating policy proposals and building a truly popular mass movement. The subjective proximity to Americans had the consequence that the Dutch became rapidly aware of dangerous trends in United States geopolitical and strategic thinking in the late seventies. Founded in 1966 by the main churches, Protestant and Catholic, the IKV launched a long-term campaign in 1977 around the slogan: 'Help rid the world of nuclear weapons. Let it begin in the Netherlands.' The idea was that although the nuclear weapons in the Netherlands were of minor military importance, a ban on them could have a disproportionate political importance by initiating a process of nuclear disarmament. As the problem of the new, long-range cruise missiles came to the fore, the IKV was soon obliged to turn its attention from the existing warheads to the deployment of cruise. The Dutch peace movement has also mounted consistent opposition to the neutron bomb, or enhanced radiation warhead, apparently earmarked to modernize two of Holland's "nuclear tasks", the Lance rocket system and the short-range nuclear artillery.

Holland was the only deployment country whose parliament actually managed to debate and vote on the NATO double decision before it was taken, and the answer was no. On 6 December 1979, the Dutch parliament voted 76 to 69 against cruise deployment. However, the Dutch government found a way round this at Brussels by supporting the decision to site American missiles somewhere in Europe, while reserving the decision as to whether to deploy them in the Netherlands until later. Since Holland is at the tail end of the schedule, with 48 cruise missiles to be installed in 1987 and 1988, Dutch governments have thus been able to adopt a policy of endless procrastinations.

Polls have indicated that a majority of the Dutch people is opposed to nuclear weapons. However, there is no challenge to the Atlantic Alliance as such, and indeed, the Dutch can hope to use their unquestionable loyalty to NATO and the West to negotiate some sort of special status. Dutch politicians can (and do) argue privately that it was, after all, Helmut Schmidt in particular, and the Germans in general, who opened the Pandora's box of 'Eurostrategic balance' with their schizophrenic suspicions of American intentions. The Dutch, for their part, always had perfect confidence in the Americans, so why should they have to pay for German neurosis? In intra-NATO politics, the basis thus exists for some sort of compromise whereby the Netherlands would be spared cruise deployment in return for exerting pressure on the Germans to accept (and help pay for) the modernized electronic battlefield in Central Europe and the tactical changes that go with it.

No two European peace movements have cooperated more than the Dutch and the West German, notably IKV and ASF (Aktions Sühnezeichen Friedensdienste), trying to overcome some of the distrust that results from history and different circumstances. The Dutch have been particularly wary of any attempt to put the 'German question' at the centre of the European disarmament problem. Instead, IKV leader Mient Jan Faber has promoted the idea of a 'détente from below' that would somehow bring together grassroots peace movements of East and West Europe.

In June 1984, the Dutch parliament approved a government package that postponed the final decision until 1 November 1985, but set conditions that in effect tied the Netherlands to the arms race between the United States and the Soviet Union. The compromise proposal unveiled on 1 June by Christian Democrat Prime Minister Ruud Lubbers stipulated that if the United States and the Soviet Union reached an arms limitation agreement by 1 November 1985, the Netherlands would accept 'its share' of cruise missiles as determined by that agreement. On the other hand, if by that date no such accord has been reached and the Soviet Union has meanwhile gone on to deploy more SS-20s, Holland will take its full allotment of 48 cruise missiles as provided in the NATO double decision of December 1979.

The third hypothetical situation — namely, that there is no Soviet–American arms limitation agreement and no further SS-20 deployments, by November 1985 — would seem to imply that Moscow is being invited to freeze its SS-20 levels in return for the cancellation of cruise missile deployment in the Netherlands. However, Dutch peace movement leaders quickly dismissed the notion of a Soviet–Dutch freeze as ridiculous, inasmuch as it would seem to suggest some sort of strategic balance between Holland and the USSR. They noted that Soviet Marshal Dimitri Ustinov had already warned that the number of SS-20s would be increased in response to cruise and Pershing-2 deployments, which the United States was trying to accelerate.

The delay in effect left time for an eventual change of policy in case the Democratic candidate should defeat President Reagan in the November 1984 presidential election in the United States. The Netherlands would be able to profit from a policy switch in Washington leading either to an arms control agreement (with perhaps fewer cruise missiles for the Netherlands) or, more dramatically, to a freeze that would hold Soviet SS-20s to their level on 1 June 1984 (no cruise missiles in the Netherlands). Dutch peace movement leaders complained that the June 1984 interim decision threw away the freedom the Dutch government had preserved until then to take some disarmament initiative of its own independently of *both* nuclear superpowers.

The Lubbers government decision was clearly designed to turn anti-missile protests against Moscow, while putting no pressure on Washington. Indeed, all the Reagan administration had to do to ensure deployment of the full Dutch quota of cruise was *not* to negotiate an arms control agreement while goading the Russians into more SS-20 deployments. Lubbers told *Newsweek* that 'our decision has deprived the Soviet Union of a propaganda tool. It is not the Dutch who are embarrassed, but the Soviets.'

Lubbers was, of course, also trying to embarrass some of 'the Dutch', namely, the leaders of IKV, like Mient Jan Faber, whose attempt to promote 'détente from below' has made them *persona non grata* in the Soviet bloc. IKV leaders have made the distinction between the United States' direct responsibility in leading every phase of the nuclear arms race, and the Soviet Union's indirect political responsibility in maintaining an "internal Cold War" within its own power sphere which frightens Western European populations and makes them susceptible to calls for military buildups. This is a distinction neither Moscow nor Washington appears prepared to appreciate. It seemed unlikely that Soviet leaders, fundamentally sceptical of Western peace movements outside their control, would make any bold, generous gesture in favour of a peace movement they particularly distrust, in a country which has always channelled its relations with Moscow through the NATO system.

The Lubbers scheme called for the eventual November 1985 missile decision to be fixed in a bilateral treaty with the United States, dealing with 'control aspects' of the cruise missile deployment. This innovation seemed designed to neutralize Labour Party opposition, first by fixing the missile decision in a treaty that would be binding on the Labour Party should it return to office before deployment is actually completed, and second by diverting politicians' attention to these negotiable 'control aspects'. Instead of *stopping* American nuclear missiles, the Dutch can be invited to take pride in being the first to *control* them.

It was no paradox that the defence minister in the Lubbers government was most reluctant to accept the cruise missiles, while the foreign minister was most eager. Dutch leaders' motivation for accepting the nuclear missiles was entirely political: they wanted to stay on as members of the NATO in-group that runs the Western World. 'They want to be taken seriously inside NATO,' explained Wim Bartels of IKV. 'They are afraid of being given "footnote status" like Greece or Denmark.' The scornful expression refers to the footnote at the bottom of NATO communiqués noting that Greece or Denmark did not agree with such and such a decision.

Dutch leaders evidently hoped to use their status as a NATO core country, plus the pressure from the peace movement, to negotiate favourable conditions for their cooperation with the United States modernization programme.

The Belgian Microcosm

The twelfth of December 1979 was a day of confusion and suspense in Brussels. While the NATO ministers were approving their famous double track, the government of the host country was on the verge of falling in its last-minute efforts to secure a mandate for NATO policy.

Although NATO headquarters was located on their territory, Belgians were kept poorly informed about the missile deployment. It was not until 16 May 1979, when the NATO decision-making mechanism was already far advanced, that the Euromissile issue was first raised in Parliament during the military budget debate by Roger Denison, military commission chairman of the French-speaking Socialist Party (PS).[1] Denison said it seemed that NATO was contemplating a fundamental transformation of its strategy 'into a veritable offensive policy'. In reply, Defence Minister Paul Vanden Boeynants confirmed the existence of a theatre nuclear forces (TNF) study within NATO and promised that the issue would be debated fully in the various European parliaments concerned. This promise was never kept. On 4 July, Foreign Minister Henri Simonet (PS) said the constitution did not require a parliamentary debate prior to government decision on the missile issue. And on 17 October, after a cabinet shakeup, Prime Minister Wilfried Martens said that 'when the time comes' the government would 'define its attitude which will be communicated without delay to parliament.'

In the weeks leading up to the NATO Brussels meeting, Belgium's political parties hastily defined their positions on the basis of incomplete information gleaned by their special study groups — only the Communist Party had opposed any nuclear arms buildup from the start. The first to take a stand was the Flemish nationalist *Volksunie* party, which on 8 November argued that it was necessary to stop the nuclear arms race and that the proposed new arms were 'attack weapons' marking an abandonment of NATO's traditionally defensive strategy. On 19 November, the country's two liberal parties (both in opposition) took conflicting positions: the French-speaking PRL supported NATO modernization, while the Flemish PVV was unable to agree. On the same day, the *Rassemblement Wallon* demanded a major debate on security policy and called on the government to take serious initiatives for mutual disarmament.

Belgium, with its old industry, its heritage of wars and working-class struggles, and above all, its endless wrangling between Dutch-speaking Flemish and French-speaking Walloons, can be seen as a microcosm of a Europe unable to surmount past quarrels and deal coherently with present challenges. If Flemish opposition to the Euromissiles has tended to be somewhat stronger than that of Walloons, this only partly reflects Dutch affinities in the North and French affinities in the South, for many Walloons resent the 'imperialist arrogance' of the French just as many Flemish condemn the 'self-righteous moral imperialism' of the Dutch. Indeed, some in the Flemish left complain that their Dutch cousins are 'incapable of making a political analysis', and that in this respect it is not the Channel but the Dutch–Belgian border that separates Anglo-Saxon attitudes from continental rationality. Be this as it may, the involvement of certain Flemish priests in the theory and practice of Liberation Theology in Central America has given the peace movement a very special impetus in Flanders. This, and the involvement of Pax Christi in the peace movement, has made Euromissile deployment a heavy cross to bear for Belgium's loyally pro-NATO Christian Democrats.

On 19 November 1979, the Flemish Socialist Party was the first of the five government coalition parties to come out against the NATO modernization. Its leader, Karel Van Miert, said any decision about new theatre nuclear forces should be postponed for serious negotiations on mutual disarmament and the creation of a nuclear-free zone. Deploring the shortage of information, the SP called for a debate in parliament.

It was only on the evening of 19 November, a mere three weeks from the NATO meeting, that top government leaders themselves were provided with a full explanation of the theatre nuclear forces (TNF) problem in an 80-page report to the cabinet jointly prepared by the Foreign Ministry, headed by Henri Simonet, and the Defence Ministry, headed by José Desmarets. It is characteristic of the whole Euromissiles affair that the arguments used to 'sell' Pershing-2 and cruise to reluctant Belgians were much more political than military and played on small-power fears of being left out of important matters. Thus the Simonet–Desmarets policy paper stressed 'the political influence our country can exercise in the Alliance', on condition that it 'assumes its responsibilities' within 'the framework of Atlantic solidarity'. Only a 'contribution' by Belgium would give it the right to 'full and complete participation in Alliance decisions'.

The blackmail was clear enough. If Belgium said 'no' to Pershing-2 and cruise, it would be banned from Alliance councils and would never again be able to have a say in superpower-dominated world affairs. That would be a shame, the policy paper implied, because so far Belgium had played a valuable role in promoting détente and various arms-control and disarmament negotiations.

The paper rejoiced that 'both East and West are looking forward to rapid ratification of SALT-II and the immediate opening of SALT-III talks, including on LRTNF' (long-range theatre nuclear forces). Brezhnev's speech of 6 October in East Berlin was cited as evidence that NATO was taking a 'realistic and firm' attitude. This was the 'best sign' that the Alliance was 'on the right track' in continuing to pursue the 'double objective of deterrence and détente'.

There were allusions to German as well as American pressures in the Simonet–Desmarets policy paper. It would be 'unfair', the paper said, and 'contrary to the interests of European construction' to allow the Federal Republic of Germany to 'bear the burden alone'. Indeed, it is possible that in this phase, pressures from Bonn were more directly felt than pressures from Washington.

The same day, Henri Simonet found himself in an isolated minority in the PS group established to study the issue. At a special general council of PS branch representatives held on 8 December Simonet presented a report in favour of the NATO Euromissiles, while military commission chairman Roger Denison presented a second report asking the government to urge a six-month NATO postponement to allow for negotiations with the Soviet Union. Denison's motion was carried with 95 per cent support. Thus two of the five government parties were on record as uncommitted to NATO missile deployment.

The next day, a broadly supported demonstration in Brussels called for the suspension of any decision on Pershing and cruise deployment, and the immediate opening of negotiations for the abolition of SS-20s and all other nuclear weapons in both Eastern and Western Europe. A number of members of parliament from both governmental and opposition parties were among the approximately fifty thousand people who marched through the Belgian capital under a driving rain.

A public opinion poll taken in late November, and published in *De Morgen* on the day of the NATO decision, showed 46.8% of Belgians 'absolutely opposed' to the installation of theatre nuclear forces on Belgian soil and 17.2% 'more or less opposed'. Only 12.4% were 'more or less in favour' and 7.8% 'fully in favour'.

The NATO defence and foreign ministers were already meeting in Brussels when the Belgian cabinet finally defined its position on the afternoon of 12 December 1979. However, the official Belgian position — which Prime Minister Wilfried Martens forced through Parliament with a large margin (130 to 48 with 8 abstentions) by calling for a vote of confidence — sounded more like the start of a disarmament process than the green light for a new round in the arms race. The Belgian government called on the NATO defence and foreign ministers to seek an immediate opening of arms limitation and reduction negotiations with the Soviet Union and made the modernization decision dependent upon their outcome. 'The application of this decision,' it stated, 'should at any moment be able to be modified or cancelled as a function of the progress of negotiations with the USSR to establish and stabilize an arms balance in this field at the lowest possible level. That is why no automatism can be accepted.' The government said it had dropped the idea of a six-month 'moratorium' after preparatory discussions with NATO indicated that a 'moratorium could also put off the opening at Alliance levels of negotiations relative to theatre weapons.' Belgium was determined not to 'create, alone in the Alliance, a division' that could harm its credibility and thus the success of negotiations.

Thus the immediate decision was justified as necessary to bring about immediate negotiations, whereas in reality the USSR had said it was ready to negotiate right away if the decision was *not* taken, and indeed refused for several months to agree to talks in the new situation.

In the newly defined view of the Belgian government, the missiles should be developed by the United States alone on its own responsibility. But implementation of the decision to modernize NATO medium-range forces would be 'suspended for six months' and even after that period it could be abandoned if arms limitation talks should yield 'satisfactory results'. At its Ministers' meeting in May 1980, NATO should examine the state of Soviet deployment and the progress of negotiations and, as appropriate, 'modify or cancel its own programme'.

All this was done so hastily, and with so little information about the real implications of NATO modernization, that it is impossible to tell from the outside which political leaders were deliberately deceiving the public and which were deceived themselves. At any event, the official Belgian position had no influence on events. A fortnight after the Brussels NATO decision, the Soviet Union invaded Afghanistan, thereby making a major contribution to the revival of Cold War. Six months later, when the six-month 'suspension period' was running out and with it the life of the Belgian coalition government, there was still no sign of negotiations. It was not possible to make a decision 'based on the progress in arms control negotiations'. The governing agreement between the six parties of Martens's new cabinet vaguely promised to 'pursue initiatives and contacts' already begun.

Public pressure against the missiles eased somewhat in 1980. Polls still showed a majority against deployment, but the numbrs of undecided had increased, perhaps influenced by a revival of fear of the Soviet Union following the invasion of Afghanistan.

The lull was temporary. The following year, 1981, was the year of a mass awakening to the Euromissile threat expressed in surprisingly large marches in various European capitals. On 25 October in Brussels, hundreds of thousands of people took part in the largest demonstration of Belgium's post-war history. By that time the Belgian peace movement was supported by such diverse forces as the Flemish nationalists, the Socialists, the Communist Party, labour organizations and the Catholic Church.

Pax Christi has concentrated on persuading the Christian Democratic labour movement to oppose the missiles. This effort was successful to the extent that many members of parliament from the labour wing of Christian Democracy took part in anti-missile marches. And yet, these same deputies turned around and voted with their party leadership for the 10 November 1983 Parliamentary resolution confirming that it was up to the government, constitutionally, to decide on the cruise missiles. At this point, the only remaining hope of the Belgian peace movement was that the Dutch would have the political courage to say 'no' or at least hedge somehow, thus reopening the question in Belgium.

Looking back on the hectic moment of the 'double decision', Socialists in several of the small NATO government coalitions felt that they had been played off against each other. In particular, Flemish Socialist leader Karel Van Miert accused Foreign Minister Henri Simonet of 'simply lying and cheating' by misrepresenting the Belgian position, notably to his Danish and Dutch colleagues, who had wanted to postpone the NATO decision for six months. According to Flemish Socialists, Simonet successively told Belgian, Dutch and Danish Socialists that they were the only ones standing in the way of the NATO decision, since the other two had already agreed. 'It's incredible but that's the way it was,' Flemish Socialist leader Louis Tobback said later. International contacts were so deficient even between the kindred social democratic parties of northern Europe that they were not familiar with each other's positions on such a crucial issue.

Finding Socialist International meetings inadequate, Dutch and Belgian socialist leaders met in late 1980 and launched the idea of a 'Scandilux' informal grouping of the Scandinavian and Benelux Socialist Parties in NATO member countries. This would meet regularly to exchange information about the state of security policy debate in the countries concerned. The first meeting was held in Amsterdam in January 1981 among leaders of the Dutch Labour Party, the two Belgian parties, the Luxembourg party and Danish and Norwegian Socialists. The German, British and French socialists were invited to send observers. The SPD regularly sent Egon Bahr, who participated actively. The British Labour Party also showed interest, sending Michael Foot or some other important leader and hosting a Scandilux meeting in London in June 1982. The French observer, Jacques Huntzinger, observed.

In the long run, if and when these parties should return to government in the Scandilux countries, and in Britain and Germany, they should be better prepared by these quarterly meetings to approach defence issues in a coherent fashion.

These exchanges contributed to the resolution passed by the Danish parliament on 26 May 1983, ordering the government to press for an extension of NATO's December 1983 deployment deadline and to work to prevent new nuclear missiles from being installed so long as negotiations continued. The parliament also suspended Denmark's financial contribution to the Euromissile deployment. The pro-missile government in Copenhagen preferred to accept these instructions rather than risk being brought down on the issue.

Divide and Rule

Scandinavia is the only region of Europe that shows signs of being able to define and unite around proposals that are not dictated by the United States. NATO members Denmark and Norway, together with neutral Sweden, practice a *de facto* denuclearization as part of their discreet defence of Finnish neutrality. Sweden is particularly well placed to take the lead in independent policies toward the Third World, as well as in sponsoring disarmament initiatives, such as the call for a nuclear-weapon-free zone in Central Europe, which may be supported by peace movements throughout Europe. Neutral Austria also has the potential to play a valuable diplomatic role in East–West disarmament.

NATO non-deployment countries in southern Europe have reacted to the Euromissile controversy in disarray, each one responding to its own inner political logic in tête-à-tête with the United States. Only Greece, under the strong personal leadership of Andreas Papandreou, has clearly opposed the NATO deployment. Papandreou has also undertaken to promote a nuclear-weapon-free zone in the Balkans. He seems quite determined to assert the specific interests of Greece, which feels threatened by fellow-NATO member Turkey rather than by the designated adversary, and which prizes its good relations with the nearby Arab world. Although these policies clearly have strong popular support, so much hinges on Papandreou's personality, and perhaps on the bargains he may be able to strike over US bases in Greece, that future developments are uncertain.

Portugal and Spain have quietly acquiesced in the NATO modernization for quite different sets of reasons.

Portugal seems to have settled back into its fairly languid existence on the periphery of Europe, as a useful power relay between the major imperialist nations and Southern Africa. Ten years after the 'carnation revolution', the situation in Portugal and in Mozambique seemed to be about where Western ruling interests meant to lead it in the early seventies, before General Antonio Spinola's reform spun off into revolution thanks to Third World ideological influence on the colonial army's junior officers. Socialist Prime Minister Mario Soares seems to look less to the West German SPD, and more to Washington, than at the start of his meteoric political career. South African pressures have forced Mozambique to abandon its revolutionary ambitions and its support to the African National Congress. Portugal has a clear place in the neo-colonialist order being promoted by the Reagan administration in Africa. To prove worthy of these African prospects, Soares denounced Soviet expansionism in Africa, and his Portuguese Socialist Party took the lead in attacking Cuba in the Socialist International and in generally disrupting Willy Brandt's attempt at an independent line toward the Third World.

If Portugal was moved by African carrots, Spain got the stick. Not only NATO missiles but NATO membership were unpopular in Spain, especially with the left voters who gave Socialist prime minister Felipe González his victory. González's Spanish Socialist Workers Party had promised a referendum on NATO membership, which was put aside after election. González even gained a new 'comprehension' for NATO nuclear missile modernization.

In contrast to Portugal, Spain seems to have little to gain in the Third World from closer association with the United States and NATO — on the contrary, this could jeopardize its excellent relations in Latin America and the Arab World. But González notoriously has a big problem which leaves him open to American pressure: a fascist officer corps which must be humoured for fear of a *golpe*. Madrid would like to recover the British enclave at Gibraltar, and good membership in NATO is supposed to promote this ambition. On the other hand, Spain has two similar enclaves on the northern Moroccan coast: Ceuta, across from Gibraltar, and Melilla, farther east. Patriotic Spanish officers would surely fly into a towering rage at any government in Madrid that betrayed the national honour by losing these proud possessions. United States influence in Morocco is considerable: presumably great enough to restrain, or *not* to restrain, any Moroccan move to recover these parts of the national territory. This situation is reason enough, if not the only reason, for González to comply with American NATO policy.

González's policy shift on NATO has not been accepted by a good part of his electorate. The restoration of political freedoms in Spain after the death of Franco was followed by a period of disenchantment and political disengagement on the left. Yet activism has begun to revive with the peace movement, which has quickly become one of the most vigorous in Europe, combining the 'Northern' virtues of cultural critique, notably anti-macho feminism, with a Mediterranean internationalism and awareness of the Third World dimension. Relatively isolated geographically, the Spanish peace movement is a most encouraging sign of the universal and unifying appeal and potential of peace issues in the recomposition of left forces.

Note

1. This story is told in *Le Dossier des Euromissiles*, published in Brussels in 1981 by the Groupe de recherche et d'information sur la paix (GRIP), directed by Bernard Adam.

6
Europe Between North-South and East-West

In four years, the Euromissiles have largely succeeded in changing the terms of political discussion in Europe. Under a smokescreen of alarm about the dangers of East–West relations, Western European governments have been drawn ever further into military involvement alongside the United States in applying force to North–South relations.

Shock Treatment

Three months before the NATO double decision, from 1 to 3 September 1979, a conference on the future of the North Atlantic Alliance was held at the Palais d'Egmont in Brussels at which some leading American foreign policy specialists attempted to apply what one of them later described as 'shock treatment' to their European allies. The conference was co-sponsored by the Center for Strategic and International Studies (CSIS), the right-wing Georgetown think-tank later largely absorbed into the upper reaches of the Reagan administration, so that while the initiative took place under the Carter administration[1], it was quite in keeping with the thinking of the presidency to follow. The event created something of a press sensation at the time, because Henry Kissinger took the occasion to say publicly that the official deterrence strategy of 'mutual assured destruction' (MAD) was not credible and should be replaced by a 'counterforce' strategy assigning credible war-fighting roles to long, medium and short-range nuclear weapons.

Kissinger said what he had not been able 'to say in office' — 'that our European allies should not keep asking us to multiply strategic assurances that we cannot possibly mean, or if we do mean, we should not want to execute, because if we execute, we risk the destruction of civilization.' Implicitly defending Carter from Schmidt's complaints, Kissinger insisted there was 'no point in complaining about declining American will, or criticizing this or that American administration' as 'weak and irresolute', since NATO was facing an 'objective crisis' of doctrine. Kissinger said bluntly that it was 'absurd in the 1980s to base the strategy of the West on the credibility of the threat of mutual suicide'. 'Just as I believe it is necessary that we develop a military purpose for our strategic forces and move away from the senseless and demoralizing strategy of massive civilization extermination, so it is imperative that we finally try to develop some credible military purpose for the tactical and theatre nuclear forces that we are building.'

Kissinger's talk included a few other deliberately tactless and provocative remarks. He suggested that 'the secret dream of every European was, of course, to avoid a nuclear war but, secondly, if there had to be a nuclear war, to have it conducted over their heads by the strategic forces of the United States and the Soviet Union.' He dismissed as 'totally wrong' the NATO doctrine developed by former Belgian foreign minister Pierre Harmel and adopted in 1968, which defined détente and defence as the Alliance's twin goals. He conceded that détente was important, but only because 'in a democracy you cannot sustain the risk of war unless your public is convinced that you are committed to peace' and it would be a mistake to 'concede the peace issue' to the other side. But he obviously shared no vision of détente as a process leading to important changes in East–West relations. As for North–South relations, he scoffed at the 'final nostalgia — that of the "noble savage", the Third World, that we're going to sweep them over to our side.'

Judging from their public reactions, European NATO leaders and editorialists were scandalized at Kissinger's suggestion that the United States might not protect Western Europe with its nuclear umbrella — so scandalized that either they did not fully believe the awful news, or were not ready to let their populations believe it. But at the same conference, Samuel P. Huntington, director of Harvard University's Centre of International Affairs, warned Europeans that 'the decline of the foreign policy Establishment' in the United States was 'clearly a fact', and that future United States foreign policy would be much more anti-Soviet and primarily concerned with restoring American power in the world.

The most blunt was 'neo-conservative' Irving Kristol, who said that as the Soviet Union approached strategic nuclear equivalence, the very notion of nuclear 'deterrence' of a Soviet aggression in

Europe by American nuclear forces had become 'preposterous'.

> It is still the official military doctrine of the United States and NATO that the use of strategic nuclear weapons is not excluded, in a case of Soviet aggression with conventional military forces — or, *a fortiori*, using tactical nuclear weapons — against Western Europe. There may even be American and NATO generals who believe this is so. They, and anyone else who believes it, are living in a world of fantasy. Under no conceivable circumstances—I repeat: under *no* conceivable circumstances—will an American government respond to such Soviet aggression in Western Europe by initiating a strategic nuclear exchange. *That* deterrence has ceased to exist, whatever some military men or politicians may officially say. The function of America's strategic nuclear weaponry today is to deter a Soviet strike against the United States itself— that and nothing but that.

Since Kristol was not Kissinger, less attention was paid to his statements, although they expressed approximately the same outlook, more clearly. In addition, Kristol gave a 'neo-conservative' political appraisal of Europe that almost certainly expresses the prevailing view among Reagan administration policy-makers.

Kristol said that what was wrong with Western Europe was 'the social-democratic temper, the inward-turning politics of compassionate reform' that had 'largely replaced the patriotic temper, the politics of national self-assertion'. This created latent problems for NATO. One was that Western Europe had no foreign policy, having apparently 'opted out of the strenuous game of world politics in order to pursue the comforts of domestic life.' Another was that a 'new American nationalism' was about to sweep away the familiar liberal 'American foreign policy establishment, which is firmly committed to a "global point of view", to the utopian notion that the ultimate and governing purpose of American foreign policy is to establish a world community of nations all living amiably under the rule of law.' The new American nationalism was not isolationist like the older one, he emphasized. 'The new nationalism . . . is based on the proposition that the United States should be *the* major and most influential world power, and as it gathers ideological momentum . . . it is going to place a strain on NATO which it can hardly cope with.' He noted that the United States was not only increasing its military budget (even under Carter), but was 'also now forming, at the insistence of Congress and the military, something called a "unilateral force" — a small army of one hundred thousand rigorously trained men with a "logistics tail" that will permit it to operate anywhere in the world *independently* of support from any existing ally. One would have to be maddened with optimism to think that no occasion will arise — in the Middle East, the Indian Ocean, Africa, perhaps South America, perhaps even Southern Europe — for this force to be used.' And when it is used, if Europe remains aloof, 'discreetly approving or sullenly disapproving', one certain consequence would be 'overwhelming support in Congress and in public opinion for the removal of American troops from Western Europe'.

The only possible alternative Kristol saw to the 'social democratization' of Western Europe — which had produced a 'risk-aversive' society without 'will to self-assertion' — would be some sort of Gaullism. 'Among contemporary European leaders, only Charles de Gaulle had a vision that rose above this level of prosaic domesticity — the nation as one vast household, whose daily problems have now been transformed into the stuff of politics. But he, most unfortunately, thought that France alone, not Western Europe in coalition, could reemerge as a major power. This was and is a chimera. Had he been able to think in European terms, had he been able to bring himself to imagine a strong NATO consisting of European powers alone, his anti-Americanism would have served a positive end — one, indeed, that would have suited American ends (in spite of American objections) better than the NATO that survives today.'

Despite the apparent paradox, despite the French refusal to recognize anything so contrary to their national mythology, the American right is, and for some time has been, 'Gaullist' in its European policy and has been trying to prod, shock or bludgeon the Europeans into being 'Gaullist' themselves.

Kristol saw hope of success in the fact that the 'social democratization' of Europe was proving to be not so solid after all.

So far from achieving greater social and political stability, accompanied by more universal tranquility, 'social-democratization' generates discontent, cynicism and 'alienation' among the citizenry. Those of us of a certain age can easily remember the hopes, which we may have shared, for a new and better world that accompanied the impulse to reform after World War II. The reforms have been effected, and the reality is disillusioning. This has a terribly important implication which we are only now beginning to perceive: *modern social democracy is an inherently unstable system*. It generates a momentum for 'equality' — in the bizarre sense of special privileges for all — which, unless firmly controlled, creates an overbearing, bureaucratic state confronting a restless and 'ungrateful' citizenry. And such firm control appears extraordinarily difficult to attain, except intermittently for relatively brief periods.

So the nations of NATO and Western Europe — social-democracies all, in their different ways — are at the point of realizing that they will have to drift either to the 'Left' or to the 'Right'.

Kristol was not wrong about the instability of social democracy, although to blame its troubles solely on factors of mass psychology is a typical conservative, or neo-conservative, explanation that leaves out such 'unmentionables' as investment capital flights from the productive job-producing sectors that finance the social democratic welfare state. Four years later, Kristol returned to the subject with an article in the *New York Times Magazine* (25 September 1983) on NATO faced with the 'basic sea change in American foreign policy'. 'The era of liberal internationalism', he wrote, 'extending from World War II until 1980, has pretty much petered out. The old liberal establishment that ran American foreign policy and that basically agreed with the European view of the world has lost, to a large degree, its credibility, its authority and its political influence. . . . The United States is becoming a much more nationalistic country, a country much more concerned about its national interest and more willing to act unilaterally if necessary to pursue its national interest.'

Europe is advised to do the same. 'To the degree that Europe has been dependent upon the United States, the European will has been corrupted and European political vitality has diminished.' What is needed is an 'all-European NATO, with its own nuclear weapons and its own military strategy'.

If it wanted intermediate-range nuclear missiles, we would provide them — but only on request. If it wanted them at sea, instead of on land, it could put them at sea. The only way the nations of Western Europe are going to regain the self-confidence that they should have — and the will to engage in international affairs in a resolute way — is if there were a European NATO with a large degree of military independence from the United States. An independent NATO, with its own nuclear deterrent, responsible for the defence of Western Europe, willing to make the sacrifices to fight (with American help, if necessary) and win a conventional war with the Soviet Union should such a war break out — that is the NATO of the future, if NATO is to survive at all.

Such a European alliance might regain its self-respect, a feeling of control over its own national destinies and, above all, it might recapture the spirit of nationalism that is indispensable to any successful foreign policy. You cannot in this century have a successful foreign policy that does not encompass the nationalist impulse. One of the problems with the involvement of the United States in NATO is that it dilutes that national impulse. Nationalism in Western Europe is up for grabs, and unless it is seized by political parties that believe in our values and traditions, it could be seized by people with less palatable aspirations.

In other words, if nationalism is not seized by the right, it could be seized by the left.

Kristol concluded that a 'new Atlantic alliance between the United States and an all-European NATO would be possible and desirable', but to achieve it, 'we must subject the NATO that now exists, a very sick NATO, to shock treatment.'

It might seem that the Reagan administration, and the press friendly to it, had already made quite an effort to provide their European allies with 'shock treatment'. The first year of the Reagan administration was marked by a series of top level statements on the possibility of nuclear war in Europe that seemed designed to produce shock. The effects were markedly different, however. In Germany, the shock helped stimulate a mass peace movement. In France, the American statements were played down, except to confirm old Gaullist suspicions about American reliablity and thus justify the *force de frappe*.

The official hints of nuclear war in Europe were followed by a stream of attacks in the American press, led by the relatively internationalist *Wall Street Journal*, against European cowardice and selfishness. American righteous indignation was especially worked up over the Polish debts and the Siberian gas pipeline. Shortly before General Jaruzelski's takeover in Poland, the *Wall Street Journal* editorialized (7 December 1981) that Western bankers should not reschedule loans to Poland but let it collapse in well-deserved bankruptcy. The newspaper noted that 'operating losses at state enterprises are suddenly bankrupting a national government that finds itself unable to take proper countermeasures without igniting just the sort of political backlash the Soviets would find intolerable.' Indeed, it was the influx of Western credits that had made possible the industrial development and provided jobs to all those workers now revolting in Solidarnosc, many of whom would find themselves out of a job or with reduced wages should ever capitalist standards of management and profit be applied. Some Solidarnosc people were quite aware of this, and indeed were counting on a sort of continued indirect subsidizing of their movement by Western banks. The *Wall Street Journal* showed that at least some American capitalists had a clearer perception of their class interests than had their European colleagues. At the WSJ, there were no crocodile tears for Solidarnosc. Since Poland is broke, let the Russians have it. 'The threat, after all, is not so much of a Soviet invastion. The Soviets are already in Poland. The threat is of a crackdown. They have a gun on the Poles, and what they're doing to the West is called extortion.'

European reluctance to punish the Russians and Poles for the sins of their economic system aroused growing exasperation on the editorial pages of the WSJ. It peaked with a widely-noted article on 15 December by an American agribusinessman named Ronald C. Nairn, who suggested flatly that: 'The time has come for the US to sever its ties with NATO.' He argued that there was no reason to fear that a Soviet conquest of Western Europe would provide America's Russian adversaries with sophisticated Western technology, since 'under Soviet domination, European technology soon would no longer be massive or sophisticated.' Let the Russians have it and ruin it — America's future lies elsewhere. 'Southeast Asia has some of the fastest developing economies in the world and has more people than all of Western Europe. Then there is East Asia, so vast in its potential as to stagger the imagination. There is also the Pacific rim of South America and beyond that South Asia and Africa await.' In comparison, wrote Nairn, 'Europe seems a puny affair. The US must begin to view itself as a true global power. In this regard, politically and philosophically, Europe has little to give and something to detract.'

This is certainly not the old-fashioned 'isolationism' that America's European allies have been dreading. It is an uninhibited view of America as dominant global power, expanding ever westward, from the saturated markets of Europe to the rest of the globe. And seen from California, Asia is no longer the old Far East but the new Far West (Secretary of Defense Caspar Weinberger has officially re-christened the former Middle East as 'Southwest Asia').

Such diatribes against Europe probably contain a measure of poker-player bluff. The readiness to write off Europe may be over-stated, but the hostility is genuine enough. To America's sunbelt capitalists, based in the non-unionized south–west and gazing over the vast non-unionized labour reserves of the Pacific basin, Europe (and to a large extent, the old industrialized sections of the north–eastern and mid–western United States as well) is the historic centre of an organized working class they are quite happy to do without. Anachronistically, American cartoonists persist in caricaturing Europe as a region of effete snobs in top hats — the upper crust of an old-fashioned class system as opposed to democratic America. Yet in the early 1980s, whether measured by the gap between rich and poor, or educational level, or participation in politics (even the simple act of voting), America is far less democratic than 'social-democratized'

Western Europe. *Seen from the sunbelt, Europe can mean, above all, a political culture that is bad for business, with its organized and demanding working class, its moralizing and influential intellectuals.*

This is why, as Nairn said, 'politically and philosophically, Europe has little to give and something to detract' when it comes to the United States's future 'as a true global power'.

Helmut Schmidt acknowledged being shaken by the vehemence of the anti-Europe (and especially anti-German) outpourings, and spent some time in the United States in 1982 trying to explain European points of view, discussing the world on the California estate of his old friend George Shultz, soon to be Secretary of State.

The more or less veiled American threats of abandonment signalled that Bonn could not rely upon American protection for an *Ostpolitik* tending toward 'convergence of the two systems'. After all, Poland was scarcely the only country over its head in debt. Nor were the causes fundamentally different from those in other developing countries: it had borrowed from Western banks to build an industry to export to Western markets which turned out not to exist. Its peculiarity, as a Communist country, was that its managers did not dare, when they saw an industry producing at a loss for lack of a market, simply to shut it down and fire the workers. This particular weakness of the Communist system bears some resemblance, in exaggerated form, to the weakness of social democracy, as seen from Reaganite America.

East–West

The Euromissiles affair, recasting East–West relations in military terms, has helped the Reagan administration to do battle against the East–West trade nexus that could eventually supply a basis for 'convergence'. In opposing the Siberian gas pipeline and other exchanges, the Americans argued that they did not want the Soviets to obtain technology susceptible to military application.

American leaders are aware of the potential importance of Eastern trade to Germany in particular. In a 1980 study of 'East–West Technology Transfer' for the Georgetown Center for Strategic and International Studies, Angela Stent Yergin recalled that 'Germany had been transferring technology to Russia for well over a century. There is a long historical tradition of Russo–German economic interdependence, characterized by the export of machinery from Germany in return for imports of Russian raw materials.' On the eve of the First

World War, Germany provided nearly half of Russia's imports. Yergin noted that thirty per cent of Germany's GNP now came from foreign trade, and that although the overall dependence on Eastern trade was small, certain sectors such as the steel industry were heavily enmeshed. 'The Soviet Union and Eastern Europe are the single largest export market for the West German machine tool industry: approximately one third of the machine tool exports from the FRG go to Communist nations, thus East–West technology trade is a significant employment guarantor for medium-sized machine tool forms. The same is true for firms producing large diameter pipe . . . '

The main limit to such technology transfer was the 'chronic Communist hard currency shortage'. Sales of natural gas do a great deal to relieve this problem. With its Siberian natural gas, the USSR will have a commodity to trade in return for German technology. The fit is obvious.

The political implications are less so. United States spokesmen profess to see Soviet–European trade as a one-way street, making only the European party more dependent. But surely the matter is more complex. For a long time, energy provision patterns enforced the post-war bloc division of Europe. Western Europe's economic growth was fed by cheap oil from the Middle East, which weaned it away from its reliance on local coal and made it heavily dependent upon American-controlled oil companies. In Eastern Europe, Soviet oil was cheap and plentiful. All this began to change in the seventies. Rising oil prices and possibilities of trade with the West opened up by détente incited the Soviet Union to cut its energy provisions to Eastern Europe and to earn hard currency by selling oil on the Western market. Because of this and other exchanges developed in the period of détente, if Soviet–German trade risked making West Germany more 'dependent' on the USSR, it also risked making Eastern Europe *less* dependent. The Polish crisis brought that lesson home.

The main thrust of United State policy toward Europe in the early eighties was to restore the East–West division. Events in Poland helped. The American coal industry, a major opponent of the Siberian gas pipeline, took advantage of Poland's production upheavals to take from it the lion's share of the Western European coal import market.

Linkage between East–West trade and American military protection became increasingly explicit. On 21 April 1983, Lawrence J. Brady, the assistant secretary of commerce and co-author, with key Pentagon hawk Richard Perle, of Reagan's East–West trade legislation, warned commercial representatives of the ten European Community countries that the United States would 'reconsider its military commitments to Western Europe' if Europeans were not more cooperative in restraining exports of high technology to the Soviet Union. The *New York Times* called this the first time any administration official had drawn a connection between NATO and European reluctance to limit trade with the USSR, although unofficial threats had been brandished for a couple of years.

The significance of Europe's East–West trade was above all qualitative. According to US State Department statistics, exchanges with Eastern Europe accounted for roughly 4% of the European NATO states' total world trade in 1980. The largest share was West Germany with 6.5%, followed by France with 4%, Italy 3.5% and Britain 2.3%. According to a January 1982 *New York Times* report, however, the small figures mask the importance of that trade. 'Most of the business (more than $8 thousand million in total West German commerce with the Soviet Union in 1980) involves major, highly technical segments of Western Europe's national economies, often the most vital segments in terms of strengthening their worldwide competitive positions. Research and new product development can be dependent on income from the East. In difficult economic periods, the Eastern connection is particularly valued; the planned Comecon economies, though inefficient, make relatively stable clients.' For West German research and development, therefore, the Eastern market might provide an alternative to the kind of strong military–industrial complex that props (and orients) American technology. Put the other way around, Germany's only alternative to the Eastern trade might be to develop a strong military-industrial complex of its own.

The dominant American thinking on arms development and East–West trade can probably be glimpsed from a December 1983 comment to the *New York Times* by New York University economics professor Melvyn B. Krauss, senior fellow at the Hoover Institution on War, Revolution and Peace, one of the influential right-wing think tanks enabling private business to formulate public policy over the heads of regular public servants. Krauss advocated a 'de-Americanization of European defence', inasmuch as the 'Americanization of European defence has led to a dangerous "new pacifism" and "new neutralism" in Western Europe.'[2] The first step would be to withdraw the American troops which 'now serve as hostages to ensure an American nuclear response in case the Russians make a move in, say, Berlin.' Although supposed to be a sign of American credibility, the

US troops 'reflect a profound European scepticism about the American nuclear umbrella.' This scepticism is increasingly justified, suggested Krauss, as peace demonstrations by European youth make Americans doubt 'whether Europe would be worth fighting a nuclear war over.'

'Far more credible to Moscow than the American nuclear umbrella would be for Europe to have its own nuclear deterrent,' Krauss reasoned. 'The obvious problems raised by a nuclear West Germany could be circumvented by the establishment of a West European defence force — so that, instead of a single finger, there would be a single hand, with five fingers, on the crucial red button. Surely a European nuclear deterrent would frighten the Kremlin more than an American one that might or might not be used to defend Europe.' There would be a bonus for United States policy, Krauss concluded. De-Americanization 'would give the Europeans more of a financial stake in the East–West struggle; as a result, they would be less likely to follow détente policies such as subsidized trade and credit that increase Soviet strength.'

The Reagan administration did not succeed in blocking the Siberian gasline deal, much less in getting West Germany to turn its back on its Eastern trade. At the height of the Euromissiles controversy, Franz-Josef Strauss himself worked out a thousand million mark credit deal with Erich Honecker, as if to make quite clear that there was a broad political consensus in the Federal Republic for German–German exchanges that was in no way enfeebled by loyalty to NATO. American strictures against East–West trade may have strengthened the West Germans' bargaining position and enhanced their influence in the East, precisely as the Germans are seen to be preserving in their chosen course despite American pressure. However, the Reagan administration's clamorous opposition to the Siberian gas pipeline cannot be considered a total failure. It helped reopen the issue of technology export to the USSR in such a way as to achieve reactivation of COCOM, the hush-hush Allied coordinating committee that meets in Paris to rule on technology exports to the Communist nations. The resulting restraints may at least help ensure that West European, and especially German, technological research and development must in future depend increasingly on military contracts within the NATO framework.

The Euromissiles are a transitional phenomenon. Their strictly military function as a close-up American 'decapitation' threat to the Soviet Union can soon be duplicated or taken over by the new generation of sea-based missiles, of comparable accuracy, deployed on submarines in Arctic waters. Meanwhile, politically, they help to 'couple' Europe to America's global strategy, while at the same time psychologically 'de-coupling' Europe from America's 'strategic umbrella' *in the way sought by American leaders.* Germany's denuclearization has been forestalled. The missiles are there on German soil, but Germans do not feel protected by them. If they want to feel protected, they must make some serious effort of their own.

American strategists evidently hope to use the Euromissile transition period to stimulate a West European arms buildup. A Soviet–European nuclear arms race could serve not only to make West Europeans wary of détente and technology transfer; it could make the Soviets just as wary. The inefficiency of the Soviet economic system already limits its attractiveness as a commercial partner. If the Russians respond to Reagan administration provocation by predictably plunging into a costly new round of the arms race, the Soviet economy is unlikely to be able to offer desirable trading conditions to Western Europe.

In compensation, Europe as nuclear power must be offered the prospect of taking part in a *de facto* imperialist restoration, preserving the 'West's' powers to monopolize advanced technology and to do as it sees fit with the lands of the South as they founder in poverty and social chaos.

North–South

At the end of the Second World War, the United States inherited the bulk of world trade, while its British, French and Dutch allies were burdened with colonial wars and rebellions. By the 1970s, American policy-makers observed that the situation had, to a considerable degree, been reversed: the United States was burdened with the military maintenance of the worldwide capitalist system, while its principal allies, notably West Germany and Japan, enjoyed a growing share of the benefits. Moreover, although American foreign policy has consistently aimed at a global capitalist economy, keeping access open to investment, resources and markets in the Third World, the Europeans have been more prone to long-term stabilizing arrangements which the American free market purists regard as cheating. The British Commonwealth, the French accords with its former colonies and the 1975 Lome Convention between the EEC and the African, Caribbean and Pacific countries — all these prefigured that European receptivity to 'North–South' dialogue or Third World demands for a 'new international economy order' which is regarded with such deep distrust and hostility by American business circles.

The Iranian revolution was a watershed event that focused American exasperation with its allies. The fall of the Shah convinced the American policy-making establishment that the Nixon policy of counting on secondary Third World powers to police the outer reaches of empire was unreliable. Europeans, with their centuries of expert experience, had to be called back to help. At the same time, the images of anti-American demonstrations in Tehran, and the impression of relative European indifference, aroused a wave of nationalist self-righteousness approaching mass paranoia in the United States, assuring the election of Ronald Reagan with a popular mandate to get tough with the whole world.

The Reagan administration thus renewed with unprecedented insistence the demand that America's European allies should pay both the economic and political price for global protection of the capitalist system, which promises to be increasingly high as bankruptcies mark the failure of the oil-profit recycling development strategy of the 1970s. Europe was put on notice that it was not to veer into friendly and profitable deals with Third World or Soviet-bloc countries while the United States, cast as the villain, defended world capitalism. Independent European policy initiatives on the Middle East or Central America were stifled.

Henry Kissinger has remarked that the United States was mistakenly anti-colonial when Europe held the colonies, just as Europe was subsequently anti-imperialist when America closed on countries Europe had been forced to leave. This reflection underlies the 'Gaullist' reconciliation between right-wing forces in Europe and the United States long recommended by a few sophisticates and finally put on the US agenda by the Iranian revolution. The fall of the Shah shattered the very principles of post-Vietnam US foreign policy: the 'Nixon Doctrine' of regional sub-powers, of course; but also the usefulness of détente, with its supposition that the Soviet Union, to earn its acceptance as a great power ('linkage'), would somehow exert a restraining influence capable of preventing such disasters; and even the whole legalistic, consultative approach to international order embodied in David Rockefeller's Trilateral Commission, inadequate to deal with fanatical mobs impervious to bankers' logic. The United States soon dropped the Law of the Sea and its official enthusiasm for human rights. In an era of national bankruptcies, with the planet's vast rural populations washing up like debris after a tropical storm on the outskirts of unmanageable cities, capitalism could no longer hope to impose order but only to protect its property. In a world of deepening chaos, sudden brutal forays of rapid deployment forces can theoretically safeguard the essential — mineral resources, mainly, starting with oil.

But the United States cannot manage this alone. The 'burden' it seeks to impose on European and Japanese allies is at once financial, political and military. Financially, whether or not they increase their own military spending as Washington urges, the allies — and the whole world — have in effect been forced, through US interest rates and the steep rise in the exchange price of the dollar, to finance the Reagan administration's armament programme. The political burden, formally accepted at Williamsburg in 1983, involves solidarity with American global action. Europeans may still try to wink at Sandinistas or Palestinians behind Uncle Sam's back, but there are to be no independent initiatives offering the peoples of the South some 'third way' out of their desperate predicament. Militarily, the apparent willingness, even eagerness, to build up the strength of such potentially formidable rivals as Japan and West Germany may seem surprisingly reckless. Rivalries between the capitalist powers have already caused two world wars in this century; similar rivalries are being revived and intensified by the long economic recession. But the planning of American leaders is not troubled by analysis of rival imperialisms as a cause of war. Ruthless competition among 'allies' is a way of life, not a threat, and part of the game is to keep all the players playing. So long as the game is the same, the American optimists are confident of winning.

The prevailing attitude toward Europe in Reagan's Washington is bullying impatience. Reagan's people don't like Europe much, but that doesn't mean they want to blow it up. On the contrary, it could come in handy. Against the Russians? Perhaps: but the real hatred, the real war plans, are directed not against the Russians but against the Third World, against those unruly peoples whom Washington strategists, in private, do not hesitate to call 'barbarians' and 'savages'. American 'Gaullism' means sending Jeane Kirkpatrick to insult the United Nations while trying to galvanize the 'civilized' nations — Europe, the far-flung English-settled nations, South Africa, Israel, Japan — for a 'Western' condominium over the backward parts of the earth. Between the white peoples of the northern hemisphere, nuclear war could break out by mistake, as the result of a failed bluff or an uncontrolled escalation. But against the 'terrorists' and 'fanatical mobs' of the southern hemisphere, nuclear war could be waged deliberately. Some see extermination as the unconscious goal of a system gone haywire. But the impulse to exterminate is in part a conscious desire stimulated by growing economic and demographic imbalance.

Worldwide Militarization

American agility in policy-making derives from an abundance of means and a readiness to use them in different ways or discard them for something new. The Euromissiles can also be multi-purpose, or discarded. They have alternative political and strategic uses. If they become redundant as a threat of nuclear decapitation directed against the Soviet Union and its western domains, notably Poland, they may still serve as a means of pressure against America's European Allies.

'As the West Germans do not want the Pershing-2s, the United States now has an opportunity to do some real bargaining with its allies,' wrote Steven Canby and Ingemar Dörfer at the end of 1983.[3] But the Germans do want cruise missiles. 'The Pershing-2 is the stick and the GLCM the carrot.' They can be used to get the Europeans to spend more money on conventional defence. 'Ironically, the INF experience may well be the cold shower, the shock NATO needs to finally get down to business.' And they add: 'The missile dispute has greatly increased Western Europe's awareness of the dangers of nuclear strategy of deterrence containing inherent uncertainties and ambiguities. As a result, the governments of smaller NATO members, such as the Netherlands and Belgium, currently under intense public pressure to resist the deployment and anxious to get off the nulear hook, are willing to strengthen their contributions to NATO conventional defence and start the alliance on the road to a credible defense strategy.'

'Dutch politicians of all political persuasions, for example, privately indicate that they would consider contributing more conventional forces to NATO,' Canby and Dörfer wrote. 'Indeed, leading Dutch socialists have for some time argued that Western Euope must begin to defend itself in order to reduce its dependence upon an increasingly bellicose United States.' What Germany wants and needs is a strong conventional defence plus linkage to the American strategic deterrent. This can be had for a price, they argued. And the price need not be exorbitant if only NATO adopts a rational 'division of labour'.

'Division of labour', NATO's post-deployment slogan, means a new round of bargaining in which the United States holds the Euromissile trumps. This is 'burden-sharing' back again, but with the United States in a still stronger position to force its Allies into military spending by a combination of carrots and sticks. These include, besides the Pershing-2 and cruise missiles, the carrot of technology transfer and the stick of a 'maritime strategy' that would abandon Europe to the Russians.

The carrots and sticks were brought into play at a second Brussels conference organized by the CSIS in January 1984, on 'The Future of NATO and Global Security'. News reports of the conference stressed what Michel Tatu of *Le Monde* called 'a combat of former partners turned enemies', the clash between Kissinger and Schmidt. Kissinger said it was 'time for our European allies to abandon the charade that their principal foreign policy goal is to moderate an intransigent America.' Schmidt retorted that Kissinger was trying to 'rationalize the lack of American ideas since 1976' and complained of the many occasions on which the United States had suddenly changed policy and obliged its allies to follow. Schmidt warned that Washington's 'egotistical economic policies' were creating an 'economic mess' much more dangerous to the alliance than the Soviet threat, harking back to the real central theme of his oft-cited and little-read 1977 London speech.

Beyond the top-level snarling, the main business of the conference was promoted by former CSIS chairman, Reagan's ambassador to NATO, David M. Abshire: namely, to ensure that the Europeans, and especially the Germans, paid up for a new generation of 'smart weapons', the AirLand Battle panoply of NATO commander in chief, General Bernard Rogers. Abshire argued that new conventional weapons would reassure European public opinion by showing that the West does not depend on nuclear war to defend itself. That was the showcase argument. The back-of-the-shop argument, explained to *International Herald Tribune* correspondent Joseph Fitchett by US officials who declined attribution, was that West Germany could be saved from industrial decline only by American technology transfer, and that the only way to secure this was to comply with US plans for NATO rearmament, including more stringent controls on exports to the Soviet bloc. 'The biggest story in Europe right now is West Germny's declining competitiveness, the stagnation of its traditional manufacturing sectors and its lack of assets in the new industries such as microelectronics,' a US aide told Fitchett. 'Unless their industry is helped to become more competitive, West Germany will become increasingly dependent on markets in Eastern Europe.' The

Americans took the position: 'Keeping Germany stable, both economically and strategically, dictates some technology-sharing.' 'US defence technology,' reported Fitchett, 'if imparted to West German industrial partners, could help revitalize the West German economy.'[4]

So much for the carrots. The main stick was that Americans would give up on Europe, turn to a maritime strategy for policing the Third World, and leave the western peninsula of the Eurasian land mass to the Russians. This stick was explained most fully by a carrot man, Robert W. Komer, who as Carter's undersecretary of defence was the first chairman of the Special Group responsible for the second track of the NATO decision. Komer told the Brussels conference that in general, 'Washington sees Third World conflict affecting US interests as much more likely to occur than overt Warsaw Pact aggression against NATO.' These interests 'and other factors such as the strong influence of ardent navalists in the Reagan administration have led to increasing debate between the advocates of what might be called a "maritime strategy" and those who (sic) they deride as Atlanticist or orthodox adherents of a more balanced force posture and strategy aimed at preserving vital US interests in Europe and the Persian Gulf. Both are schools of conventional strategy, though neither propose to abandon nuclear deterrence. Both favour a forward strategy based on strong US force projection capabilities, though they strongly disagree over whether the United States should settle for a sea-control navy or build one designed primarily for offensive maritime force projections into high-threat areas. Tacitly acknowledging Soviet conventional predominance on the Eurasian land mass and stressing instead US exploitation of the medium it can most readily dominate — the sea — the navalist school advocates allocating the bulk of conventional US investment to flexible naval and marine forces able to deal with Third World area conflict or to launch carrier strikes against the Soviet Union itself.' The United States, added Komer, 'seems to be drifting by default toward a force posture that would dictate a predominantly maritime strategy.' And he warned that 'the fatal flaw in a primarily maritime US strategy is that it could not adequately protect those vital interests in the Eurasian rimlands that could be dominated by Soviet power even if the US Navy chased every Soviet ship from every one of the seven seas.'

Komer's personal carrot was a multiple rocket launcher to be produced by a five-nation consortium of the USA, France, Britain, West Germany and Italy. Komer, Abshire and other US arms specialists busily toured Allied countries in early 1984 drumming up European investment for joint ventures, with the promise of trying to make NATO arms procurement a 'two-way street'. This conventional rearmament using new technologies will evidently bind Europe into a new phase of global militarization largely controlled and arbitrated by the United States.

In July 1984, Holland's old cold warrior Joseph Luns was replaced as NATO general secretary by Lord Peter Carrington, who brought a more soothing tone to East–West and Europe–US relations. Lord Carrington called for a 'sweet-and-sour approach to Moscow' as a 'tactical necessity'.[5] In his view, the 'economy and ideology of Communism are moribund', but the West must let them die a slow death rather than try to finish them off in a hurry. 'Our policy in Eastern Europe, as elsewhere, must be to encourage reform rather than revolution.' Moscow leaders should be made to understand 'that new opportunities for cooperation could arise if they were to put a stop to expansionism.' Since Moscow's system is 'moribund' in Europe, such 'expansionism' must lie elsewhere: in the Third World, in the form of aid to Third World revolts and revolutions. Here Carrington returns to Kissinger's concept of 'linkage' which, Mike Davis has written, 'in the jargon of Kissinger meant the US codification of the strategic arms status quo in exchange for Soviet ratification of the socio-political status quo in the Third World.'[6] Arms control and parity mean that the West holds back from threatening to use its political and technological advantages to destabilize the USSR's Eastern European buffer zone.

In Brussels, Kissinger himself again defended linkage, complaining that the USSR in recent years had 'missed no opportunity to undermine Western positions' in Angola, Ethiopia, Aden, Afghanistan, Indochina and Central America. 'The Soviet Union must decide whether it is a country or a cause,' Kissinger declared.

Carrington advocates the 'division of labour' in NATO. 'We should look for ways in which each country can be allowed to specialize in an area where it naturally excels,' he suggested to the IISS. 'For Britain, for self-evident historical and geographical reasons, the emphasis would be on the Navy.'

If Britain gets the sea, what will Germany get? Not, probably, as Heine suggested, the realm of the clouds — that should go to the French, with their dreams of space-ships. Germany can specialize in soldiering, for which it is historically renowned. The new, highly complex weapons systems provide possibilities for eventual export of training and specialized military skills to client countries in the Third World. This is already beginning, through exports of sophisticated military equipment, such as the anti-aircraft systems requiring specialized personnel that were sold to Saudi Arabia in 1984.

AirLand Battle: The Land

In August 1981, with the issuance of an updated version of Field Manual 100–5 (FM 100–5), the United States Army adopted a new official doctrine called 'AirLand Battle'. One year later, a document titled 'AirLand Battle 2000' was published under the joint signatures of US Army Chief-of-Staff General Edward C. Meyer and General Meinhard Glanz, Army Inspector of the Federal Republic of Germany. The foreword stated: 'The United States Army and the German Army agree in principle to the jointly developed concept "AirLand Battle 2000", as far as the operational and tactical aspects of land warfare are concerned.' This document, and the fact that it was signed by General Glanz, caused a political uproar in Bonn when it was brought to public attention in the summer of 1983. The basic concept of an electronically controlled battlefield integrating conventional, nuclear and chemical weapons, all used early to gain advantage in the first stages of a conflict, with deep strikes behind enemy lines, seemed to abandon NATO's traditional defensive doctrine in favour of an offensive posture that could raise Soviet suspicions and tensions in Central Europe. General Rogers himself said the AirLand Battle concept was not appropriate for Central Europe. Where then was the battlefield envisaged? And what was the Bundeswehr Inspector doing signing a concept 'jointly developed' for use outside the NATO area? Embarrassed Bonn officials said General Glanz was not taking responsibility for what the Americans might plan to do elsewhere in the world. It is true that one purpose of the concept is to 'provide a focus for existing technology, and research and development efforts', and thus it is possible to hope that the only real battlefield will be one of procurement and military contracting. However, the most interesting part of the document, describing 'trends' in the 'Environment 2000', suggests a multitude of real battlefields . . . in the Third World.

'AirLand Battle 2000' notes that 'security interests of the Alliance are affected by events outside the geographical boundaries of NATO.' This is because a 'significant portion of the energy required by the Western European nations of the Alliance is imported. Although requirements of the Western World are expected to decrease slightly, lesser developed countries, beginning to require more energy with increased industrialization, will demand an increased share of petroleum.' The document states (although this is contested), that the Soviet Union and Eastern Europe are expected to become oil importers. 'Additionally, industrialized members of the Alliance are dependent on strategic minerals, particularly those imported from sub-Sahara Africa. The Alliance imports over ninety per cent of its critical minerals from sources outside of its geographical boundaries.'

The polar terms of the split between 'first' and 'third' worlds are changing from 'industrialized' and 'undeveloped' to 'high-tech' and 'newly industrialized'. The document continues: 'As the developing countries aided by their relatively low wage scales become increasingly competitive in traditional manufacturing industries, the developed nations are rushing to dominate the high technology sector, hoping to provide the jobs and exports they will need for the future. The Third World will continue to increase its production capacity and by the end of the century may provide more than a quarter of the world's industrial production.' With its new industry, the Third World consumes more petroleum. It also purchases weapons. 'Emerging nations are beginning to acquire more lethal weapons systems and to develop larger armed forces. The Soviet Union has sponsored much of the growth in military potential in the lesser developed countries.'

Since oil, rare mineral resources, new industries and well-equipped armed forces are all piling up in the Third World, the NATO countries must evidently make the most of their technological advantage to stay in control of the whole business. The document warns that 'emerging Third World countries create a greater imbalance of power. These nations may align themselves with more hostile states and resort to terrorism, blackmail or limited war to attain an *equal share of resources*' (my emphasis). In the oil-producing Middle East and in mineral-rich Africa, two threats are foreseen: 'Soviet intrusion or intervention to secure control', or else 'political intransigence and instability of governments in the area'.

These threats are, of course, wholly imaginary, in that Third World countries, revolution or no revolution, never seek to withhold their resources from Western buyers. At most, they may try to obtain a fair price for them, which is only normal 'market' behaviour. In reality, this fantasy projects the fear of Western oil and mining companies that they will lose control of nationalized deposits, and the broader fears born of repressed awareness in the West that the planet's resources are being exhausted by current rates of consumption — by the United States, first of all. This exhaustion will proceed even if weapons are perfected to exterminate all the intrusive Third World populations who might dare demand 'an equal share'. The only real remedy would be to curb Western, and especially American, greed — but that would require a movement of self-limitation, of self-restraint, wholly alien to a culture which prefers an aggressive, expansive solution to every problem.

AirLand Battle: The Air

On an official visit to The Hague on 7 February 1984, President Mitterrand suggested that 'a European space community would to my mind be the most appropriate response to the military realities of tomorrow.' This was Mitterrand's most spectacular bid for European investment capital to develop joint high-technology projects in which France could play a major part. 'One must already look beyond the nuclear if one does not want to be late for a future that is closer than people think,' the French president said. 'Should Europe be capable of launching into space a manned station which would allow her to observe, transmit and thus to counter any eventual threat, she would have made a big step toward her own defence.'

Commentators tended to dismiss this idea as unrealistic, on the grounds that a European satellite could be easily disabled by the Soviet Union in case of conflict. But that is to assume that such a European satellite would be designed for use in a conflict with the USSR — an assumption only made because such costly and ambitious arms projects are always justified in terms of East–West defence needs. But upon examination, this project in particular makes sense only in terms of North–South conflict.

Since the late seventies, it has been reported in specialized journals[7] that France was planning to develop satellite support for her cruise missile programme. What this would mean was explained in an authoritative article[8] written by Richard Burt, Reagan's director of politico-military affairs at the State Department (and Komer's successor in charge of the Special Group), while he was working as the *New York Times* military correspondent. After noting that the 'usefulness of force in international politics seems to be on the rise, particularly in the regions of the non–aligned, or the Third World', Burt observed that the new cruise missiles have 'high accuracy at relatively long ranges' and could thus be of use in Third World conflicts, which Burt calls 'local conflicts'. But the guidance system poses a problem. The Tomahawk cruise missiles stationed in Europe use TERCOM, terrain contour matching, a system which requires thorough prior mapping of the target route. Eastern Europe and the USSR are being thoroughly mapped, said Burt, but mapping the whole world would be 'incredibly costly'.

'For contingencies in the Third World, then, it might be preferable to rely for guidance on precision-positioning technology. Delivery vehicles, whether missiles or aircraft, would receive signals from radio beacons, which would enable the on-board guidance equipment to establish the position of the vehicle in relation to the target so that course corrections could be made,' Burt explained. 'By the mid 1980s, the United States is scheduled to have deployed the global-positioning system, an arrangement in which NAVSTAR satellites in high orbits will enable ships, aircraft and ground forces to determine their location within ten metres. The global positioning system will be vulnerable, in theory, to anti-satellite attacks and thus not ideal for strategic or theatre nuclear roles. *But Soviet use of anti-satellite systems in local conflicts is unlikely,* so global positioning technology might provide a more efficient and less costly alternative to TERCOM guidance for the use of cruise missiles outside Europe or the Soviet Union.' (My emphasis.)

Here the value of 'linkage' is particularly clear. If the Russians understand that they are 'a country and not a cause', they will mind their own business while the West wages 'star wars' against rebellious natives interfering with the 'West's' oil and other natural resources. But there is also a danger that 'linkage' will work the other way round, said Burt: arms control agreements with the Soviet Union 'could impinge on the use of cruise missiles in Third World conflicts.' (Later, as head of the Special Group, Burt was responsible for NATO arms control policy.)

Burt noted that although cruise missiles can carry either conventional or nuclear warheads, 'at more than $1 million per copy, cruise missiles in non-nuclear conflicts would be too costly.' He doubted they could do more than gain time for other forms of intervention in a limited local conflict such as Angola. On the other hand, he thought they could prove effective in an intense war among well-armed adversaries, as might take place in the Middle East or the Persian Gulf. ''Perhaps overdesigned for most conventional roles, the new generation of cruise missiles is particularly well suited to theatre warfare and to nuclear and chemical weapons delivery, as their small size and launch weight offer mobility and their high accuracy makes possible limitation of collateral damage,' he wrote. 'Development of a new generation of binary chemical agents and insertable nuclear components may allow missiles earmarked for conventional missions to be used for nuclear and chemical roles.'

Burt observed that despite the proliferation to Third World countries (especially the rich oil-producers) of many high-tech weapons, there was no real danger of cruise proliferation in the foreseeable future. A weapons system dependent on satellite-borne global positioning is out of reach for all but those few powers able to launch and control their own satellites. The satellite-guided cruise missiles thus seem to be recommended as the ideal weapons system for the high-tech elite countries to use in wars for control of the Gulf oil resources.

It seems a relatively easy matter for American enthusiasts to sell the advantages of this system to leading allies with strong imperialist traditions of their own. During the Falklands–Malvinas war, for example, while Margaret Thatcher and a chorus of archaic chauvinists raved on about unbeatable British character standing up victoriously for principle even against faint hearts in Washington, the United States was secretly using its satellite technology to save Britain from defeat. 'The British operation to recapture the Falklands in 1982 could not have been mounted, let alone won, without American help,' the *Economist* disclosed in an authoritative article nearly two years after the events.[9]

President Mitterrand evidently shares the fantasy of a planet controlled by satellite. The whole French ruling elite is desperately eager to secure its place in the second rank of this new technological world order.

Of course one may argue, plausibly, that such missile systems will not work as planned. But they *are* working already politically and culturally. The Utopia of global electronic security will not create order tomorrow, but it is creating disorder today. The military fantasy is also a *political* fantasy, the fantasy of a world hierarchy established by technology.

AirLand battle, the rapid deployment forces and cruise missile fleets guided by satellite are the imagined instruments for transferring the class struggle into geostrategic terms, as a new division of labour is created between the 'brain' nations, those that think, plan and control (electronically), and the 'brawn' or proletarian nations, who dig up minerals or work in factories.

Of course the Third World proletarian nations must have their elites too. This worldwide militarization implies a devolution method. Wars and armaments create Third World hierarchies that are 'modernized' and 'Westernized' through their contact with increasingly sophisticated weapons systems. Electronic technology becomes the decisive initiation. An unnatural selection of persons whose harmony with electronic devices exceeds their harmony with their fellow creatures favours the emergence of a new sort of feudalism. Ethnic hierarchies may be determined or reinforced through mastery of technological instruments of power. Well-armed, dependent ruling classes may weed out and trim their own populations, eliminating rebels, population excess and old humanist cultural remnants. The violent disorder of this process may even be interpreted to confirm the 'West's' sense of cultural superiority and to justify further militarization as an effort to bring 'order' to turbulent parts of the world.

This description of technological feudalism is not a prediction of the future. It is, rather, the negative Utopia whose pursuit directs the present like an undercurrent. It is El Salvador today, Lebanon today, Southern Africa today.

In the 'first world', this dark vision has been rapidly occupying cultural space and influencing the terms of political debate. In France especially, the Left's assumption of the Gaullist heritage has produced a virtual media monopoly devoted to promoting France's place in the new technological hierarchy led by the United States. As reflected in book publication and sales, there has been a notable shift from intellectual interest in the Third World as an area of human and political problems (witnessed in the sixties by the success of the publisher François Maspéro) to *strategy*, which sees those areas in terms of natural resources and military movements. Populations are of interest only as their movements may affect power relations. This attitude became generalized in the intelligentsia as part of a *post facto* rejection of 'third worldism', after certain events, notably in and between Cambodia and Vietnam, were taken to prove that revolutionaries are no better than those they replace and even worse when it comes to 'human rights'. With so many starving people in the world, concern has become increasingly selective and politicized. Words like 'misérabilisme' have come into fashion to help stigmatize and chase away certain subjects of concern. 'Strategy' is a more comforting subject because it permits, indeed practically demands, identification with the triumphant powers. It has very largely replaced the Marxist-Leninist identification with oppressed peoples. By this switch to strategy, much of the French intelligentsia has crossed the class battle-lines to become at least aspirant 'organic intellectuals' of electronic imperialism.

Gaullist Proliferation

By accepting the new American strategy for NATO, European ruling-circles have not (as peace movement activists sometimes conclude) simply agreed to prepare for nuclear holocaust in Europe out of servility to the United States. These leaders are not suicidal and, despite the required public alarms over the SS-20, do not consider war with the Soviet Union in Europe to be a very serious possibility. They are tempted, rather, by a share in world dominance, by a sort of European 'Gaullism'.

The new 'Gaullism' promoted by the American right involves essentially three things: a revival of European nationalisms to defeat socialist and left-wing tendencies; an ostentatiously 'independent' form of neo-colonialism characterized by unperturbed duplicity; and a technological and industrial development linked to ambitious and expansionist arms production. This policy paves the way for a fundamentally Spenglerian ruling class to make a last effort to hold off the barbarian hordes. It is European upper-class pessimism taking refuge under the wing of an American optimism it frequently denounces and despises, the better to play its specific role as, if not 'good cop' on the imperialist beat, then 'smart cop'. At home, militarization seems to offer a way to absorb idle male youths and manage the transition to a new high technology society in which the domestic proletariat will be too small and controlled ever to threaten the social order.

Politically and ideologically, as Thatcher's Falklands war showed, this 'Gaullism' helps ruling classes to gain the sympathy of the less privileged segments of their own populations while skewing a new phase of economic development against them. On the other side of the Atlantic, in addition to their simple material motivation (make the Europeans pay!), American strategists make a political assumption in promoting this new Gaullism: namely, that a Europe with more diplomatic and military responsibilities will be a more right-wing Europe; or, to put it the other way around, that dependence on America has fostered an unhealthy identification with subjected peoples that may be dissipated by a few assertions of national might in the Third World. This assumption is by no means groundless. The kind of Europe being encouraged by American policy could turn out to be much nastier than the United States itself.

'AirLand Battle 2000' foresees an on-going arms proliferation: the East–West arms race will be carried on in the southern hemisphere. 'Industrial nuclear proliferation increases the likelihood that materials become more available for the development of weapons,' the document observed. 'Smaller countries, especially in critical areas like the Middle East and Africa, can be expected to acquire at least a limited nuclear capability in addition to increasing military capabilities. Nuclear weapons offer cheap alternatives to conventional forces, and the threat of nuclear blackmail looms greater than ever before.' Thus the Pentagon seems to be sacrificing any attempt to maintain the 1970 Nuclear Arms Non-Proliferation Treaty, counting instead on its ability to keep ahead of the pack. Proliferation has been finding its apologists. 'We need not fear that the spread of nuclear weapons will turn the world into a multipolar one,' Kenneth N. Waltz concluded, in his 1982 book for the London International Institute for Strategic Studies, *The Spread of Nuclear Weapons: More May Be Better*. And in July 1983, after a guided tour of the French nuclear submarine base at Brest, American columnist William Pfaff gave a favourable report and came out in support of nuclear proliferation. 'Given that a return to nuclear innocence, to a disarmed world, is beyond possibility, it is arguable that the road toward security (a goal which will never be reached) is to so generalize national nuclear systems as to make the active threat, or the use, of nuclear weapons impossibly risky. The British and French deterrents point that way. It is not a very inviting route, but it may prove the best we have.'[10]

A major political task of the Reagan administration has been to lure Japan into this free-for-all. Post-war Japan provided a model of rapid development geared to civilian consumption, striking proof that technological innovation could flourish without a burdensome military–industrial complex. By the early eighties, it was frequently argued that heavy military investment, far from providing useful spin-offs for American consumer industry, had held back American civilian technology while the Japanese rushed ahead in key fields. The Reagan administration therefore brought heavy pressure to bear on the Japanese government to transfer military-related technology to US defence contractors. The Japanese Ministry of International Trade and Industry strongly opposed such technology transfer. Moreover, the Japanese government had a policy established in 1967 to ban all arms exports.

In November 1983, after three years of resistance, the government of Prime Minister Yasuhiro Nakasone finally agreed to allow selective transfers of military technology to the United States. As usual, the showcase argument was Japan's duty to help the United States, its protector against the 'Soviet threat'. The back-of-the-shop argument was that an uncooperative Japan could not expect its goods to be allowed unhindered into the essential American market. The disproportionate US share of 'the world market' was a potent reason for Japanese and European governments to play along with American military policies at a time when worldwide recession was constricting many markets.

At the same time, the United States exerted strong pressure on Japan to increase military spending beyond the self-imposed limit of one per cent of GNP. Many observers were amazed to see the Americans stubbornly bullying such a potential competitor as Mitsubishi Heavy Industries to move into the arms export business. At the 1984 Brussels CSIS conference, *Asahi Shimbun* defence correspondent Shunji Taoka said that if Japanese were asked what kind of military role their country could play for the security of Western Europe, 'they might cynically reply that by keeping Japan's defence forces relatively small and its arms industry internationally non-competitive, Japan might be promoting the overall security of Western Europe.' For the present, at least, Japanese arms manufacture depends heavily on US licences.[11] American arms-control legislation gives Washington a veto power over weapons sales to another country by a recipient of US defence technology such as Japan. This leash on the potentially ruinous Japanese dragon can only increase Washington's clout with its European allies.

Political Conclusions

This analysis suggests a few tentative political conclusions.

1. In military or strategic terms, the NATO Euromissiles do not contribute to the defence of Western Europe, but are designed to strengthen United States capacity for intervention in the Third World, by holding the Soviet Union in check. They also initiate the changeover from massive deterrence weapons to a proliferation of smaller and more accurate nuclear (and sub-nuclear) weapons.

2. The Gaullist rationale for possession of nuclear weapons — that they 'sanctuarize' national territory, thus making it safe to take part in Third World conflicts without fear of superpower retaliation — is an incitement to nuclear proliferation. As the Soviet Union has consistently opposed proliferation, it is Western strategists, American and 'Gaullist', who seem to have concluded that proliferation would be advantageous for the Western side. A point is reached where the world must move toward nuclear disarmament or nuclear proliferation. The Western nuclear powers evidently prefer proliferation, which will justify their own forces and enable the countries allied to

the United States (the principal European powers, but also Israel, South Africa, Australia) to gain global preponderance over the USSR.

3. Justified ideologically by the East–West conflict, the arms race is largely financed by massive arms sales to Third World countries. This tendency fosters the militarization not only of social orders but also of problem-solving strategies.

4. Headlong proliferation of weapons of all kinds is accompanied by a promise that the United States will be able to stay on top techno-logically, notably in space. This is a promise of endless, escalating worldwide war.

5. None of the stated motivations for this process — from defence of the 'free world' against the 'evil' Soviet empire to protection of the routes to 'our' oil — are reasonable or convincing. Aside from the propaganda about freedom, the objective which counts most in the discussions of strategists is to guarantee 'access to resources'. But not only is this inadequate to justify such a monstrous development, it does not even make sense. The only real threat to oil and other 'strategic' resources is the alarming rate at which the industrialized countries in general, and the United States in particular, are using them up. This exhaustion is then accelerated by the wasteful military production supposedly required to 'protect' them. Moreover, it is simply untrue that Third World revolutions, whether or not they are backed by the Soviet Union, threaten Western access to resources. On the contrary, post-revolutionary Third World countries have proved eager to develop and market their resources, but usually run up against punitive American boycotts.

Thus it is not 'access to resources' that United States militarization seeks to guarantee, but rather *control* of those resources. It is not the 'free world market', but a distorted world market in which American power can influence the terms of trade. This is perhaps the basic thread of rationality — but how thin — running through a process that is largely out of rational or political control.

6. The export of the East–West conflict to the southern parts of the globe is producing a free-for-all which does not obey any political logic. East and West arm both sides in the endless Iraq–Iran war. The West backs Pol Pot in Cambodia after accusing him of genocide. The United States sees Islamic fundamentalism as prime enemy in Iran and the Gulf, but backs it in Afghanistan and supports dictatorial regimes in Pakistan and Sudan when they attempt to force unwilling populations to obey Islamic law. By going into the guerrilla business itself, South Africa has forced major political concessions from the victorious national liberation movements of the former Portuguese

colonies Mozambique and Angola. It takes a heavy dose of ideological certitude (such as Maoism provided in its heyday) to remain
tranquilly persuaded that all this murderous confusion is leading
inexorably toward human progress, enlightenment and liberation.
Thus even supporters of armed Third World liberation struggles
must take an interest in promoting a world environment where
changes could take a more peaceful form.

7. The Euromissiles are a political instrument for the Reagan
administration to involve European allies in its Rapid Deployment
Force strategy in the Third World. Here the temptation is dangerous
for European leaders. In the short run, global militarization may
appear to offer irresistible advantages: (1) an occupation for the most
active part of a generation without career prospects; (2) access to
technological development; (3) preservation of social hierarchies and
privileges; and (4) an ideology of superiority (racial, cultural, technological) to console European peoples recently deprived of other
expectations.

8. European refusal to comply with this strategy could make a
difference. But that would require more than rhetorical condemnation of 'blocs' and 'superpowers', more than a European patriotism
which would merely found yet another nuclear superpower, yet
another bloc — probably without effectively escaping American
domination. The real test of European independence will lie in the
capacity to advance alternative social models, technological development and North–South relations.

9. The frontline of peace movement struggle is to stop the proliferation of nuclear and other weapons. Calls for a freeze or for nuclear-free
zones may help. But strong political pressure must be brought to bear
on the nuclear powers to take the first steps toward disarmament.
Peace movements must face up to the complexities of these issues, or
risk seeing their followers confused and their slogans recuperated by
clever new apologists for militarization; such as the 'build-down'
theorists. For example, in late 1983 and early 1984, the nuclear
disarmament movement felt reinforced by widely-publicized scien-
tific studies[12] warning that full-scale nuclear war with existing
arsenals would produce climatic changes that could destroy all life on
earth. However, the conclusions drawn from these studies bore a
disturbing resemblance to the arms modernization goals of the US
military establishment. Professor Carl Sagan reached 'one apparently inescapable conclusion: the necessity of moving as rapidly as
possible to reduce the global nuclear arsenals below levels that could
conceivably cause the kind of climatic catastrophe and cascading

biological devastation predicted by the new studies.' How is a peace movement to relate to proposals that might make global nuclear holocaust impossible, while making nuclear war 'safer' and thus more likely? Fear of the end of the world is not sufficient to combat the limited nuclear war strategies.

10. The peace movement needs to be more than a single-issue movement. The peace issue has the potential of providing a central point for the recomposition of the Left in the developed countries. One of the historic weaknesses of the revolutionary working-class movement has been the scant interest of workers themselves in 'workers' control'. Except for heady moments of revolt, the majority do not want to take part in long discussions for the sake of something as abstract as 'socialism' or 'autogestion'. To promote such abstract ideas, without clear, concrete proposals as to the purpose of control, is probably to put the cart before the horse.

The surrounding society must inspire its workers to care about what they are doing and making, to want to control their work for the social good. Society at large must take its needs to producers, while showing attention to their problems. This is where the new social movements come in. They can define concrete needs that producers could meet. The issue of industrial conversion from war to peaceful needs, democratically defined, can be the driving wedge in the battle to bring the economy under democratic control.

Notes

1. CSIS chairman David M. Abshire was in charge of the 'national security' group of the transition team, headed by Ed Meese, which managed the power turnover in the American administration after the election of Ronald Reagan in November 1980. The 'national security' group covered the State Department, the Pentagon, the CIA and all agencies handling international affairs. CSIS staff members Chester Crocker, specializing in Africa, and Michael Ledeen, specializing in Italy, were among those getting high administration posts. Abshire himself was later made US Ambassador to NATO.

2. *International Herald Tribune*, 12 December 1983.

3. Steven Canby and Ingemar Dörfer, 'More Troops, Fewer Missiles', *Foreign Policy* 53, Winter 1983–4.

4. Joseph Fitchett, 'Conventional Arms for NATO: Who Will Pay?' *International Herald Tribune*, 18 January 1984.

5. Lord Peter Carrington, Alastair Buchan Memorial Lecture to London International Institute for Strategic Studies, 21 April 1983.

6. Mike Davis, 'Nuclear Imperialism and Extended Deterrence', in *Extermination and Cold War*, Verso/NLB, London 1982.

7. *Flight*, 23 July 1977, p. 262, cited in Desmond Ball, 'The Costs of the Cruise Missile', *Survival*, November–December 1978.

8. Richard Burt, 'Local Conflicts in the Third World', in *Cruise Missiles: Technology, Strategy, Politics*, edited by Richard K. Betts, Brookings Institution, 1981.

9. *The Economist*.

10. *International Herald Tribune*, 18 July 1983.

11. Jack Burton, 'US Puts Subtle Pressure on Japan to Export Arms,' *International Herald Tribune*, 19 March 1984.

12. See Carl Sagan, 'Nuclear War and Climatic Catastrophe: Some Policy Implications', *Foreign Affairs*, Winter 1983–84.

Index